The Well-Read Muse

The Well-Read Muse

Present and Past
in Callimachus and the Hellenistic Poets

PETER BING

Michigan Classical Press

Michigan Classical Press
PO Box 130194
Ann Arbor, MI 48113 USA

Revised edition copyright © 2008 by Peter Bing
All rights reserved.
Library of Congress Control Number
2007940078
ISBN 978-0-9799713-0-3

Printed in the United States of America
2011 2010 2009 2008   4 3 2 1

First edition published 1988 by Vandenhoeck & Ruprecht, Göttingen

∞ Printed on acid-free paper

No part of this publication may be reproduced, stored in a retrieval system, or transmitted in any form or by any means, electronic, mechanical, or otherwise, without the written permission of the publisher.

www.michiganclassicalpress.com

Preface to the 2008 Edition

"Nothing is more cold than the invocation of a muse by a modern," says the narrator in Henry Fielding's *Tom Jones* of 1749, citing Lord Shaftesbury, and "nothing can be more absurd. A modern may with much more elegance invoke…a mug of ale," since that is a better source of inspiration "than all the liquors of Hippocrene or Helicon" (VIII 1).[1] This renunciation of the Muse is so witheringly absolute, so dauntingly confident in its proscriptive sweep, that it is a wonder that any Enlightenment "modern," or subsequent author, should ever have dared to invoke a Muse again. Yet Fielding's provocative dismissal of the Muses can hardly be taken at face value. It more likely reflects the 18th century social satirist's pose of rationality – indeed, his reaction to their ongoing (irritating?) prevalence – than any sense in which these goddesses were truly obsolete. On the contrary, Muses are among the most resilient creatures of western literature, and there can be little doubt that they remained ubiquitous.

Consider only Walt Whitman's vibrant, industrial-age Muse from *Leaves of Grass* ("Song of the Exposition," parts 2–3), whom the speaker implores to "migrate from Greece and Ionia"…

> Placard 'Removed' and 'To Let' on the rocks of your
>   snowy Parnassus;   15
> Repeat at Jerusalem – place the notice high on Jaffa's gate,
>   and on Mount Moriah;
> The same on the walls of your Gothic European
>   Cathedrals, and German, French and Spanish Castles;
> For know a better, fresher, busier sphere – a wide, untried
>   domain awaits, demands you.

That "wide, untried domain" is Whitman's mid-19th century New York, packed with immigrants and in the thick of the industrial revolution, which the poem proudly proclaims on the occasion of the Fortieth Annual Exhibition of the American Institute in 1871. Here, the Muse makes her grand entrance as

---

[1] This passage is cited by E.R. Curtius in his useful chapter on "The Muses" of the medieval era in his *European Literature and the Latin Middle Ages* (W.R. Trask, trans., New York, 1953) 228-46, 245.

> ...the illustrious Emigré, (having, it is true, in her day,
>   although the same, changed, journey'd considerable,)
> Making directly for this rendezvous – vigorously clearing a path for
>   herself – striding through the confusion,
> By thud of machinery and shrill steam-whistle undismay'd,
> Bluff'd not a bit by drain-pipe, gasometers, artificial
>   fertilizers,
> Smiling and pleased, with palpable intent to stay,
> She's here, install'd amid the kitchen ware!

As Whitman so inventively conveys in this captivating poem, the Muse is perpetually welcomed by poets into ever-new historical circumstances, reimagined and transformed to suit her novel surroundings – "having...in her day,...changed, journey'd considerable." Each era envisions the Muses in its own way.

So, too, with the Hellenistic Age. This book, *The Well-Read Muse*, reprinted here twenty years after its initial release, began with the straightforward observation that this era's goddess seemed unlike her earlier manifestations: notably, she had acquired the ability to read and write, was knowledgeable not just about events but about books, was invoked now to aid the poet in composing his verse on the written page. All this appeared to reflect something fundamentally new in the poetry of the age. Clearly, for many poets of the time, especially those among the élite, the impulse was not, as in Fielding, to reject the Muse as the outmoded convention of an earlier age. Rather, like Whitman, they sought to integrate her into a new world, replete with newly prominent technologies (here, those of a culture of reading), and to modify her traits so as to keep pace with a changing conception of poetry and of the poet. In the book, I suggested that this conception of the Muse bespoke a more generally heightened awareness among poets with regard to the materiality of the text. Compared with their predecessors, the Hellenistic poets had a different, notably bookish conception of their craft. From the moment of "inspiration," through the process of composition, and on to their poems' reception and preservation, these poets continually and strikingly drew attention to the practices of writing and of reading. By highlighting the image of a well-read Muse, I tried to provide a heuristic tool that would be useful in helping to crystallize the difference between Hellenistic and earlier poetry, a difference Classical scholars had often sensed, but had not always been able or disposed to articulate in a comprehensive way.

How did this difference arise? In the book, I argued that it was rooted in the fact that many of these poets were also engaged in work as scholars and editors, particularly at the Library of Alexandria, and not least of all in editing their own verse. From the literary-historical standpoint, this was very much a new thing, and the marriage of these previously discrete activities – scholarship and poetry – in an environment in which books were uniquely privileged and plentiful certainly affected poets' idea of themselves and of what poetry should be.

A further factor shaping their conception of verse was an altered political landscape and a new geography. Following Alexander's conquests, a world of new possibilities opened up for Greeks. Many of the most gifted artists and thinkers left their native lands, streaming to the newly Hellenized kingdoms of Alexander's successors, in particular to that of the Ptolemies in Egypt, with its recently established capital of Alexandria. Thus, as in the case of Whitman's Muse, theirs became an "illustrious Emigré," one who had "journey'd considerable" to seek out "a better, fresher, busier sphere – a wide, untried domain." This physical dislocation from their lands of origin, each rich in its own heritage and cultural practices, encouraged a sense of artistic dislocation as well: the poets came to view themselves as latecomers, at a remove from the great achievements of the poetic past. That sense of belatedness finds expression in various ways: in the setting of monuments for past literary greats (the many fictitious epitaphs; the establishment of a literary canon), in the poets' fascination with aetiological- and ktisis-poetry (close kin to scholarly projects of cultural recuperation going on in the Library), and in their obsessive evocation of literary antecedents by means of learned allusion.

At the same time, artistic dislocation offered poets creative space to attempt something new: one manifestation thereof was that heightened attention to the technologies of writing and reading mentioned before, including the still-new challenge for poet-editors of arranging their individual poems, or those of others, into aesthetically coherent books. For those enjoying Ptolemaic patronage, another was their manner of accommodating the needs of monarchs, who were themselves constantly navigating between traditional Greek and Egyptian conceptions of monarchy, translating each so as to govern a multi-ethnic, multi-lingual state. In support of their patrons' political objectives, some poets incorporated traditional Egyptian conceptions of kingship in their poems. That was true, above all, for Callimachus, the representative literary figure of the Age.

These are some of the themes that I developed in *The Well-Read Muse*, and happily my approach has proven fruitful, contributing to, and helping to shape, the discussion of Hellenistic poetry. Since the volume's initial publication, scholars have become increasingly interested in the phenomena that caught my attention. A reader's experience of the text as material object, for instance, lies at the heart of Doris Meyer's *Inszeniertes Lesevergnügen* (2005), and the aesthetic of the poetry-book has been memorably treated in Kathryn

Gutzwiller's *Poetic Garlands: Hellenistic Epigrams in Context* (1998). Indeed, the publication of the Milan Posidippus papyrus has now made Hellenistic poetry-books a hot topic, and added fuel to the debate. Similarly, the intervening years have seen important work on the Hellenistic poets' relationship to the literary past, with such studies as R. Hunter's *Theocritus and the Archaeology of Greek Poetry* (1996), Benjamin Acosta-Hughes' *Polyeideia: The Iambi of Callimachus and the Archaic Iambic Tradition* (2002), and M. Fantuzzi and R. Hunter's *Tradition and Innovation in Hellenistic Poetry* (2004). Ptolemaic patronage of Hellenistic poets, and especially their accommodation of Egyptian concepts of kingship, have been the subject of the remarkable *Alibis* by D. Selden (1998), and S. Stephens' *Seeing Double: Intercultural Poetics in Ptolemaic Alexandria* (2003).

In my own work, I have elaborated any number of threads laid out in *The Well-Read Muse*. To name just a few, I have pursued in more detail the shift from public staging of poetry to its reception in the solitary act of reading, particularly in the tantalizing questions it raises about the poet's "I," and about voice in general: previously embodied by a separate performer, the speaking voice in a poem now resides on the page, and might rely on the reader for its actualization. Callimachus, for one, was clearly intrigued by the resultant ambiguities, which allowed him to play with varying degrees of readerly participation and identification, especially in his *Hymns*.[2] Or again, in a series of essays about epigram, I have explored the question of how readers experience verse under varying conditions and in diverse media: for instance, how does a wayfarer apprehend an epigram inscribed on a monument within a landscape as he passes it by, and how is that different from what happens when he experiences that text on the page, divorced from its physical setting? Some Hellenistic authors wrote epigrams with an eye toward their reception in more than one medium: What different demands could that poet place on his readership in the one setting as opposed to the other? And what expectations did readers bring to the text in either medium?[3] Further, in several articles about the new Posidippus papyrus I have extended my investigations of the poets' role in celebrating and articulating the policies of the Ptolemaic court.[4] Yet here too, and throughout, my overriding concern has been with

---

2 Thus, for example, in my essays on "Impersonation of Voice in Callimachus' *Hymn to Apollo*," and "Callimachus and the *Hymn to Demeter*."

3 Such questions lie at the heart of my essays, "Ergänzungsspiel in the Epigrams of Callimachus," "Between Literature and the Monuments," "The Un-Read Muse: Inscribed Epigram and Its Readers in Antiquity," "Allusion from the Broad, Well-Trodden Street: The *Odyssey* in Inscribed and Literary Epigram," etc.

4 For instance in "Posidippus and the Admiral: Kallikrates of Samos in the Epigrams of the Milan Posidippus Papyrus," "Posidippus' Iamatika," and "The Politics and Poetics of Geography in the Milan Posidippus."

the reader's experience in the act of reading. Those who wish to sample in more detail the ideas that grew out of *The Well-Read Muse* may now turn to my collection of essays old and new, *The Scroll and The Marble: Studies in Reading and Reception in Hellenistic Poetry* (Ann Arbor, 2008), which includes all the articles cited above, in revised form, and with updated bibliography.

Let me express my gratitude to Ellen Bauerle, and the editorial board of the Michigan Classical Press, for their interest in reprinting *The Well-Read Muse* and making it available to a new generation. It is my fond hope that readers will continue to find it useful, and that it will stimulate them to explore further the delights of Hellenistic verse.

Peter Bing
Emory University
November 2007

Acknowledgments

A great many friends and colleagues have helped me with this monograph, and it is a pleasure to acknowledge them by name – though mere enumeration cannot possibly convey the extent of my debt. As a Junior Fellow at the Center for Hellenic Studies, in Washington, D.C., I enjoyed the friendly criticism of Professors Sheila Murnaghan, Kevin H. Lee, Simon R. Slings, and Frank Romer. The Alexander von Humboldt foundation allowed me to spend eight productive months at the University of Tübingen, where I discussed several drafts with Volker Uhrmeister, Lutz Käppel, Helmut Krasser – always with profit. Likewise in Tübingen, Prof. E.A. Schmidt and Dr. Graham Zanker read sections of the work, and provided me with many valuable suggestions. It was at this stage, too, that Prof. H. Lloyd-Jones read the manuscript and gave me his advice on many points. I should add that the Humboldt Foundation has made a generous contribution towards printing costs. I owe a debt of thanks to the University of Pennsylvania for allowing me this leave of absence, and to its Research Foundation for an additional grant towards printing costs. And I must thank Case Western Reserve University for a last minute subvention. While doing revisions back in Philadelphia, I often pestered my colleagues, Professors Ralph Rosen and Joseph A. Farrell, Jr., with yet another version of a particular passage, and they responded with characteristic kindness and acuity. Further, my conversations with Professor Rip Cohen were crucial in helping me formulate certain sections in chapter two. But throughout my work on this book, from its inception right through to publication, my greatest debt has been to two men, Prof. Ludwig Koenen of the University of Michigan and Prof. Richard Kannicht of the University of Tübingen. Each of them has, through his scholarly generosity and unstinting encouragement, been of decisive influence both on this work and on my scholarly development. They have my gratitude and affection. And it is to them that I dedicate *The Well-Read Muse*.

Contents

Preface to the 2008 Edition	v
Acknowledgments	xi
Abbreviations	xiv
Poetic Inspiration and the Poet's Self Image in Hellenistic Greece	10
Rupture and Revival. The Poet's Link to the Literary Past	50
Callimachus' *Hymn to Delos*	91
Conclusion	144
Structural Diagram of the *Hymn to Delos*	146
Bibliography	147
Index Locorum	155
Subject Index	162

Abbreviations

Bornmann	F. Bornmann, *Callimachi Hymnus in Dianam* (Florence 1968)
DK	H. Diels, W. Kranz, *Die Fragmente der Vorsokratiker*, 3 vols. (Berlin[6] 1951)
FGE	D. L. Page, *Further Greek Epigrams* (Cambridge 1981)
FGrHist.	F. Jacoby, *Die Fragmente der griechischen Historiker* (Berlin 1923-1930, Leiden 1940-1958)
Dicht. u. Phil.	H. Fränkel, *Dichtung und Philosophie des frühen Griechentums* (Munich 1976)
Dover	K. J. Dover, *Theocritus Select Poems* (London 1971)
Fraser, *Ptol. Alex.*	P. M. Fraser, *Ptolemaic Alexandria*, 3 vols. (Oxford 1972)
GLP	D. L. Page, *Select Papyri III. Literary Papyri (Poetry)* (Cambr. Mass. 1942)
Gow	A. S. F. Gow, *Theocritus*, 2 vols. (Cambridge[2] 1952)
G-P	A. S. F. Gow, D. L. Page, *The Greek Anthology, Hellenistic Epigrams*, 2 vols. (Cambridge 1965)
HD	U. von Wilamowitz-Moellendorff, *Hellenistische Dichtung in der Zeit des Kallimachos*, 2 vols. (Berlin 1924)
Hopkinson	N. Hopkinson, *Callimachus. Hymn to Demeter* (Cambridge 1984)
Lichtheim *AEL*	M. Lichtheim, *Ancient Egyptian Literature*, 3 vols. (Berkeley 1973-1980)
McLennan	G. R. McLennan, *Callimachus. Hymn to Zeus. Introduction and Commentary* (Rome 1977)
Mineur	W. H. Mineur, *Callimachus. Hymn to Delos. Introduction and Commentary* (Leiden 1984)
Pfeiffer	R. Pfeiffer, *Callimachus*, 2 vols. (Oxford 1941, 1953)
Pfeiffer, *Hist.*	R. Pfeiffer, *History of Classical Scholarship* (Oxford 1968)
PCG	R. Kassel, C. Austin, *Poetarum Comicorum Graecorum Fragmenta* (Berlin 198-...)
Powell	J. U. Powell, *Collectanea Alexandrina* (Oxford 1925)
Reinsch-Werner	H. Reinsch-Werner, *Callimachus Hesiodicus: die Rezeption der hesiodischen Dichtung durch Kallimachos von Kyrene* (Berlin 1976)
SH	H. Lloyd-Jones, P. Parsons, *Supplementum Hellenisticum* (Berlin 1983)
Urk.	K. Sethe, W. Helck, *Urkunden des ägyptischen Altertums* IV, Fasc. 1-22 (Leipzig, Berlin 1906-1958)
Williams	F. Williams, *Callimachus. Hymn to Apollo. A Commentary* (Oxford 1978)

„sed quasi poeta, tabulas quom cepit sibi,
quaerit quod nusquam gentiumst, reperit tamen,
facit illud veri simile quod mendacium est,
nunc ego poeta fiam."

        Plautus, *Pseudolus* 401–404

Poetic Inspiration and the Poet's Self Image in Hellenistic Greece

In his 1950 film, *Orphée*, Jean Cocteau dreamt up a rather startling source of inspiration for his poet-hero Orpheus. As with many poets of the past, Cocteau's hearkens to a voice from the beyond. In this case, however, that voice is not of the traditional kind. For it comes to him in his Rolls Royce – over the car radio. What is more, its utterances, inspired by B.B.C. broadcasts to France during the German occupation, are suitably avant garde. An example: "The bird sings with its fingers. Twice. I repeat. The bird sings with its fingers." Avidly jotting down the words on a pad, Orpheus spends his every free moment with the Rolls. "This car is the only thing that matters to you," complains Eurydice, his wife. "I could die and you wouldn't even notice."

What amuses us in this scene is the intrusion of modern technology onto time-honored notions of poetic inspiration and the creative process. For Cocteau, such notions no longer adequately reflect contemporary experience. They must be revised. Not, to be sure, so radically as to break with tradition entirely (Cocteau's obvious affection for his classical model precludes such a course), but just enough to jar the viewer, provoking in him a smile of recognition at a world transformed by the advent of the electronic age.

Such revisions, of course, are nothing new. But they are of particular interest when coinciding with and reflecting a period of intense societal change. Film, radio, video, television and telephones have propelled us into just such a time and, under their influence, we have entered a phase of what literacy experts call "secondary orality," a shift of emphasis from the written to the spoken word. A poet inspired by the radio – this is one rather radical manifestation of that shift.

In the following pages I wish to examine the view of poetic inspiration and the Muses among the ancient Greeks, likewise at a cultural turning point, namely that between the Classical and Hellenistic Ages. Here, in the first generation of poets after the death of Alexander the Great in 323 B.C. we shall find a crucial role played by the book. Although in Greece the "primary oral culture" ("a culture totally untouched by any knowledge of writing or print")[1] had long since

---

[1] W.J. Ong's definition, *Literacy and Orality* (New York 1982) 11.

changed into a literate one, with writing fully interiorized by about the early 4th cent. B.C., this inward change found outward expression in the poet's self-image only in the new Age. Writing now came to dominate intellectual activity, scholarly *and* poetic. While oral culture declined, the book rose to a position of unexampled prominence, becoming, as Rudolph Pfeiffer has said (*Hist.* p. 102) "a characteristic sign" of the Hellenistic Age.[1a]

The new prominence of the "written" word had many consequences. It led, for one, to amusing clashes between modern, self-consciously literate poetic conventions, and those of the old oral culture – clashes not unlike those used by Cocteau. But further, it substantially altered the traditional view of poetic activity. Poets rethought their methods, modified their goals and, in so doing, created a new aesthetic which affected not only subsequent Greek authors, but the Latin poets of the Augustan Age as well. These are some of the consequences we shall trace.

But before turning to the Hellenistic Age, we must briefly discuss the way earlier poets described inspiration, the role of the Muse and the creative process. Here it is of utmost importance to recognize that the view which proved decisive in shaping the subsequent tradition was that of a "primary oral culture." To be sure, the Greeks adopted the Phoenician alphabet already in the 8th century B.C.[2] and widespread literacy followed soon after. Their poetry, however, inherited the conventions of Homer. And although the *Iliad* and *Odyssey*, as we know them, probably also date from the 8th century, their origins go back many generations to a pre-literate age: for they are both demonstrably products of a long oral tradition;[3] their poet may himself have been illiterate as was the world he portrayed. There is only one instance of writing in Homer (*Il.* 6.168-9).

The manner in which the oral poet described inspiration and for what it was used may best be seen in the most elaborate invocation of the Muses in Homer, namely that before the catalogue of ships (*Il.* 2.484-92):

[1a] Cf. now also G. Zanker, "The Nature and Origin of Realism in Alexandrian Poetry", *A&A* 29 (1983) 125f. who says "It has become a cliché of modern criticism to call the Alexandrian age 'bookish'" p. 129.

[2] And far earlier perhaps, cf. the studies of J. Naveh, *Early History of the Alphabet. An Introduction to West Semitic Epigraphy and Palaeography.* (Leiden 1982) 175-186, who argues for a date ca. 1100 B.C. But cf. W. Burkert, *SB Heidelberg.* I (1984) 30 ff.

[3] Concerning the Oral Poetry debate, it will suffice here to refer the reader to J. Latacz' survey of its history, "Tradition und Neuerung in der Homerforschung" in *Homer,* Wege der Forschung CDLXII (Darmstadt 1979).

> Tell me now, Muses, who have your homes on Olympos
> For you are goddesses, and are there, and you see all things
> and we have heard only the rumor of it and know nothing.
> Who then were the leaders of the Danaans and their lords?

As Maehler and others have observed, the poet appeals to the Muses not for help in achieving a particularly lovely affect, i.e. not for his *form*, but for a precise accounting of the facts, for his content.[4] The Muses, in turn, can oblige because they are eyewitnesses to everything beyond the poet's personal experience (ὑμεῖς γὰρ θεαί ἐστε, πάρεστέ τε, ἴστέ τε πάντα, / ἡμεῖς δὲ κλέος οἶον ἀκούομεν οὐδέ τι ἴδμεν v. 485-6). Put somewhat differently, they are "daughters of Memory" (so first in Hes. *Th.* 54, cf. West ad loc.) and, with their assistance, the poet enjoys total recall. One easily sees how this was the function of a culture with no written records.

Though modified in some details, this orally determined view of poetic inspiration went virtually unchallenged by the poets themselves right through the Classical Age. Inspiration did not come to them as it did already in the early 6th century B.C. to Ezechial, who ate the scroll and thus received God's message (2.8-3.3; cf. also Jeremiah 15.16). The Jews were people of the book. Not so the early Greeks. Even when writing came to be used by the poets, it was never, or at most indirectly, acknowledged.[5] The poets persisted in calling themselves "singers" (ἀοιδοί, the old epic designation) or "makers" (ποιηταί, a 5th century innovation), but never "writers".

In the meantime, literacy was changing the world. This process has been dealt with at length by J. Goody and I. Watt.[6] Their findings show

---

[4] H. Maehler, *Die Auffassung des Dichterberufs im frühen Griechentum* (Göttingen 1963) 18 f., cf. P. Murray, "Poetic Inspiration in Early Greece", *JHS* 101 (1981) 87 f., esp. 90-94, who admirably surveys much of the previous literature on the subject.

[5] By the 2nd quarter of the 5th century, writing becomes a common metaphor for recollection in lyric and tragedy with the image of the tablets of memory, cf. Pind. *Ol.* 10.1 f.; Aesch. *Choe.* 450, *Eum.* 273-5; Soph. *Triptolemus* fr. 597 (Radt); etc. For further examples cf. Groeneboom ad Aesch. *PV* 789. On this development generally cf. R. Pfeiffer, *History of Classical Scholarship* (Oxford 1968) 25-6, Ph. E. Legrand, *Étude sur Théocrite*, Bibliothèque des Ecoles Francaises d'Athènes et de Rome 79 (Paris 1898, repr. 1968) 429-436, D. Sansone, *Aeschylean Metaphors for Intellectual Activity*, Hermes Einzelschr. 35 (1975) 59-63, and C. Segal, "Greek Tragedy: Writing, Truth, and the Representation of the Self" in *Mnemai. Classical Studies in Memory of Karl K. Hulley*, ed. H. D. Evjen (Chico 1984) 46.

[6] Cf. "The Consequences of Literacy" in *Literacy in Traditional Societies*, ed. J. Goody (Cambridge 1968) 27-68. On the question of literacy/orality generally, cf. E. A. Havelock's *Preface to Plato* (Cambr. Mass. 1963), *The Literate Revolution in Greece and Its Cultural Consequences* (Princeton 1982), and *The Muse Learns to Write* (New Haven 1986). Important contributions have also been made in three articles by W. Rösler: "Die

that "literacy fixed permanently and made available to a wider audience previously fluid descriptions: the evasions and reinterpretations of the oral tradition ceased, and the resulting gap between written statement and actual experience led to the formation of a critical approach to life based on a notion of the essential rationality of all aspects of reality, public and private" [O. Murray, *Early Greece*, (Sussex 1980) 97].

Thus, by the end of the 5th century, the rational investigations of philosophy were enjoying enormous growth. Poetry, on the other hand, was in a crisis of confidence. "Blessed is he", laments Choirilos of Samos, "who was skilful in song at that time, a servant of the Muses, when the meadow was still uncut. But now, when all has been apportioned and skills have their limits, we are left behind like the last in a race. Nor is there anywhere, even when one searches all around, to drive a new-yoked chariot" (*SH* 317). So too Aristophanes, in his comedy "The Frogs", was well aware that a door had been closed on an era: with the deaths of Euripides and Sophocles, tragedy too had died. But he also saw why: the best young minds were flocking to Socrates. Plato is said to have burned his verse because of Socrates (Diog. Laert. III 5).

The crisis of poetry and the rise of philosophy were indispensible for poetry's rebirth in the Hellenistic Age, for while poetry was in decline, philosophy appropriated the Muses. Plato's Academy and Aristotle's Lyceum contained prominent shrines of the Muses, "mouseia", and philosophical discourse there was probably considered to be under the aegis of these goddesses.[7] But music itself acquired a new meaning. "Philosophy", says Socrates in the *Phaedo* (61 a), "is the best music." Not only were the poets banished from Plato's Republic, they had little place in the philosophical schools. Instead, the Muses' domain now included scholarly debate, scientific research and the gathering of books into libraries. Walter J. Ong is certainly not far from the mark when he calls this "the point when alphabetic literacy first clashed head on with orality" (*op. cit.* n. 1 above, p. 24) and, following E. A. Havelock, describes Plato's aversion to poets as a "rejection of the ... oral-style

---

Entdeckung der Fiktionalität in der Antike", *Poetica* 12 (1980) 283-319, "Schriftkultur und Fiktionalität. Zum Funktionswandel der griechischen Literatur von Homer bis Aristoteles," in *Schrift und Gedächtnis. Beiträge zur Archäologie der literarischen Kommunikation* eds. A. and J. Assmann, and Chr. Hardmeier (Munich 1983) 109-122 and "Alte und neue Mündlichkeit. Über kulturellen Wandel im antiken Griechenland und heute", *Der altsprachliche Unterricht* 28 (1985) 4-26. Cf. also W. Schadewaldt, "Der Umfang des Begriffs der Literatur in der Antike", *Literatur und Dichtung* (ed. H. Rüdiger, Stuttgart, etc. 1973) 12-25 and R. Harder, "Bemerkungen zur griechischen Schriftlichkeit", *Die Antike* 19 (1943) 86-108 = *Kleine Schriften* (Munich 1960) 57-80.

[7] Cf. P. Boyancé, *Le Culte des Muses chez les Philosophes Grecs* (Paris 1937) 262 *et passim*, as well as J. Lynch, *Aristotle's School* (Berkeley 1972) 108-116.

thinking perpetuated in Homer in favor of the keen analysis of dissection of the world and of thought itself made possible by the interiorization of the alphabet in the Greek psyche" (*op. cit.* n. 1 above, p. 28).

This sets the stage at last for the Hellenistic Age, and we herewith turn our attention to the literary developments that occurred in the city of Alexandria in Egypt. Previously the site of an insignificant village, this city had been founded by Alexander the Great as an administrative center for the Greeks after his conquest of Egypt. He was drawn here perhaps because it was the scene of a famous episode in Homer where Menelaus wrestled the sea-god Proteus into submission – Proteus, who soon came to be identified as an Egyptian pharaoh (at least since Herodotus II 112 f.). The scene's symbolic value would certainly not have been lost on Alexander, who had himself forced Egypt to its knees.

Alexander hoped that this city would become the gateway to Egypt for the Greeks. But after his death in 323, his successor, Ptolemy the 1st Soter, soon realized that it would take more to attract and keep a Greek population – the basis of his power – in such unfamiliar surroundings where they would never be more than a small minority. The hero, Menelaus, had after all continued on to Sparta. How could one bind these Greeks, who were drawn from the furthest corners of the Greek world, each with its own tradition, to a city essentially traditionless?

Ptolemy's answer was grandiose. He resolved to bring that vast tradition to Egypt.

With a reverent eye towards Alexander and his tutor, Aristotle, he established a Museum – literally a shrine of the Muses – elaborating on, and institutionalizing, the important status of the Muses in the philosophical schools;[7a] and for this Museum he lured some of the most gifted minds away from Greece. The cornerstone of the project was the great library, built through an aggressive policy of buying which deliberately sought out the obscure and the remote, and thus created a kind of microcosm of Greece on Egyptian soil. The Museum was a beehive of intellectual activity, where scholarly disputes and rivalries flourished. The poet Callimachus likened the contentious scholars to a swarm of

---

[7a] Lynch, *op. cit.* (n. 7 above) 122, explains the official, organizational role of the Muses at the Alexandrian Museum *vis-à-vis* their earlier function in Aristotle's school as follows: "It is clear...that the Museum was not simply an Alexandrian Peripatos. For in Egypt, long before the Alexandrian Museum was founded, learning was associated with the priestly class (cf. Aristotle, *Metaphysics* I 1, p. 981 b 24; Isocrates, *Busiris* 21-23); in Egyptian society, priests traditionally were the teachers and they kept books in temples. It is only to be expected, therefore, that an institution of higher learning founded in this tradition would be presided over by a priest and have a marked religious dimension." Egyptian influence was not restricted to the Museum, moreover. In chapter 3 (p. 128 ff.) I shall argue that it is central to the view of kingship put forth in Callimachus' *Hymn to Delos*.

angry wasps, or flies about a goatherd, or Delphians greedily grasping for a portion of meat at the sacrifice (*Iambos* 1.26 f.).

In one important respect, the Museum differed from its philosophical model: among its most prominent members were poets. What is more, it seems that these poets were required to engage in some form of scholarship, for it is difficult to explain their nearly total participation in this activity if not as the result of policy. Poetry, then, for the first time became grounded – institutionally – in the written word.

How did this affect the view of the creative process and the Muses? What became of those venerable traditions and conventions that reached back to the era of oral song? Some examples may help to shed light on the problem.

Poseidippus, a poet active in Egypt in the 280's and '70's B. C., wrote a programmatic elegy to open a collection of his epigrams (*SH* 705). The beginning will raise no eyebrows: "Now (Muses), sing along with Poseidippus a song of hateful age" (νῦν δὲ Ποσε[ι]δίππῳ στυγερὸν ϛυναείσατε γῆρας v. 5). A perfectly orthodox invocation by a poet who refers to himself and his Muses as "singing". But in the next line the Muses are to sing with the poet, "having inscribed (the song) in the golden columns of writing-tablets" (γραψάμεναι δέλτων ἐν χρυσέαις ϛελίσιν v. 5-6). It seems that the Muses have learned to write![8] Having aroused the most conventional expectations, then, the poet follows up with an innovative twist, achieving an affect at once amusing and disquieting for the reader. And I use the word "reader" deliberately since poetry was now largely experienced through books. Our evidence is the sudden efflorescence of purely visual phenomena: pattern poems (short works written in the shape of what they describe) and acrostics containing the poet's name or a key word (our earliest acrostich is that of the tragedian Chairemon, F 14 b Snell, in the second half of 4th cent., on which cf. B. Snell, *Szenen aus griechischen Dramen*, Berlin 1971, p. 159-160, 166-168. On the Hellenistic vogue, see E. Vogt, *A & A* 13, 1967, p. 80-95). But the poet's self image is now also geared to the reader. Just a few lines on, Poseidippus hopes that a statue of himself will be set up in the market place of his home town, depicting him "unwinding a book-roll with both hands" (ἔϛμι δὲ βίβλον ἑλίσσων / †ἀμφωτ† λαοφόρωι κείμενος εἰν ἀγορῆι v. 16-17). The distinctive emblem by which the poet wishes to be remembered is now his book.[9]

---

[8] Inspiration was connected with writing much earlier, but by those who were not poets. Thus, Democritus states ποιητὴς δὲ ἄσσα μὲν ἂν γράφηι μετ' ἐνθουσιασμοῦ καὶ ἱεροῦ πνεύματος, καλὰ κάρτα (*DK* 68 B 18). Cf. Segal, *op. cit.* (n. 5 above) p. 53.

[9] Cf. Segal, *op. cit.* (n. 5 above) p. 45 n. 16.

We can gauge the significance of this innovation by recalling the weight of tradition that stood against it. Poets had been content to picture themselves in the received manner throughout the Classical Era, yet book-rolls appear as attributes of the Muses in vase-painting as early as ca. 459 B. C., i. e. 130 years before the Hellenistic Age.[10] And in sculpture, they are first found in the Mantinea reliefs of the mid fourth century.[11] These artisans were apparently able to reflect the historical reality of the roll because they were less burdened by literary precedent than were the poets.[12]

This rift, it appears, emerged even within poetry itself. Solon, for instance, in his capacity as lawgiver refers to himself as "writing" (θεσμοὺς δ' ὁμοίως τῶι κακῶι τε κἀγαθῶι / εὐθεῖαν εἰς ἕκαστον ἁρμόσας δίκην / ἔγραψα, fr. 36.18-20 W), for this technology was evidently an acknowledged part of legislation by the early 6th century B.C. As poet, however, Solon speaks only of song (cf. fr. 20.3 W). The same is still true nearly two centuries later when Critias says of his motion for Alcibiades' return: γνώμη δ' ἥ σε κατήγαγ', ἐγὼ ταύτην ἐν ἅπασιν / εἶπον καὶ γράψας τοὐργον ἔδρασα τόδε (DK 88 B 5). Conversely, when speaking of song he uses traditional terms: καὶ νῦν Κλεινίου υἱὸν Ἀθηναῖον στεφανώσω / Ἀλκιβιάδην νέοισιν ὑμνήσας τρόποις (DK 88 B 4).[13]

But literary precedent alone cannot account for this strange dichotomy. To Pindar it is apparently of no inherent interest that a work was written, but for the Hellenistic poets it is crucial. Why should this be so? It would seem that the relative importance of performance is a key. Public performance persisted as the primary reality in creating and experiencing verse at least through the late 5th cent.; writing, though

---

[10] Cf. H.R. Immerwahr, "Book Rolls on Attic Vases", *Classical, Mediaeval and Renaissance Studies in Honor of Berthold Louis Ullman*, ed. Ch. Henderson (Rome 1964) and idem, "More Book Rolls on Attic Vases", *Ant. K.* 16 (1973) 143-7; cf. also O. Bie, *Die Musen in der antiken Kunst*, (Berlin 1887); Th. Birt, *Die Buchrolle in der Kunst*, (Leipzig 1907); W. Schubart, *Das Buch bei den Griechen und Römern*[3] (Heidelberg 1962); and, for a summary of the history of books in Greece, J. Platthy, *Sources on the Earliest Greek Libraries*, (Amsterdam 1968).

[11] Cf. Roscher, s.v. Musen, p. 3250-4.

[12] We might, of course, have a different picture if we possessed the lost plays on the Muses by Phrynichus (31-5 Meineke = 31-5 Kock), Polyzelus (7-10 Meineke = 7-10 Kock), Euphron (8 Meineke = 8 Kock), Ophelion (I 415 Meineke = II p. 294 Kock).

[13] Critias' iconoclasm took another form, of course, namely the insertion of an iambic line in an otherwise elegiac poem in order to accommodate Alcibiades' name. This and other innovations justify Pfeiffer's assessment: "Critias...holds an important position in the middle between the *poetae philosophi* of the past and the *poetae docti* of the future." (*Hist.* p. 55).

probably utilized, was incidental.[14] The audience, its expectations attuned to spectacle, would be largely oblivious, and therefore indifferent, to the textual dimension in the work. Thus, Pindar frequently refers to the circumstances of performance;[15] this was the theme that mattered.

By Hellenistic times, however, it mattered very much less. The coherent fabric of the polis-community had disintegrated, supplanted by the remote, dislocated mass of the Oikoumene. Poetry, in concert with this change, became a private act of communication, no longer a public one. Through reading, the literary community too was broken down into individual readers responding to a given text in isolation (or at best in circumscribed groups). Performance might now appear as a self-conscious fiction, as in the so-called "mimetic" hymns of Callimachus (2, 5 and 6), where the narrator, indeterminately now master/mistress of ceremonies, now celebrant, now poet, vividly describes a ritual that is clearly a literary evocation.[16] By their very artificiality, these poems underline a decisive shift. At that point when performance can be an illusion, no longer a datum, it becomes inevitable that the illusion will be broken – antiquarian interest alone cannot sustain it in the absence of a living performative tradition. The dominant medium of communication will assert itself.

Clear evidence of such assertion may be seen in the efflorescence of epigram. Epigram is a genre inextricably tied to its inscribed quality. Yet, like Callimachus' "mimetic" hymns, it now, characteristically, appears at one remove from its original chiseled setting.[17] It no longer has to be inscribed since all poetry has moved in the direction of epigram: a poem is always now an inscription. This is obvious in verses

---

[14] Cf. J. Herington's analysis of the "song culture" of early Greece in *Poetry into Drama. Early Tragedy and the Greek Poetic Tradition* (Berkeley 1985) 3–40 *et passim*. Cf. also R. Merkelbach, "Sappho und ihr Kreis", *Philologus* 101 (1957) 5–6 and B. Gentili, "Oralità e scrittura in Grecia", in *Oralità Scrittura Spettacolo*, ed. M. Vegetti (Torino 1983) 37–43. It should be recalled that even in the 5th cent., texts were not as common as one might think. Socrates, for instance, finds it worthy of note that Euthydemus owns a complete Homer (Xenophon, *Mem.* IV 2.10), and see also Polybius III 32.1; but cf. Gentili, *op. cit.*, "Poeta e musico in Grecia" (quoted in n. 59 below), who properly stresses that performative poetry did indeed continue to exist throughout this period, but that it did so in an entirely separate sphere.

[15] Cf. H. Fränkel, *Dicht. u. Phil.* (Munich 1962) 488 and n. 7.

[16] Cf. Ph. E. Legrand, "Problèmes alexandrins 1: Pourquoi furent composés les hymnes de Callimaque?", *REA* 3 (1901) 293; H. Herter, *RE* Suppl. V 434; H. Erbse, "Zum Apollonhymnus des Kallimachos", *Hermes* 83 (1955) 411–28; N. Hopkinson, *Callimachus, Hymn to Demeter* (Cambridge 1984) 3–4, 35–37.

[17] Uninscribed epigrams appear occasionally as early as the 5th century B.C. (cf. Wilamowitz, *HD* I 129–32), but with the Hellenistic period they become typical.

that must be read to be understood, such as the pattern-poems and acrostics mentioned above, but is in some way true for poetry as a whole in this age.

Perhaps the most telling confirmation of this truth may be found in those instances in which a written text is simply assumed. In fragment 7 of his *Aetia*, for instance, Callimachus employs the traditional notion that a poem composed with the favor of the Graces will endure over a long period of time. Thus, previously, Pindar (*N*. 4.6-8) had said that "the word lives longer than the deed, whenever the voice brings it forth from depths of the mind with the Graces' favor" (ῥῆμα δ' ἐργμάτων χρονιώτερον βιοτεύει, / ὅ τι κε σὺν Χαρίτων τύχᾳ / γλῶσσα φρενὸς ἐξέλοι βαθείας). Now, however, the poet implores the Graces to "wipe your annointed hands on my elegies" (ἐλέγοισι δ'ενιψήσασθε λιπώσας / χεῖρας ἐμοῖς fr.7.13-14) so that they may survive for many a year. How, we may ask, can one wipe one's hands on an *orally* communicated work? This is an odd - indeed a bizarre - request, unless we conceive of the elegies as being on tablets or scrolls.

A less obvious case in which a written text is assumed occurs in Callimachus' *Hymn to Artemis*, where the poet addresses the following prayer to the goddess: "O queen, may my care forever be song / and therein (i.e. in that song) shall be Leto's marriage, therein shall be your name often, / therein shall be Apollo, and therein all your labors, / and therein your hounds and your bow and your chariots" (ἄνασσα, μέλοι δέ μοι αἰὲν ἀοιδή· / τῇ ἔνι μὲν Λητοῦς γάμος ἔσσεται, ἐν δὲ σὺ πολλή, / ἐν δὲ καὶ Ἀπόλλων, ἐν δ' οἵ σεο πάντες ἄεθλοι, / ἐν δὲ κύνες καὶ τόξα καὶ ἄντυγες v. 137-140). The conspicuous repetition of "therein" (ἐν in the Greek) is a traditional feature of Greek poetry. But all examples outside Callimachus refer to a concrete object (a shield or a cloak) or place (cf. Sappho 2.5 and 9 L-P) and never to something so incorporeal as song.[18] Or is it incorporeal? Another passage in Callimachus gives us a clue. In the tale of Acontius and Cydippe in Bk. 3 of the *Aetia*, the poet discusses the work of the 5th cent. Cean chronicler, Xenomedes, using the same repetition to set out the content: "*In* it the insolence and the lightning death, and *in* it the wizards Telchines; and Demonax who foolishly paid no heed to the ... gods he put *in* - to his tablets" (ἐν δ' ὕβριν θάνατόν τε κεραύνιον, ἐν δὲ γόητας / Τελχῖνας μακάρων τ' οὐκ ἀλέγοντα θεῶν / ἠλεὰ Δημώνακτα γέρων ἐνεθήκατο δέλτ[οις fr. 75.64-66). What was left unspoken in the *Hymn to Artemis*, is here

---

[18] Cf. D. Fehling, *Die Wiederholungsfiguren und ihr Gebrauch bei den Griechen vor Gorgias* (Berlin 1969) 194-197, esp. 196.

made explicit. Song is indeed now a concrete object in the form of papyrus or tablets.[18a]

This concretization is particularly stark in another Hellenistic text,[19] namely the prooem to the Batrachomyomachia: ἀρχόμενος πρώτης σελίδος χορὸν ἐξ Ἑλικῶνος / ἐλθεῖν εἰς ἐμὸν ἦτορ ἐπεύχομαι εἵνεκ' ἀοιδῆς / ἣν νέον ἐν δέλτοισιν ἐμοῖς ἐπὶ γούνασι θῆκα, "starting with the first column of writing, I pray that the chorus come down from Helikon into my heart on account of the song which I have recently written in the tablets upon my knees" (v.1-3).[20] Muses were traditionally invoked at the start of epic recitation. Here the convention has been visualized. Their proper place is not the temporal beginning of a song, but its concrete manifestation in space, the πρώτη σελίς on the page.[20a]

Even the Muses' foes (such as Thamyris was at *Iliad* 2.594-600) no longer attack the goddesses' *singing*: by the time of Euenus (1st cent. B.C.?) that creature most hateful to them – is the bookworm! ἐχθίστη Μούσαις σελιδηφάγε (*AP* IX 251.1 = 1.1 *Garl. Phil.*).

[18a] Cf. also the pseud-Epicharmean fragment (by Axiopistus? ca. 300 B.C.) in Powell p.219 v.1-6: τεῖδ' ἔνεστι πολλὰ καὶ παντοῖα.../ v.4... αἴτε τις / ἀλλ' ἔχει κακόν τι, καὶ τούτοισι κέντρα τεῖδ' ἔνο. / ἐν δὲ καὶ γνῶμαι σοφαὶ τεῖδ',..."

[19] On the dating of the *Batrachomyomachia* cf. H. Wölke, *Untersuchungen zur Batrachomyomachie* (Meisenheim 1978) 46-70 and R. Pfeiffer, *Hermes* 63 (1928) 319 = *Ausgewählte Schriften* (Munich 1960) 113.

[20] Note that while Poseidippus (in the programmatic elegy mentioned above) invoked the Muses to sing with him (συναείσατε) after they have penned his song (γραψάμεναι), the poet of the animal epic has written his work alone; he calls the goddesses into his heart perhaps just to inspire his performance. Such devaluation of the Muses is taken to its limit by Varro, *De Re Rustica* I, 1.4-7, who explicitly rejects an invocation in the style of Homer and Ennius, calling rather on the twelve "Dei Consentes" (*advocabo eos, nec, ut Homerus et Ennius, Musas, sed duodecim deos Consentis*, 1.4), the patrons of rural life, whom he presents in a catalogue clearly modelled on that of the Hesiodic Muses. A second, parallel catalogue lays bare the source of his inspiration: i.e. those "qui Graece scripserunt...Hi sunt, quos tu habere in consilio poteris, cum quid consulere voles" (1.7f.). On the text πρώτης σελίδος (found only in O²) rather than πρῶτον (or -ως, -ος) Μουσῶν, cf. Wölke, *op. cit.* (n.19 above) p.257-8.

[20a] There is evidence that the concretization of song may also have altered the sense of a traditional form of poetic closure, namely the conventional announcement of a new theme at the end of many Homeric Hymns. It has been pointed out that the final verse of the 'Epilogue' of the *Aetia* (fr. 112.9 αὐτὰρ ἐγὼ Μουσέων πεζὸν [ἔ]πειμι νομόν) recalls and varies such hymnic endings as αὐτὰρ ἐγὼ...ἄλλης μνήσομ' ἀοιδῆς or μεταβήσομαι ἄλλον ἐς ὕμνον (thus Pfeiffer *ad loc.*). Whereas these formulae indicate the transition from the hymn (as *prooimion*) to epic recitation in the context of *performance*, Callimachus' words – if we believe, as I think we must, Rudolf Pfeiffer's interpretation (cf. *Philol.* 87 [1932] 226 = *WdF* p.150-151) – appear to mark the transition between the *Aetia* and the *Iambi* in the final *published* edition of these works, i.e. the transition on the scroll of papyrus. As Pfeiffer himself points out, however (*op. cit. ad* n.121), this interpretation has not gained universal acceptance.

It is no coincidence, then, that reading and writing suddenly emerge as conspicuous parts of the poet's self-image; rather their prominence reflects a fundamental change in approach: poetry is now chiefly composed and experienced in writing. Accordingly, in an epigram of Asclepiades, who flourished about 275 B.C., we hear that the poem "Lyde" was "co-written" by the Muses and Antimachus: τὸ ξυνὸν Μουσῶν γράμμα καὶ Ἀντιμάχου (32 G-P). In the 1st cent. B.C., Crinagoras imagined a similar collaboration in writing between poet, Muses or Graces (ἔγραψεν ἢ Μουσέων σὺν μιῆι ἢ Χαρίτων, AP IX 513.2 = 49 Garl. Phil.) and between poet and Passions (ἔγραψεν ἢ παρ' οἶνον ἢ σὺν Ἱμέροις, AP IX 239.4 = 7 Garl. Phil.). As often, these passages rely for their effect on the pleasant jolt caused by departure from a traditional literary commonplace. Each draws on the old theme of the poet's cooperation with the goddesses of song (which we find, for instance, in Bacch. 5.9: ἢ σὺν Χαρίτεσσι βαθυζώνοις ὑφάνας / ὕμνον or Pind. N. 9.53f.: Ζεῦ πάτερ / εὔχομαι ταύταν ἀρετὰν κελαδῆσαι / σὺν Χαρίτεσσιν),[21] but each simultaneously transforms it by portraying the singer as writer, his goddesses as fellow scribes.

A startling mutation on the theme of "poet and Graces" may be found in Theocritus' 16th *Idyll*, the "Charites". Here, in a vivid mime, we meet the Graces as personified scrolls, and the poet quasi as their dealer: storing the poems in a coffer, sending them off to prospective clients for perusal - a frank portrayal of the Hellenistic poet's life (v. 5-12).

> Τίς γὰρ τῶν ὁπόσοι γλαυκὰν ναίουσιν ὑπ' ἀῶ
> ἡμετέρας Χάριτας πετάσας ὑποδέξεται οἴκῳ
> ἀσπασίως, οὐδ' αὖθις ἀδωρήτους ἀποπέμψει;
> αἳ δὲ σκυζόμεναι γυμνοῖς ποσὶν οἴκαδ' ἴασι,
> πολλά με τωθάζοισαι ὅτ' ἀλιθίην ὁδὸν ἦλθον,
> ὀκνηραὶ δὲ πάλιν κενεᾶς ἐν πυθμένι χηλοῦ
> ψυχροῖς ἐν γονάτεσσι κάρη μίμνοντι βαλοῖσαι,
> ἔνθ' αἰεί σφισιν ἕδρη ἐπὴν ἄπρακτοι ἴκωνται.

> Now, who of all who dwell beneath the blue dawn
> will gladly open up and receive our Graces
> in his house, nor send them back again without gifts?
> - when they come bare-foot home complaining,
> jeering at me that their journey was in vain;
> and cowering again in the bottom of the empty chest,
> they wait, head bent over cold knees,
> their usual abode when they return unused.

---

[21] Cf. D.E. Keefe, CQ 32 (1982) 237-8.

This bold scene is all the more striking for the manner in which it deviates from and develops a Classical model: for in depicting his Χάριτες, i.e. his poems, as stored in a chest, Theocritus is plainly alluding to a pun related to us in an anecdote (Stob. III 10.38, etc. Cf. Gow *ad* v. 10ff.) about Simonides. According to the story, the poet had been asked to compose an encomium for pay (χάρις). On subsequently being told that he would get thanks (χάρις) but no money for his labor, he said that he had one chest for thanks (χαρίτων), another for money, and that when he opened the former he found in it nothing useful.

By making Simonides' chest a scroll-box, his χάριτες its written contents, Theocritus plunges his readers into the contemporary world of books; or differently, by reference to the past, he underlines the intervening change: a heightened awareness of the medium of writing. "Theocritus' papyrus calls itself a papyrus", as F.T. Griffiths has said (*Theocritus at Court* p. 24). The Simonidean pun is thereby given an added dimension. All the "thanks" (χάριτες) *or* "pay" (χάρις) that Theocritus receives is simply the return of his Χάριτες, his papyrus rolls, which lie in his chest unused, unrealized in their function as dispensers of glory, a constant rebuke to the poet (cf. N. Austin, *TAPhA* 98, 1967, 5 and 11 n. 19).

Like changes occurred in other spheres of poetic activity. Crinagoras mentioned the topos of wine and song. As early as Archilochus, we find that these two go hand in hand: "I know how to lead the dithyramb, the lovely song of lord Dionysus, when my brain is thunderstruck with wine" (ὡς Διωνύσου ἄνακτος καλὸν ἐξάρξαι μέλος / οἶδα διθύραμβον οἴνωι συγκεραυνωθεὶς φρένας, fr. 120 W = 117 Tarditi). Their usual setting was the symposium where one might hear exhortations such as Ion's ("let us drink, let us play, let song go through the night", πίνωμεν, παίζωμεν· ἴτω διὰ νυκτὸς ἀοιδή, fr. 27.7 W) or that in Pherekrates' *Persai* ("fill up the cup and raise the cry of the triple paian, as our custom is", ἔγχει κἀπιβόα τρίτον Παιῶν' ὡς νόμος ἐστίν, fr. 131.5 Kock).[22] By the 3rd cent. B.C., however, we find an exhortation of another kind. Instead of urging his friend to drink and sing, Hedylus (6 *G-P*) urges him to drink and *write*: καὶ γράφε καὶ μέθυε (v. 6). Coming as it does in the very last words of a poem which is traditionally sympotic in every other way,[23] this exhortation acts as a punchline, aimed to unsettle – as it did Gow and Page, who comment (on v. 4) "γράφε ... does not suggest a symposium".[24]

---

[22] We find further instances of singing and drinking in Alcaeus fr. 58.12 L-P, Anacreon *PMG* 356b, Theognis 533 W, etc.

[23] Cf. Giangrande, *Entretiens Hardt* 14 (1968) 158-63.

[24] For writing while drinking cf. Catullus 50.1-6: *Hesterno, Licini, die otiosi / multum lusimus in meis tabellis, / ut convenerat esse delicatos. / scribens versiculos uterque nostrum /*

Writing brought innovation even to the theme of novelty. To create something new - that is what poets had desired for centuries. And it was a commonplace to claim to have achieved it. Thus already Hesiod told of how he and Homer sang at Delos, ἐν νεαροῖς ὕμνοις ῥάψαντες ἀοιδήν ("stitching song in new hymns" fr. 357.2 M-W) and Pindar, referring to his own poem, could write that "there are songs in every style, but to put a new one to the touchstone for testing is all danger" (πολλὰ γὰρ πολλᾷ λέλεκται, νεαρὰ δ' ἐξευρόντα δόμεν βασάνῳ / ἐς ἔλεγχον, ἅπας κίνδυνος· N. 8.20-1). Perhaps Timotheos asserted his claim with the most aggressive self-confidence: "I sing no ancient stories, for new themes are better; new is the king who is reigning, Zeus, but Cronos ruled in olden times; away with the outdated Muse" (οὐκ ἀείδω τὰ παλαιά, / καινὰ γὰρ ἁμὰ κρείσσω· / νέος ὁ Ζεὺς βασιλεύει, / τὸ πάλαι δ' ἦν Κρόνος ἄρχων· / ἀπίτω Μοῦσα παλαιά, PMG 796, cf. also Timotheos PMG 791.202f. and Anon. PMG 851b).

The Hellenistic poets likewise pursued the new, but in keeping with their altered circumstances they perceived novelty in bookish terms. Thus, in the opening elegy of Meleager's Garland (AP IV 1.55 = 1.55 G-P) recent poems are ἔρνεα πολλὰ νεόγραφα ("a rich harvest, newly written"), and later, in the corresponding poem of the Garland of Philip, the poet is described as "reaping a sheaf of recent columns" (καὶ σελίδος νεαρῆς θερίσας στάχυν, AP IV 2.3 = Garl. Phil. 1.3, cf. Hesiod's νεαροῖς ὕμνοις mentioned above), a lovely play on the equivalence of poetry and papyrus plant.

Likewise with metrical innovation, Boiskos of Kyzikos identifies himself as a "writer" in introducing the iambic tetrameter distich with second verse catalectic: Βοίσκος ἀπὸ Κυζικοῦ, καινοῦ γραφεὺς ποιήματος, / τὸν ὀκτάπουν εὑρὼν στίχον, Φοίβῳ τίθησι δῶρον ("Boiskos of Kyzikos, writer of this new poem, inventor of the eight-footed line, gives it as a gift to Phoebus", SH 233). And in the prooimion to his Hymn to Demeter, Philikos of Corcyra offers his novel stichic choriambic hexameters as "written" (καινογράφου συνθέσεως) specifically for "readers", "men of letters", γραμματικοί (καινογράφου συνθέσεως τῆς Φιλίκου, γραμματικοί, δῶρα φέρω πρὸς ὑμᾶς, SH 677).

Wilamowitz disparaged these novelties as "nichtig", seeing in them merely "die Sucht, seinen Namen durch die Erfindung eines angeblich neuen Verses zu verewigen ...; ob es schon so hohe Summen von Choriamben oder Iamben gegeben hatte, wie sie zu einem Verse verei-

---

ludebat numero modo hoc modo illoc, / reddens mutua per iocum atque vinum. But although these verses portray two poets having a drink while writing, this can hardly be called a symposium where one is urged to get drunk, μεθύειν, and write.

nigten, war wirklich einerlei".²⁵ Though Wilamowitz accurately describes how this metrical innovation consists simply of adding feet to existing meters, his condemnation obscures what might be of some interest, namely the cause: for such verses characterize an Age when, to an ever greater extent, the primary experience of literature was through books, and poets, because they had fewer and fewer opportunities to hear lyric meter, were no longer perfectly at ease with its complexities. They therefore either avoided such forms entirely – witness the strange elegiac epinicians of Callimachus (*SH* 254–269 and fr. 384 Pf.) –, or simplified them, as in Theocritus' non-stanzaic imitation of Sapphic and Alcaic Greater Asclepiadian.²⁶ The appeal of the added feet was clearly less to the ear than to the eye. And that is not cause to disparage. For taken on its own terms, that is within the confines of the page (the new location of poetic discourse), the obvious pride of Philikos and Boiskos in their inventions is neither cynical nor petty. Indeed, the phenomenon itself is of considerable cultural significance.

The examples of Philikos and Boiskos should make it very clear that even in that most traditional form, the hymn, the written word brings change. This is nowhere more evident than in the remarkable *Hymn to Pan* by Kastorion of Soloi (*SH* 310):²⁷

σὲ τὸν βολαῖς νιφοκτύποις δυσχείμερον
ναίονθ' ἕδραν, θηρονόμε Πάν, χθόν' Ἀρκάδων
κλήσω γραφῇ τῇδ' ἐν σοφῇ πάγκλειτ' ἔπη
συνθείς, ἄναξ, δύσγνωστα μὴ σοφῷ κλύειν,
μωσοπόλε θήρ, κηρόχυτον ὅς μείλιγμ' ἱείς.

You who inhabit a wintry, snow gust-beaten
place, herdsman Pan, the Arcadians' land,
I will celebrate in this learned text, having composed
a poem of all-renown, lord, hard for one not learned to understand,
O serving-beast of the Muses, who utters a melody moulded of wax.

"Daß auch schon leere Spielereien vorkamen," said Wilamowitz in writing of Hellenistic meter, "dafür sind Iamben eines Kastorion ein unerfreulicher Beleg"²⁸ and his verdict set the tone for the understand-

---

²⁵ *Griechische Verskunst* (Berlin 1921) 127. Cf. also Ph. E. Legrand (*op. cit.* n. 5 above) 434–435.
²⁶ Cf. Gow's preface to Theocr. 28: "In lyrics intended to be sung to a tune which repeats itself stanza-form is necessary, but if, as seems likely, T. meant his lyrics... not for singing but for reading, it is conceivable that he should have deliberately discarded stanza-form as no longer relevant or necessary."
²⁷ The following reproduces, in a substantially abbreviated form, my analysis of this hymn in *AJPh* 106.4 (1985) 502–509.
²⁸ *Griechische Verskunst* (Berlin 1921) 126.

ably few critics that have mentioned Kastorion since.[29] Merely a fragment, the beginning of his *Hymn to Pan* is known to us through Athenaeus (X 454 f.) citing Klearchos Περὶ Γρίφων (fr. 88 Wehrli). But though γριφοειδής indeed, a closer look at the hymn reveals that it is anything but "leer".

Self-avowedly "literate" - a γραφὴ σοφή (v. 3) intended for σοφοί (v. 4) - the poem challenges the reader to understand its art fully: δύσγνωστα μὴ σοφῷ κλύειν. Yet understanding seems easy. The language of the hymn, while consistently elevated,[30] and having two hapax legomena in five lines (νιφοκτύποις and πάγκλειτ'), is never an impediment to comprehension. The meter is iambic trimeter in the severe style of Lycophron and Hellenistic tragedy:[31] Resolution occurs only in polysyllabic words with several shorts, on any longum except in the last metron. Porson's bridge is uniformly observed. Caesura falls on the penthemimeres or hepthemimeres throughout - except in the first line, which, because νιφοκτύποις and δυσχείμερον coincide with their respective metra, has no regular caesura.[32] This verse, inelegantly chopped into three equal parts, is the clue to that part of the puzzle which was solved already in antiquity (cf. Athenaeus X 454 f.): namely that each metron is metrically equivalent and interchangeable with any other, for each begins with a consonant and ends with a consonant or long vowel. Thus verse one, according to Athenaeus, could just as well be read: νιφοκτύποις σὲ τὸν βολαῖς δυσχείμερον. It was further recognized that each metron has exactly eleven letters, a feature that could only be experienced visually through reading.[33]

---

[29] See Wilamowitz again in *HD* II (Berlin 1924) 149 n. 2 (cited in n. 34 below), W. Kroll, "Kastorion" *RE* Suppl. IV 1880: "Das Fragment ist eine törichte Spielerei"; O. Kern, *Die Religion der Griechen* III (Berlin 1963) 131 n. 2; L. Lehnus, *L'Inno a Pan di Pindaro* (Milano 1979) 99-100.

[30] δυσχείμερον already in Homer (*Il.* 2.750 of Dodona); ἕδραν cf. Pind. *P.* 11.63 etc.; for the poetic periphrasis χθόν' Ἀρκάδων cf. *LSJ* s. v. χθών II; κλήσω cf. Hes. *WD* 1 ἀοιδῇσιν κλείουσαι as opposed to κλήσω γραφῇ here; μωσοπόλε cf. Sappho 150.1 *L-P*; μείλιγμ' see Theocr. 22.221.

[31] Cf. P. Maas, *Greek Metre* (Oxford 1962) #102 and M. L. West *Greek Metre*, (Oxford 1982) 159-160.

[32] Recognized already by Porson in his preface to the *Hecuba* (Leipzig 1824) p. XXIX when he compared Kastorion's observance of penthemimeral and hepthemimeral caesura to that in Tragedy: "*Verum, si versus istos recte metieris, Tragicorum regulae unum modo adversantem reperies. Secundus enim, quartus et quintus pertinent ad caesuram Ba, tertius ad Ad, Sed primi similem Tragico scribere nunquam, ut opinor, permissum erat.*"

[33] This led Wilamowitz, *Kleine Schriften* VI (Berlin 1971) 504 n. 3, to suggest that the poem was written in monometers, στοιχηδόν, i. e.:

ΣΕΤΟΝΒΟΛΑΙΣ
ΝΙΦΟΚΤΥΠΟΙΣ
ΔΥΣΧΕΙΜΕΡΟΝ

We are dealing, then, with a hymn whose metra can be freely reshuffled. And I should stress that this process is conceivable *only* in writing inasmuch as the audience, in order to work out all the possibilities, must keep track not only of the six possible combinations in each line, but of how each of these in turn would fit with the six possible combinations of each line that precedes *and* follows it. Such a work would seem to attack the very foundations of the genre – and this, perhaps, explains why critics have generally doubted that the poem is in fact a hymn.[34] For hymnic convention dictated that the god be invoked either with the first word – so in the majority of cases – or, less commonly, elsewhere in the first line; the invocation was usually linked to a verb of singing; the divinity was then glorified with a recitation of its attributes or in a relative clause which attempted to grasp the essence of its being.[35]

The interchangeability of the metra is indeed the key to Kastorion's poem, but not in the sense that we initially assume, that is not as the "törichte Spielerei" (as Kroll called it, *RE* Suppl. IV 880) that substi-

ΝΑΙΟΝΘΕΔΡΑΝ
ΘΗΡΟΝΟΜΕΠΑΝ
ΧΘΟΝΑΡΚΑΔΩΝ
ΚΛΗΣΩΓΡΑΦΗΙ
ΤΗΙΔΕΝΣΟΦΗΙ
ΠΑΓΚΛΕΙΤΕΠΗ
ΣΥΝΘΕΙΣΑΝΑΞ
ΔΥΣΓΝΩΣΤΑΜΗ
ΣΟΦΩΙΚΛΑΥΕΙΝ
ΜΩΣΟΠΟΛΕΘΗΡ
ΚΗΡΟΧΥΤΟΝΟΣ
ΜΕΙΛΙΓΜΙΕΙΣ

but if this were so, neither the eleven letters nor the interchangeability of the metra would be very puzzling as they would be visually obvious. Such a reading is antithetical to the challenge of v. 4. An earlier example of interchangeable verses is the epitaph of Midas (*AP* VII 153, cf. Plato *Phaedr.* 264 d) which, however, functions on an exclusively aural level. Imperial times brought a refinement on Kastorion's eleven letter metra, the ἰσόψηφος poem in which the numerical value of all the letters in a verse are equal, cf. D. Page, *Further Greek Epigrams* (Cambridge 1981) 504-6, 508-10.

[34] Cf. Wilamowitz, *HD* II 149 n. 2: "Ein Hymnus auf Pan, wenn man so sagen darf" and O. Kern, *op. cit.* (n. 25 above) p. 131 n. 2: "die Iamben des Kastorion von Soloi, die man nicht als Hymnos, sondern nur als metrische Spielerei bezeichnen darf". A similar attitude may be found in a more recent work, L. Lehnus, *op. cit.* (n. 25 above) p. 100, where we read that Kastorion's poem is "in realità un griphos … cui l'assetto esteriormente innico dell' esordio non toglie carattere e finalità da virtuosismo metrico."

[35] On hymnic features cf. E. Norden, *Agnostos Theos* (Leipzig 1913) 143-76; H. Meyer, *Hymnische Stilelemente in der frühgriechischen Dichtung* (Würzburg 1933) 19 *et passim*; R. Janko, "The Structure of the Homeric Hymns: A Study in Genre", *Hermes* 109 (1981) 9-24; W. H. Race, "Aspects of Rhetoric and Form in Greek Hymns", *GRBS* 23 (1982) 5-8.

tutes clever chaos for traditional order; rather by making us compose the hymn anew – and I refer the reader to my analysis in *AJPh.* 106.4 (1985) 502–509, where every possible combination of metra within each verse is put to the test – Kastorion leads us to a reaffirmation of hymnic convention and of his particular composition which, as it turns out, can be changed very little without being diminished. That which is δύσγνωστα μὴ σοφῷ κλύειν is, in other words, the order in which the metra are to be put together.[36]

The poem thus takes us through a two-fold process, the first part of which is to discover that the hymn consists of metrically equivalent and interchangeable metra of eleven letters each. Consequently we appear to enjoy free rein in reshaping the hymn as we please – such was Athenaeus' instinct – casting Pan and hymnic convention for the most part aside, and rejoicing in yet another example of Hellenistic ingenuity – and of our own! But the second part of our reading reveals a deeply conservative, traditional – though no less ingenious – perspective.[37] For the ostensible *embarras de choix* turns out to be illusory, and we arrive finally at the inescapable conclusion that there are only so many variables in addressing a god, and that Kastorion's achievement in this regard is consummate and would be the less so for any change.

The fragment thus embodies the old tension between originality and tradition in a peculiarly Hellenistic way. For, on the one hand, the written word creates the possibility of transforming the traditions of the literary past, in this instance by visual manipulation of the words on the page (the poem is thus a flamboyant, virtually emblematic example of the method which most Hellenistic poets were using to compose their verse). Yet, the very freedom that writing provides has here another function, namely to affirm the continued validity of the tradition.[38] A

---

[36] This gives special point to the choice of the word συνθείς (v. 4) since it thus refers to the task of both poet and reader which consists precisely of "putting together" the discrete metra.

[37] Certain, of course, only for the five verses that survive – though I doubt that the hymn was very long: riddling poems such as the epitaph of Midas, the ἰσόψηφος poems (cf. n. 33 above) or technopaignia are invariably short. It would be surprising to find a device such as interchangeable metra of eleven letters spread over a poem of great length.

[38] Our conclusion bears on another aspect in the problem of innovation and tradition. We have been dealing here only with Kastorion's *Hymn to Pan*, yet the critics' scepticism vis-à-vis this hymn typifies the modern stance generally towards the Hellenistic hymn qua hymn: Literary virtuosity is thought to be incompatible with religious intent. Callimachus' *Hymn to Apollo* is thus "concerned primarily not with politics or religion, but with literature" (F. Williams, *Callimachus, Hymn to Apollo*, Oxford 1978, p. 3); we are warned that that same poet's "Götterhymnen sämtlich einem Geiste entspringen, der an die persönlichen Götter als Lenker irdischer Geschicke nicht mehr glaubt" (A. Körte and P. Händel, *Die Hellenistische Dichtung*, Stuttgart 1960, p. 21). Philikos' *Hymn to Demeter*, mentioned

naturally conservative medium, writing advanced an artistic renewal that, in its innovations – the characteristic use of learned allusion, a taste for the obscure and the remote, etc. –, defined itself as never before by reference to the recorded past.

We have already seen that the Muses had learned to write. But that is not all. For Callimachus, they are no longer the old epic goddesses who knew each thing because they were there; rather, his is a well-read Muse. The story of Acontius and Cydippe mentioned above is said to have come to his Muse through the writings of Xenomedes (ἔνθεν – scil.

---

above, exhibits "an obvious lack of genuine religious feeling, but since the piece is a confessed literary exercise, this is hardly surprising, even if it accords ill with Philicus' position as a priest of Dionysus at the time of the great procession of the reign of Philadelphus" (P. M. Fraser, *Ptolemaic Alexandria*, Oxford 1972, p. 651-2, cf. Callixenus in Athenaeus 198b. For Philikos' role in the procession, cf. E. E. Rice, *The Grand Procession of Ptolemy Philadelphus*, Oxford 1983, p. 52-58).

More recently, Anthony W. Bulloch has examined Callimachus' religious attitude in the Hymns ("The Future of a Hellenistic Illusion. Some observations on Callimachus and religion", *MH* 41, 1984, p. 209-230), finding that the poet, while not "rejecting religion out of hand" (p. 229), nonetheless presents a "distrustful view" (*ibid.*) in which "the orderliness assumed by traditional religion is illusory... the religious illusion has broken and does not seem to have much of a future" (*ibid.*). Living in "confusing" times (p. 214), Callimachus, according to Bulloch, was a "realist" (p. 229) whose "'education to reality' involves facing the contradictions which orthodox religion often tries to ignore" (p. 230). Religion, for him, "is found *not to connect* with the adult world in which we, his audience, try to live our lives" (p. 229). Indeed, the ancient poet may be "in the process of forming his own 'personal neurosis'" (p. 230 n. 32).

It seems as if Bulloch has projected, in undisguisedly modern psycho-analytic terms, a problem typical of the twentieth century onto a poet of the third century B.C. (cf. p. 215 n. 13). There is little room, on this view, for levity either in Callimachus or in Greek religion more generally. Thus humorous, fanciful moments, such as when baby Zeus' umbilical cord falls off and becomes the aition for the name of the Omphalian plain, or when an entire landscape takes to its heels before Leto as she tries to find a birthplace for Apollo, appear as products of a "very disturbed, even fractured... state of mind", a "febrile wit", "a very bizarre, and one might say frenzied, imagination" (p. 219). But are these images of the divine significantly more irreverent or burlesque than those that we can find in the *Iliad*, the *Odyssey* or the *Homeric Hymn to Hermes* (cf. N. Hopkinson's sensible remarks concerning this problem in "Callimachus' Hymn to Zeus", *CQ* 34, 1984, p. 147-148)? Further, without wishing to seem reactionary and assert that the hymns were composed for performance at specific religious festivals – this has been the tendency of French scholarship on Callimachus' Hymns, e. g. Cahen, *Callimaque et son Œuvre Poétique*, Paris 1929, p. 281: "C'est aux lieux mêmes ou la fête célébrée qu'aurait été déclamé chacun des hymnes" before "un public de dévots"; see also P. Bruneau, *Recherches sur Les Cultes de Délos à L'Époque Hellénistique*, Paris 1970, p. 16 with regard to the *Hymn to Delos*: Il a sûrement été écrit pour une cérémonie délienne"; or C. Meillier, *Callimaque et son Temps*, Lille 1979, p. 94 on the *Hymn to Apollo*: "l'œuvre littéraire intégrée dans le culte" –, one might ask of what a sophisticated scholar-poet's "religion" might consist. Was continued use of traditional genres merely cynical? Could there be for the poet a more personal sign of devotion than the product of his involvement in the intense literary experiments and innovations of the age?

from Xenomedes' tablets – ὁ πα[ι]δός / μῦθος ἐς ἡμετέρην ἔδραμε Καλλιόπην fr. 75.76-7). Similarly, in the third mime of Herodas, who flourished about the same time, we hear that a student, if properly flogged, may read better than Klio, the Muse, herself (3.92). If such statements are metaphorical, there is nevertheless a fresh conception behind them – a conception dictated by the new primacy of the book. The "reading" Muse apparently became so common that it caused ancient scholars to misinterpret earlier literature. For example, Pindar's 10th Olympian Ode was composed ca. 474 B. C., that is nearly a century and a half before the developments of which we are speaking. It begins with a command to read out the victor's name (τὸν Ὀλυμπιονίκαν ἀνάγνωτέ μοι / Ἀρχεστράτου παῖδα, πόθι φρενός / ἐμᾶς γέγραπται v. 1-3). Thereafter, Pindar turns to the Muse, who is clearly a *new* addressee (ὦ Μοῖσ', ἀλλὰ σὺ ... v. 3). The scholia (1 a), however, which are largely Hellenistic, debate whether the command that the name be read is addressed to the Muse. Thus, although the syntax precludes the possibility, the convention is now so strong that Hellenistic scholars project it onto the previous age.[39]

---

[39] In this context it is important to mention Pindar *Ol.* 6.154, which seems to contain an image that would associate the Muses with writing. The poet addresses the chorodidaskalos, Aineas, as ἄγγελος ὀρθός ἠυκόμων σκυτάλα Μοισᾶν. Ancient commentators on the passage largely took σκυτάλη to be the Spartan message stick (Schol. Pind. *Ol.* 6.154 b, d, e, f, h) which was used for secret dispatches: the sender and recipient each had a staff of equal diameter and length, along which the former would wind a strip of leather. He would then write his message on the strip while it was on the staff. When the leather was subsequently unwound, the order of the letters would no longer be apparent, so that a messenger could bring the strip without fear that the message would be deciphered. Once the strip was delivered, its recipient would in turn wind it around his stick, thus bringing the letters back into order (cf. J. Oehler, "Skytale," *RE* III A 691-2 and Ch. Daremberg, Edm. Saglio, *Dictionaire des Antiquités Grecques et Romaines* IV 2 [Paris 1911] s. v. Scytale). Such an interpretation of Pindar's σκυτάλα Μοισᾶν (as is to be found in virtually all modern scholars, e. g. Slater s. v., or Farnell ad loc.) implies a conception of message-writing Muses.

But is it really necessary to interpret the phrase in this way? The only earlier known instance of σκυτάλη occurs in a famous fragment of Archilochus (fr. 185 W = 188 Tarditi): ἐρέω τιν' ὕμιν αἶνον, ὦ Κηρυκίδη, / ἀχνυμένη σκυτάλη, ... This ἀχνυμένη σκυτάλη was a source of debate already in antiquity. Apollonius of Rhodes discussed the tradition of the message stick in a book on Archilochus (Athen. X 451 d) and Aristophanes of Byzantium devoted a whole work to the fragment entitled Περὶ τῆς ἀχνυμένης σκυτάλης (Athen. III 85 e). But Denys Page is surely correct in finding that "we have no idea what is meant by ἀχνυμένη σκυτάλη, and no reason to suppose that it has any connection with the practice of wrapping an inscribed role of leather round a staff" ("Archilochus and the Oral Tradition" in *Archiloque,* Entretiens Hardt X, Geneva 1964, p. 163). In fact, the earliest instance in which σκυτάλη means message stick is Thuc. 1.131 (cf. thereafter Xen. *Hell.* III 3.8-9, V 2.34). It seems to me more likely, therefore, that in both Archilochus and Pindar the word appears in its basic sense, "staff" or "stick" (cf. Chantraine s. v.),

The other side of the "reading" and "writing" Muse, i.e. the "singing" or "talking" book, had already made its appearance early on. In Euripides' *Erechtheus,* for example, the chorus, longing for peace and song, expressed the wish: δέλτων τ' ἀναπτύσσοιμι γᾶρυν / ἇι σοφοὶ κλέονται (fr.60.6-7 in C.Austin, *Nova Fragmenta Euripidea in Papyris Reperta* (Berlin 1968) 32, cf. also the complementary notion of the "writing" voice at Eur. *Alc.* 966f.: οὐδέ τι φάρμακον / Θρήσσαις ἐν σανίσιν, τὰς / Ὀρφεία κατέγραψεν / γῆρυς.). And Theseus, upon reading the tablets left by Phaedra in the *Hippolytus,* exclaimed: βοᾶι βοᾶι δέλτος ἄλαστα· ... οἷον οἷον εἶδον· γραφαῖς μέλος / φθεγγόμενον τλάμων (v. 877-881, cf. also v. 864-865: φέρ' ἐξελίξας περιβολὰς σφραγισμάτων / ἴδω τί λέξαι δέλτος ἥδε μοι θέλει.). To this largely undeveloped idea the Hellenistic poets, true to their bookish bent, brought a cheerful willingness to experiment and elaborate. One result is an entirely new kind of poem: the (presumably) fictitious book inscription.[40]

Characteristically, these inscriptions are not written by the authors of the works which they purport to represent. All the same, they undertake to provide those works with a seal (σφραγίς), identifying its author, giving some small indication of its content and commenting on its quality.[41] The book that speaks in Asclepiades' epigram (32 G-P =

---

here as the attribute of the herald (cf. Hermes' ῥάβδος in *Od.* 5.47 and *H.H.Hermes* 529f. In the 5th cent. we also find the word κηρύκειον). In both poets it is used metaphorically for herald, appositively playing upon or elaborating the previous words: in Archilochus, the speaking name Κηρυκίδης; in Pindar, the ἄγγελος ὀρθός.

It would appear then that, as in the case of *Ol.* 10.1f., the idea of the writing Muse is anachronistic. And as one might expect, Hellenistic poets and scholars frequently mistook their literary past in this way. Thus, in an epigram celebrating Ptolemy IV Philopator's establishment of a temple for Homer (probably between 217-205 B.C.), the poet is described as τῶι πρὶν Ὀδυσσείας τε κ[αὶ Ἰλ]ιάδος τὸν ἀγήρω / ὕμνον ἀπ' ἀθανάτων γραψ[α]μένωι πραπίδων (*SH* 979.4-5). An accidental acrostic, ΛΕΥΚΗ, in the initial letters of *Iliad* 24.1-5 was taken as deliberate by the grammarians and, as J.M.Jacques convincingly argues (*Rev. d. Ét. Anc.*, 62, 1960, 48-61, cf. esp. 49-51), was echoed by Aratus in the acrostic ΛΕΠΤΗ in the *Phaenomena* (v.783-7, for a similar acrostic from roughly the same time cf. Philostephanus of Cyrene in Page, *FGE* p. 21). Such misunderstandings come from the same mentality that produced "die kindische Einteilung" of Homer into the 24 letters of the alphabet (thus K.Lachmann, *Berichte über die Verhandlungen der Akademie der Wissenschaften,* 1846, p. 30 = *Betrachtungen über Homer's Ilias,* ³1874, p. 93).

[40] See, for example, Asclepiades 28 G-P on Erinna's *Distaff*; Leonidas of Tarentum 101 G-P on Aratus' *Phaenomena*; Anon. *AP* 9.190 = Page *FGE* p. 345 on Erinna's *Distaff*; the epigram of Crinagoras (*AP* 9.545 = *Garl. Phil.* 11) may actually have been written in a copy of Callimachus' *Hecale* as it is addressed to a specific reader. On these poems generally cf. M.Gabathuler, *Hellenistische Epigramme auf Dichter* (St.Gallen 1937) 50.

[41] It is interesting to note that, as far as we can see, none of these works had a σφραγίς internal to itself.

AP 9.63) is Antimachus' *Lyde*: "I am Lyde by race and by name, more revered than any of Kodros' line because of Antimachus. For who has not sung me, who is there who has not read Lyde, the joint writing of the Muses and Antimachus?" (Λυδὴ καὶ γένος εἰμὶ καὶ οὔνομα, τῶν δ᾽ ἀπὸ Κόδρου / σεμνοτέρη πασῶν εἰμι δι᾽ Ἀντίμαχον· / τίς γὰρ ἔμ᾽ οὐκ ἤεισε; τίς οὐκ ἀνελέξατο Λυδήν, / τὸ ξυνὸν Μουσῶν γράμμα καὶ Ἀντιμάχου;). Cleverly exploiting the homonymy of title and heroine, the epigram first poses as Lyde herself. By the third line, however, Lyde has merged with her eponymous book. A more straightforward, though no less clever, example of a book taking voice is Callimachus' epigram VI Pf. = 55 G-P in which the poem poses as the *Oichalias Halosis* and, ironically, comments on its own disputed authorship (v. 3-4 ... Ὁμήρειον δὲ καλεῦμαι / γράμμα. Κρεωφύλῳ, Ζεῦ φίλε, τοῦτο μέγα.).[42]

Such epigrams represent an interesting departure from an old tradition. Greeks had long written poems for which they claimed the authorship of others (e.g. Homer, Theognis, etc.), but unlike these, the book inscriptions, while in themselves not proclaiming the identity of their own authors, must nevertheless have circulated freely with little doubt as to their authorship. For although, on one level, they provide their books with a useful σφραγίς, they also represent a seal of approval (or disapproval) from their creators which might amount to a programmatic stance. An identifiable point of view was thus essential. We appreciate the full force of Callimachus' attack on Antimachus in fr. 398 (Λυδὴ καὶ παχὺ γράμμα καὶ οὐ τορόν) only by recognizing that it simultaneously attacks Asclepiades' attitude in Λυδὴ καὶ γένος εἰμὶ καὶ οὔνομα.[43] The fact that, starting in the 3rd cent., a discussion like this (or that about the *Oichalias Halosis*) could transpire within the medium of book inscriptions is a measure of how closely a work was now identified with its written form. Epigrams on a poet might occur from Plato onwards, but epigrams concerning, and - allegedly - inscribed within, a book were new.

A further, though much later, example of a talking book is in Straton *AP* XII 208 (ca. 150 A.D.):

> Εὐτυχές, οὐ φθονέω, βιβλίδιον· ἦ ῥά σ᾽ ἀναγνοὺς
> παῖς τις ἀναθλίβει πρὸς τὰ γένεια τιθεὶς
> ἢ τρυφεροῖς σφίγξει περὶ χείλεσιν ἢ κατὰ μηρῶν
> εἰλήσει δροσερῶν, ὦ μακαριστότατον·
> πολλάκι φοιτήσεις ὑποκόλπιον ἢ παρὰ δίφρους
> βληθὲν τολμήσεις κεῖνα θιγεῖν ἀφόβως.

---

[42] Cf. W. Burkert's persuasive and balanced judgement on this poem, "Die Leistung eines Kreophylos", *MH* 29 (1972) 76f.

[43] Cf. Pfeiffer *ad* fr. 398: *Asclepiadis ipsa verba ad ridiculum convertit.*

πολλὰ δ' ἐν ἠρεμίῃ προλαλήσεις· ἀλλ' ὑπὲρ ἡμῶν,
χαρτάριον, δέομαι, πυκνότερον τι λάλει.

Happy little book, I don't begrudge you; some boy reading you
  will rub you, holding you under his chin,
or press you against his delicate lips, or wind you down
  over his dewy thighs, O most blessed of books!
Often you will wander into his lap or, tossed down on the chair,
  you will dare to touch those things without fear.
And all alone you will chat of many things to him. But little book, I beg,
  say something now and then on my behalf.

This epigram, which adds startling emotional resonance to the word "bibliophile", is a bookish variation on the old theme of the lover who imagines what it would be like to be something with which the object(s) of his desire comes into close physical contact. This is most often expressed in the form of a wish (as, for example in the skolion *PMG* 900: εἴθε λύρα καλὴ γενοίμην ἐλεφαντίνη / καὶ με καλοὶ παῖδες φέροιεν Διονύσιον ἐς χορόν, "would that I were a beautiful ivory lyre and the beautiful boys might carry me into the chorus of Dionysus"), or a makarismos (as in our poem, cf. Meleager *AP* XII 52.3-4 = 81 G-P, where the beloved is at sea: τρὶς μάκαρες νᾶες, τρὶς δ' ὄλβια κύματα πόντου, / τετράκι δ' εὐδαίμων παιδοφορῶν ἄνεμος, "thrice blessed ships, thrice happy waves of the sea, four times lucky wind that carries my boy"). The poet's art, in such poems, consists of varying the object imagined[44] – and the details of the physical contact.[45]

Straton can top past practitioners in this topos simply by using an object – the text – which, unlike those used before, could communicate and, because it was now so utterly familiar (note the tone in the diminutives βιβλίδιον v. 1 and χαρτάριον v. 8), could be readily personified. The book as "friend" – no other object could compete with that![46]

Though shrouded in controversy, an intriguing "paignion" by Philetas of Cos (10, p. 92 Powell) may be an instance of a talking book:[47]

---

[44] For example, *PMG* 901 (a gold ornament); *AP* V 83 (the wind); *AP* V 84 (a rose); Theocr. 3.12-14 (a bee); Rhianos 10 G-P = *AP* XII 142 (a bird); Longus 1.14 (syrinx and goat); Meleager 36 G-P = *AP* V 174 (sleep), 35 G-P = *AP* V 171 (a cup), 81 G-P = *AP* XII 52 (a dolphin); and finally the extreme case of Anacreontea 22 West (a mirror, a gown, water, myrrh, a fillet, a pearl, a sandal). Cf. O. Hiltbrunner, *Gymn.* 77 (1970) 286-287.
[45] For this topos and examples in Latin cf. F. Boemer ad Ovid *Met.* 8.36-7.
[46] It is surprising only that this particular variation on the old theme does not appear earlier. Did Straton find it in a source now lost to us?
[47] Cf. also my expanded discussion in *Rh. M.* 129 (1986) 222-226.

Οὔ μέ τις ἐξ ὀρέων ἀποφώλιος ἀγροιώτης
αἱρήσει κλήθρην, αἱρόμενος μακέλην·
ἀλλ' ἐπέων εἰδὼς κόσμον καὶ πολλὰ μογήσας
μύθων παντοίων οἶμον ἐπιστάμενος.

The speaker identifies herself as a κλήθρη, an alder tree, asserting that no benighted (ἀποφώλιος),[48] mattock-toting[49] mountain rustic will take her, but rather the typical Hellenistic poet who, through his own hard work (πολλὰ μογήσας v. 3), is skilled in song. Alder-wood is fit for a variety of furniture or woodwork. But what does a poet want with the tree; or the tree with a poet? As Stobaeus (II 4,5) locates the poem among the παίγνια, we can expect some sort of "play" to be involved.

The most appealing solution, to my mind, is that the speaker is no tree at all, but a writing tablet made of alder-wood.[50] αἱρήσει κλήθρην, then, is deliberately vague. For in reading the first two lines, κλήθρη is unproblematic: there is no need to take it as anything but a tree, and the fact that ἐξ ὀρέων can go with αἱρήσει rather than ἀγροιώτης reinforces that view. But the second couplet is troubling – as Wilamowitz saw in a literal-minded way: "Wer da gemeint hat, es rede ein Baum, ... der hat ... daran ... nicht (gedacht), daß Philitas keinen Baum fällte,

---

[48] ἀποφώλιος (and by extension the entire paignion) may recall *Od.* 8.167-177. There, the word appears without a negative for the only time in early epic and, as in Philetas, a contrast is drawn between physical ability and skill with words:

οὕτως οὐ πάντεσσι θεοὶ χαρίεντα διδοῦσιν
ἀνδράσιν, οὔτε φυὴν οὔτ' ἂρ φρένας οὔτ' ἀγορητύν.
ἄλλος μὲν γὰρ εἶδος ἀκιδνότερος πέλει ἀνήρ,
ἀλλὰ θεὸς μορφὴν ἔπεσι στέφει, οἱ δέ τ' ἐς αὐτὸν   170
τερπόμενοι λεύσσουσιν· ὁ δ' ἀσφαλέως ἀγορεύει
αἰδοῖ μειλιχίῃ, μετὰ δὲ πρέπει ἀγρομένοισιν,
ἐρχόμενον δ' ἀνὰ ἄστυ θεὸν ὣς εἰσορόωσιν.
ἄλλος δ' αὖ εἶδος μὲν ἀλίγκιος ἀθανάτοισιν,
ἀλλ' οὔ οἱ χάρις ἀμφιπεριστέφεται ἐπέεσσιν·   175
ὣς καὶ σοὶ εἶδος μὲν ἀριπρεπές, οὐδέ κεν ἄλλως
οὐδὲ θεὸς τεύξειε, νόον δ' ἀποφώλιός ἐσσι.

cf. also *LfgrE* s. v. ἀποφώλιος.

[49] αἱρόμενος μακέλην must be taken as a generalizing epithet (parallel to and contrasting with πολλὰ μογήσας for the poet), as was seen by G. Kuchenmüller, *Philetae Coi Reliquiae* (Berlin 1928) p. 61 and 63. Because he tried to imagine the rustic chopping down the tree with a mattock, Wilamowitz thought that the text needed emendation (cf. *HD* I p.116).

[50] Thus first F. Jacobs, *Animadversiones in epigrammata Anthologiae Graecae* I, 1 (Leipzig 1798) 388, followed by Wachsmuth in his apparatus criticus to the passage in Stobaeus and by Kuchenmüller, *op. cit.* p.61. An alternative solution is that the speaker is a poet's staff made from alder-wood. This was the suggestion of E. Maass, *De tribus Philetae carminibus*, Ind. Lect. Marp., 1895, p.96. Cf., however, Bing *Rh. M.* (*op. cit.* n. 47 above) 224-5. For the scholarly literature on this poem cf. I. Cazzaniga, *Riv. di Fil.* 90 (1962) 238-9.

wenn er neue codicilli brauchte" (*HD* I p. 116 n. 1). The answer (as Kuchenmüller saw, *op. cit.* p. 61) is to take κλήθρη as metonymy. Euripides had used πεύκη metonymously for writing tablets at *I. A.* 39 and *Hipp*, 1253 f., and Philetas does so here with the alder. Wilamowitz objected on another ground as well, however. He flatly denied (*op. cit.* p. 116 n. 1) that tablets could be made of alder. While Kuchenmüller could point to the variety of objects for which the alder was used, and could ask "why not for tablets?" (*op. cit.* p. 62), he could not produce an example. We, however, are now in a position to do so. For alder-wood tablets (early 2nd cent. A. D.) were found in great quantity during the mid 1970s at Vindolanda in England.[51] With these objections set aside, then, we can interpret this poem as a special case of the "talking book", that is to say the "talking tablet";[52] but more, to the extent that it is a riddle the poem marks the ties that now exist between writing and song in a particularly dramatic and involving way. It does not merely state the fact of those ties; rather it relies for its affect on their active recognition and acceptance by the reader who wishes to solve the puzzle.

The personifacation was not limited to the book as a whole, but could extend to its parts. Thus, we find the "singing" papyrus columns of Sappho (φθεγγόμεναι σελίδες) in one of Poseidippus' epigrams (17.6 G-P).[52a] The complementary "silenced" papyrus column appears somewhat later in Aceratus (*AP* VII 138.3-4 = *FGE* p. 3): σοῦ δὲ θανόντος, / "Εκτορ, ἐσιγήθη καὶ σελὶς Ἰλιάδος.[53]

Perhaps the most extraordinary development occurs at the end of the *Garland of Meleager* (ca. 100 B. C.) when – for the first time ever, so far

---

[51] Cf. A. K. Bowman and J. D. Thomas, *Historia* 24 (1975) 471-2; A. K. Bowman, *ZPE* 18 (1975) 244-8, and R. Meiggs, *Trees and Timber in the Ancient Mediterranean World* (Oxford 1982) 296.

[52] A late instance of a talking tablet, likewise riddling, is in *AP* XIV 60 (cited by Kuchenmüller, *op. cit.* p. 62):

Ὕλη μέν με τέκεν, καινούργησεν δὲ σίδηρος·
εἰμὶ δὲ Μουσάων μυστικὸν ἐκδόχιον·
κλειομένη σιγῶ· λαλέω δ', ὅταν ἐκπετάσῃς με,
κοινωνὸν τὸν Ἄρη μοῦνον ἔχουσα λόγων.

And even the wax on the tablet takes voice, though again at a late date, in *AP* XIV 45:

Εἰμὶ μέλας, λευκός, ξανθὸς ξηρός τε καὶ ὑγρός·
εὖτε δὲ δουρατέων πεδίων ὕπερ ἐντανύσῃς με,
Ἄρει καὶ παλάμῃ φθέγγομαι οὐ λαλέων.

[52a] Cf. Callimachus *Aetia* fr. 92: Λε]ανδρίδες εἴ τι παλαιαί / φθ[έγγ]ονται[ ]υφαν ἱστορίαι.

[53] Further examples of σελίς are listed by Page in *FGE* p. 342 ad v. 1198.

as I can see - a diacritical sign, the coronis,[54] assumes a persona and speaks for itself (*AP* XII 257 = 129 *G-P*):

Ἁ πύματον καμπτῆρα καταγγέλλουσα κορωνίς,
ἑρκοῦρος γραπταῖς πιστοτάτα σελίσιν,
φαμὶ τὸν ἐκ πάντων ἠθροισμένον εἰς ἕνα μόχθον
ὑμνοθετᾶν βύβλῳ τᾷδ' ἐνελιξάμενον
ἐκτελέσαι Μελέαγρον, ἀείμνηστον δὲ Διοκλεῖ
ἄνθεσι συμπλέξαι μουσοπόλον στέφανον.
οὖλα δ' ἐγὼ καμφθεῖσα δρακοντείοις ἴσα νώτοις
σύνθρονος ἵδρυμαι τέρμασιν εὐμαθίας.

I, who announce the final lap's finish, the coronis,
  trustiest keeper of the bounds of written columns,
I declare that Meleager has finished, he who enrolled
  in this book the labor of all poets gathered
into one, and that it was for Diocles he wove with flowers
  a wreath, whose memory is evergreen.
But I, curled in coils like the back of a snake, am fixed here
  enthroned beside the limits of this learned work.

Meleager has here devised an extremely artful poem in which he has suited style to the peculiarity of the speaker, structure to theme, and the theme itself - by means of word-play - to his book as a whole. In the first place, the "ingeniously complicated" phrasing of v. 3f. (thus Gow-Page *ad loc.*) in which Meleager's work is described, is not an "ineptus tumor" as Graefe put it.[55] On the contrary, it could hardly be more apt: for it reflects the self-avowedly convoluted nature of the coronis: οὖλα δ' ἐγὼ καμφθεῖσα δρακοντείοις ἴσα νώτοις v. 7.

As to structure, there is in this epigram a simple symmetry. The coronis presents itself in the first and last distichs - the two ends of the poem made vivid by the agonistic image of turning post (καμπτήρ v. 1) and finish line (τέρμα v. 8) - while the central verses (3-6) characterize Meleager's Στέφανος. But the word κορωνίς itself gives added point to the form. For a fragment of Stesichorus' *Helen* teaches us that this word can mean "wreath": *PMG* 187.3 καὶ ῥοδίνους στεφάνους ἴων τε κορωνίδας οὔλας. Indeed, Meleager may be alluding to this verse with κορωνίς v. 1 and οὖλα v. 7. In this light, the first and last distichs do not just frame, they set a wreath around Meleager's work. And, by a playful twist which rounds out the agonistic image, the wreath crowns the wreath (στέφανος v. 6) which Meleager has just completed.

That it actually became common to place coronis-poems at the end of a scroll is suggested by the undistinguished example at the end of an

---

[54] On the coronis generally cf. G. M. Stephen, *Scriptorium* 13 (1959) 3f.
[55] Cf. Gow-Page's introduction to the poem.

Iliad papyrus, P. Lit. Lond. 11, of the 1st cent. A.D. The text is that of A. Wifstrand, *Hermes* 68 (1933) 468:

ἐγὼ κορωνίς εἰμι γραμμάτων φύλαξ.
καλαμός μ' ἔγραψε, δεξιὰ χεὶρ καὶ γόνυ.
ἄν τινί με χρήσῃς, ἕτερον ἀντιλάμβανε·
ἐὰν δὲ μ' ἀλείφῃς, διαβαλῶ σ' Εὐριπίδῃ.
ἄπεχε.

I am coronis, guardian of letters.
The reed wrote me down, the right hand and the knee.
If you lend me to anyone, put another in may place;
but if you soil me, I will slander you to Euripides.
Keep away!

For our part, we may mark the end of this sectioin with a 1st cent. B.C. epigram by Philodemus (*AP* XI 41 = *Garl. Phil.* 17) which, it has been argued, was itself intended to crown a collection (cf. A.H. Griffiths, *BICS* 17 [1970] 37-38). The poem brings us back to the lettered Muses, whom the poet here beseeches to write a coronis (i.e. put an end) to his amatory sufferings: αὐτὴν ἀλλὰ τάχιστα κορωνίδα γράψατε, Μοῦσαι, / ταύτην ἡμετέρης, δεσπότιδες, μανίης. Such metaphorical use of the "writing" Muse bespeaks just how familiar she was to the literary scene (cf. also Martial X 1.1). But her familiarity surpassed even that. As early as the 2nd cent. B.C., she had filtered down to inscriptions for the common man. An epitaph of an ephebe from Chios says that he died while blossoming – not with the Muses' song, but with the columns of their *writing* (ἄρτι δ' ἐφηβείας θάλλων Διονύσιος ἀκμαῖς / καὶ σελίσιν Μουσῶν ἤλυθον εἰς Ἀΐδαν *GV* 945 Peek).[56]

Having traced the new importance of the book, its impact on the poet's self-image, the consequent emergence of the writing and reading Muse, we now turn to some of the implications. Here, the reading Muse is of special importance. For the ability to read will mean that the Muse may provide a poet with that which he may readily acquire with his own two eyes – by reading himself – and it is only a short step before the Muses' inspiration and the written record become one and the same.

Is this in fact what happened? Had the Muses become no more than an emblem for the written tradition?

On a purely concrete level – leaving the Muses aside for a moment – we know that poets could indeed now find their inspiration in books. Aratus of Soloi wrote a didactic poem on astronomy (the *Phaenomena*)

---

[56] See also now the epitaph of a doctor from Arcadia, 2nd cent. B.C., who says ξυνὸν ἐγὼ δόξας ἑλόμαν ἐν παισὶ ἄεθλον, / Πιερίδων ἱεραῖς τερπόμενος σελίσιν v. 1-2, cf. G.J. M.J. Te Riele, *Chiron* 14 (1984) 238-243.

based on a prose treatise by Eudoxus of Cnidus. This is our first example of a poem based on a book. Aratus himself, according to Cicero (*De Orat.* I 69), had no practical experience of astronomy whatsoever. Callimachus wrote an epigram on the *Phaenomena* in which he praises the delicate verses, calling the work "a token of sleeplessness" (σύμβολον ἀγρυπνίης *Ep.* 27.4 Pf. = 56 *G-P*). The reference, of course, is to the long nights spent by Aratus watching the stars. The attentive reader, however, will catch the ironic point: the stars that Aratus watched during his long sleepless nights were mainly those in the book of Eudoxus.

One is tempted to see a famous fragment of Callimachus in this light as well. Here he states: "I sing nothing that is unattested" (ἀμάρτυρον οὐδὲν ἀείδω fr. 612). To a Homeric singer, this would certainly mean that the Muses were there, that they witnessed the event described. But what would it mean to the Hellenistic poet? Nothing unattested by whom? By the Muse? By the written record? Both, perhaps? We cannot know since the context of the fragment is lost.

We are beset by similar questions in an invocation from the *Hymn to Artemis* (v. 183–186).

>   τίς δὲ νύ τοι νήσων, ποῖον δ' ὄρος εὔαδε πλεῖστον,
>   τίς δὲ λιμήν, ποίη δὲ πόλις; τίνα δ' ἔξοχα νυμφέων
>   φίλαο καὶ ποίας ἡρωίδας ἔσχες ἑταίρας;
>   εἰπέ, θεή, σὺ μὲν ἄμμιν, ἐγὼ δ' ἑτέροισιν ἀείσω.

>   Which then of islands, what mountain gives most delight,
>   which harbor, what city? Which of the nymphs do you especially
>   love and what heroines did you take as companions?
>   Speak, goddess, you to me, and I will sing it to others.

Callimachus' model is evidently Pindar's invocation of the Muse in fr. 150 (Snell-Maehler): μαντεύεο, Μοῖσα, προφατεύσω δ' ἐγώ ("Speak the oracle, Muse, and I will act as interpreter"). Yet by a bold stroke the Hellenistic author drops the Muse and turns with his questions to the very topic of his work, the goddess Artemis. In cross-examining his theme, however, is he still addressing a goddess? Is this Artemis? or her embodiment in the written tradition? Can one still distinguish between them? A single passage in earlier epic is comparable, *Iliad* 16.692f. where the singer, here the Homeric bard, likewise invokes his theme:

>   ἔνθα τίνα πρῶτον, τίνα δ' ὕστατον ἐξενάριξας,   692
>   Πατρόκλεις, ὅτε δή σε θεοὶ θανατόνδε κάλεσσαν;
>   Ἄδρηστον μὲν πρῶτα καὶ Αὐτόνοον καὶ Ἔχεκλον…
>   τοὺς ἕλεν· οἱ δ' ἄλλοι φύγαδε μνώοντο ἕκαστος.   697

Poetic Inspiration and the Poet's Self Image 37

Which then did you slay first, which last,
Patroklos, when the gods summoned you deathwards?
Adrastos first, then Autonoos and Echeklos...
These he killed, but the others' thoughts turned to flight.

The startling similarity between these passages provokes us to ponder all the more the gulf in time and technology that lies between them. For it is improbable that the mentality of two poets separated by over 400 years should have remained the same. May we see, then, in the question put to Patroklos an invocation of the oral-, in that to Artemis an invocation of the written tradition?

Perhaps a closer look at the life of a poet in this "bookish" Age, as Pfeiffer calls it (*Hist.*, 102 f.), will help us towards an answer. The artist most clearly epitomizing his time is one we have often mentioned already: namely Callimachus. Like most of his contemporaries, Callimachus was not raised in Alexandria. It was the prospect of royal patronage in a stimulating cultural milieu that drew him away from his native Cyrene in Libya. Nor was he disappointed. Having won the favor of the king, he soon had access first to a circle of scholars and poets who were participating in an exciting controversy on poetic theory; and then to the Ptolemaic court itself with its political intrigues, its religious and governmental statecraft. His position was that of "cataloguer" in the library of Alexandria; his greatest scholarly achievement was the system of lists, or "Pinakes", which arranged the books not simply by author, but generically. Callimachus thus fits perfectly the description in an epigram by Poseidippus (*AP* XII 98 = 6 G-P), where the poet is seen as the traditional Μουσῶν τέττιξ (v. 1) but his ψυχή is ἐν βύβλοις πεπονημένη (v. 3).

One might go so far as to say, then, that the real world for such a scholar or poet was largely the world of books. And we sense this because distinctions that had previously held true when the outside world was primary are here no longer valid. Regional boundaries, for instance, can now be stressed, now ignored. A person or place can exist wherever one finds it in a book.

Thus, in the prologue to Poseidippus' epigrams (mentioned above), the poet bids the Muses come to Pipleian Thebes: εἰς δὲ τὰ Θήβης / τεί- χεα Πιπ[λ]είης βαίνετε †...αλαδες † (v. 7-8).[57] Whether this Thebes was

---

[57] This is the text of Lloyd-Jones, *JHS* 83 (1963) 75 f., constituted from new photographs of the wax tablets in Berlin and with the palaeographical assistance of J. W. B. Barns (cf. his notes on the reading of v. 8, p. 79). It accords basically with that of W. Schubart, *Symbolae Philologicae O. A. Danielsson octogenario dicatae* (1932) 290 f., D. L. Page, *GLP* I #114 p. 470 f., and E. Heitsch, *Abh. d. Ak. d. Wiss. in Göttingen, phil.-hist. Kl., dritte Folge* 49 (1961, 1) 21, all three of whom thought, as do I, that Πιπ[λ]είης is attrib-

in Egypt or Boeotia,[58] Pipleia, the Muses' birthplace, was far away in Thrace. Poseidippus invokes the goddesses, however, as "fellow-citizen Muses", Μοῦσαι πολιήτιδες (v. 1), because to his mind Thebes is a second Pipleia. The systematic gathering of isolated local traditions under one roof, that is in a library, effectively freed those traditions from their purely regional significance and meant that Pipleia, for instance, existed wherever it was experienced in the written word.[59] It now also becomes clear how Callimachus, in his 13th *Iambos,* can refute his critics when they complain that he writes iambic poetry in the style of Hipponax without having gone to Ephesus (home of Hipponax) or mingled with Ionians.[60] Hipponax is in Alexandria, for Callimachus conjures him up as a ghost for his poem (fr. 191).

---

utive with Θήβης. In v. 8, Lloyd-Jones and Parsons (*SH* 705) are more circumspect, printing only τείχεα Πιπ[ ]...ς βαίνετε...αλαδες. This reading appears to reflect Lloyd-Jones' conviction that Πιπ[λ]είης was more probably "followed by either a noun meaning something like 'daughters of', 'dwellers in', or (likelier) 'ones born in' (sc. Pipleia), or else perhaps an adverb or a group of words containing an adjective or adverb on which Πιπ[λ]είης depended" (*JHS op. cit.* p. 86), for – as noted in the app. crit. of the *SH* ad v. 8 – he considers Pipleian Thebes, "id est 'Pipleis Musis acceptae'", a "mira locutio". Yet in the twenty years between the article in *JHS* and the *SH*, he was unable to find a satisfactory supplement for -αλαδες to support his interpretation. His assessment, moreover, will appear to be based on too narrow an understanding of Pipleian Thebes.

[58] For this discussion cf. Lloyd-Jones, *JHS* 83 (1963) 86.

[59] This is not to say that regional distinctions died out. On the contrary, the great majority of Hellenistic poets continued to write works of mainly local interest, often for popular consumption, that celebrated the history and achievements of particular communities and of their rulers; such was the thesis of K. Ziegler's book, *Das hellenistische Epos: ein vergessenes Kapitel der griechischen Dichtung* (Leipzig 1934, rev. 1966), now clearly confirmed through the multitude of regional poems collected in the *SH*, cf. Lloyd-Jones, *SIFC* 77 (1984) 58.

This popular, local poetry had a separate existence from that produced in the Alexandrian Museum or other places in which libraries became the focal point of literary production. B. Gentili, "Poeta e musico in Grecia" in *Oralità Scrittura Spettaculo, op. cit.* (n. 14 above) p. 73, has eloquently described the dichotomy: "Accanto a questa cultura più propriamente letteraria ed erudita, che fiorì nell'ambito ristretto delle corti e dei cenacoli, patrimonio esclusivo di un'élite di intellettuali, ebbe vita autonoma un'altra forma di cultura, che con termine moderno potremmo definire 'popolare' o 'di massa', nel senso che era destinata a larghe fasce di fruitori e trasmessa oralmente in pubbliche audizioni, da parte di recitatori, cantori e attori itineranti (*rhapsoidoi, kitharoidoi, auloidoi, tragoidoi, komoidoi* etc.), che esercitavano la loro professione ottenendo compensi e onori negli agoni e nelle feste istituite dalle diverse città del mondo ellenizzato. Dunque, una cultura itinerante, che aveva la funzione d'intrattenere larghi uditori, diffondendo il sapere relativo ai miti panellenici o ai miti locali, da cui prendeva le mosse la storia delle singole città."

[60] The primary meaning of this complaint is that Callimachus does not follow his model, Hipponax, closely enough (cf. D. L. Clayman, *Callimachus' Iambi*, Leiden 1980, p. 45). But the notion that poets made "pilgrimages" to places especially connected with those they wished to emulate, is not just a metaphor. Aspiring tragedians visited the tomb

A radical manifestation of this trend to liberate poetic themes from their native soil is the Hellenistic vogue for fictitious epitaphs and votive inscriptions to commemorate every kind of person and object from all corners of the Greek world. A dramatic instance appears in a pair of "sepulchral" epigrams by Dioscorides (active in Egypt, late 3rd cent. B. C.). In the first, a statue of a satyr standing atop the tomb of Sophocles and holding a tragic mask relates to a passerby the evolution of Tragedy out of Satyr Play, and Sophocles' role therein (*AP* VII 37 = 22 G-P):

> Τύμβος ὅδ' ἔστ', ὤνθρωπε, Σοφοκλέος, ὃν παρὰ Μουσῶν
>   ἱρὴν παρθεσίην ἱερὸς ὢν ἔλαχον,
> ὅς με τὸν ἐκ Φλιοῦντος ἔτι τρίβολον πατέοντα
>   πρίνινον ἐς χρύσεον σχῆμα μεθηρμόσατο
> καὶ λεπτὴν ἐνέδυσεν ἁλουργίδα. τοῦ δὲ θανόντος
>   εὔθετον ὀρχηστὴν τῇδ' ἀνέπαυσα πόδα...

> This is the tomb of Sophocles, friend, whom the Muses entrusted,
>   a sacred pledge, to my consecrated hands.
> It was he who, when I was still treading the rude threshing sledge
>   in Phlius, adapted me to the golden show
> and dressed me in delicate purple. But now that he's dead
>   I have stayed here the foot that danced so well...

In the second (*AP* VII 707 = 23 G-P), the speaker is likewise a satyr-statue, this time astride the tomb of the Hellenistic dramatist Sositheos:

> Κἠγὼ Σωσιθέου κομέω νέκυν, ὅσσον ἐν ἄστει
>   ἄλλος ἀπ' αὐθαίμων ἡμετέρων Σοφοκλῆν,
> Σκιρτὸς ὁ πυρρογένειος· ἐκισσοφόρησε γὰρ ὡνήρ
>   ἄξια Φλιασίων, ναὶ μὰ χοροὺς, Σατύρων
> κἠμὲ τὸν ἐν καινοῖς τεθραμμένον ἤθεσιν ἤδη
>   ἤγαγεν εἰς μνήμην πατρίδ' ἀναρχαΐσας...

> I too, Frisky the red-beard, stand guard at a tomb, the tomb of
>   Sositheos,
>   Just as one of my brothers in town stands guard
> over Sophocles. For Sositheos carried the ivy crown,
>   a man worthy – yes, by the chorus – of satyrs from Phlius.
> And me, who had already been nurtured in modern ways, he made me
>   recall my homeland by reverting to archaic practice...

With the words κἠγώ, "I too" (v. 1), the satyr explicitly refers to his kin on the tomb from the previous poem. As he goes on to praise

---

of Aeschylus (*Vita* A 11), and the poetess Nossis (*AP* VII 718 = 11 G-P) assumes that people journey to Mitylene to be "inspired" by Sappho's graces (cf. Gow-Page's n. ad ἀναυσόμενος v. 2, and generally M. Treu, „Selbstzeugnisse alexandrinischer Dichter", *Miscellanea di studi alessandrini in memoria di A. Rostagni* (Torino 1963) 277-281.

Sositheos for having restored Satyr Play (or Drama in general) to its original form, i.e. for having accomplished precisely the opposite of his Classical counterpart, it becomes clear that the poem offsets and complements the one about Sophocles. In short, they are meant to be read as a pair, and moreover in sequence. Now if these are genuine sepulchral inscriptions, we must assume that they stood sufficiently close to permit such concrete and sequential cross-reference. Yet close physical proximity is challenged from within: ἐν ἄστει, "in town" (v. 1, second poem), implies that while Sophocles was buried in the city (i.e. in Athens), Sositheos was not. And further doubt is cast when we recall that, in the *Vita*, Sophocles was not interred "in town" at all, but at Decelea with his ancestors, and on his tomb was no satyr but either a Siren (cf. Paus. I 21.1) or a swallow made of bronze (cf. Gow-Page, intro. to *AP* VII 37 = 22 G-P). The inscriptions, then, are a fiction. Their sequential connection – κἠγώ, "I too" (v. 1) – is that between neighboring texts *on the page*. No real tomb, statue or inscription need come into play any more: implicit in the unassuming καί of κἠγώ is nothing less than the entire transformation of the world into an interior, literary landscape.

Thus, not just the poet's life, which we looked at before, but also their works offer a clear sign that these poets existed in a world of books. Is it not significant, then, that that world itself was situated, as it seems, in the Muses' domain, that is in their shrine, the Museum of Alexandria?[61] The implications of the "reading" Muse, namely that the goddess' inspiration and the written record could become very nearly the same, are made the more substantial through the coincidence of the Muses' domain and the book-world of the poet. Together, they strongly suggest that books have become the vehicle, at least, of poetic inspiration, if not its equivalent. But perhaps they are now even that:

In his *Hymn to Delos* (v. 55 ff.), Callimachus tells of Leto's search for a place to give birth to Apollo, her son by Zeus. But Hera, Zeus' wife, does her utmost to prevent this, and, to that end, intimidates the localities into refusing asylum for Leto. Wherever Leto appears, the localities flee. Callimachus here plays with the tradition that all places have their eponymous gods, from which they are virtually indistinguishable. By pressing this to its humorous extreme, he shows that it is problematical: what, asks the poet, if an entire landscape suddenly took to its heels and no place was left for Apollo's birth?

This amusing, yet unsettling experiment is brought to a climax when the nymph Melie is sent reeling from the dance upon seeing her tree endangered by the flight of Mt. Helikon. Here, as though no longer

---

[61] For the strong probability that the library was located in the Museum cf. P. M. Fraser, *op. cit.* (n. 38 above) p. 324–5 with n. 145, and p. 335.

able to bear the uncertainty, the poet breaks into the narrative in mid-verse (v. 82) and demands that his Muses set him straight:[62] "did trees really come into being at the same time as nymphs?" (ἦ ῥ' ἐτεὸν ἐγένοντο τότε δρύες ἡνίκα Νύμφαι; v. 83, a play on the name "hamadryads"), i.e. is the life of a place and its god really one?

The interpretation of the next two lines (v. 84-85) which, as we shall see, has direct bearing on the distinctions we have been trying to draw between the Muses' inspiration and the written record, is problematical. Yet the difficulty is belied by the outward form of the couplet, which is lucid and symmetrical:

Νύμφαι μὲν χαίρουσιν, ὅτε δρύας ὄμβρος ἀέξει,
Νύμφαι δ'αὖ κλαίουσιν, ὅτε δρυσὶν οὐκέτι φύλλα.[63]

The Nymphs rejoice when rain makes the oaks grow tall
The Nymphs lament when there are no longer leaves on the oaks

With the symmetry of these verses, Callimachus stresses the special sympathy between nymphs and trees. The behavior of the nymphs in the first half of each line is linked causally to the condition of the trees in the second, and the corresponding phrases in the two lines reflect a relationship that is constant even under changing circumstances. Each verse begins with the same word (Νύμφαι); μέν corresponds to δ' αὖ. There is deliberate assonance between χαίρουσιν and κλαίουσιν. After a penthemimeral caesura, both lines begin with the same words (ὅτε

---

[62] This unusual and strongly adversative mid-verse switch from third person narrative to direct address is all the more startling as it deliberately breaks with old epic convention in which the Muses were invoked only at the start of a poem or section. In the words of E. Howald and E. Staiger, Die Dichtungen des Kallimachos (Zürich 1955) 101, "das ist wohl der Gipfel des unverfrorenen Spieles mit der Tradition, der gewagteste Mißbrauch der epischen Muse."Cf. H. Reinsch-Werner, Callimachus Hesiodicus (Berlin 1976) 191. For Callimachus' uses of direct speech generally in the hymns, cf. G. R. McLennan, Callimachus, Hymn to Zeus (Rome 1977) Appendix II p. 144-149.

[63] The reading of P. Alex. 547 by A. C. Mancini, Ann. d. Sc. Norm. Sup. di Pisa, Cl. di lett. e filos., ser. III 2 (1972) 502-5, pl. XXXV, and Pap. Lett. Greci, ed. A. Carlini etc. (Pisa 1978) 12, pl. V, assures the final ν in δρυσίν and hence confirms οὐκέτι of the MSS. Pfeiffer's μηκέτι is based on the appearance, in one papyrus, of δρυσιμ[(P. Oxy. 2225), which might easily be an error. Perhaps Pfeiffer was thinking of the Hellenistic tendency to substitute μή for οὐ (Schwyzer II 594, cf. e.g. Call., Hymn III 64-5: κείνους [scil. the Cyclopes] γε καὶ αἱ μάλα μηκέτι τυτθαί / οὐδέποτ' ἀφρικτὶ μακάρων ὁρόωσι θύγατρες. and Bornmann's n. ad loc: "in età ellenistica si preferisce decisamente μή a οὐ"), a freedom that extended to causal and temporal clauses (cf. Schwyzer II 595, bottom of page, and KG II 188c). We cannot, however, argue that μηκέτι is lectio difficilior, as does Mineur ad loc., because for the scribe writing P. Oxy. 2225 in the 2nd cent. A.D. - by which time the preference for μή would have been well established - the reverse might very well have been the case. Thus, though we cannot rule μηκέτι out, the weight of the evidence, that is the occurence of οὐκέτι in a papyrus and the undeviating testimony of

δρύας / ὅτε δρυσί), ending at the bucolic diaeresis.[64] All word ends come at the same position except ὄμβρος and οὐκέτι (though perhaps "Wortbild"). Both lines consist of 15 syllables each.[65] Yet the sympathy, which is manifest even in the outward form of the lines, does not mean that nymphs and trees are identical or live coterminous lives. On the contrary, it makes all the more critical the uncertainty which Callimachus has caused (and which it is in his interest to maintain) with the flight of the localities.

That uncertainty is exacerbated by the further difficulty of knowing to whom to attribute these lines. Wilamowitz and Pfeiffer set the verses in quotation marks, taking them to be the Muses' reply. And indeed, they have a wise and traditional ring that befits the goddesses of song. On the other hand, no speaker is indicated and we cannot assume, as Wilamowitz does (*HD* II 67), that the change would have been felt in the reciter's intonation. One might well take the couplet as a gnome, added asyndetically, with which the poet supports his question.[66] In that case, the Muses would give no answer at all, the question would remain open and the strange effect of the localities' flight simply continue.[67]

A third possibility is that the uncertainty of attribution is natural. Perhaps it does not matter whether the couplet is a gnome or the utterance of the Muses. For, at a time when Mnemosyne's daughters characteristically assist a poet in recalling the "recorded" past, the difference will in fact be very small. With its venerable, apophthegmatic quality, the couplet has the appearance of something sanctioned by the literary tradition, which to a large extent is what the Muses now embodied.

If this is so, it may be of help in explaining the cultivated ambiguity in the sense of the couplet. For that ambiguity faithfully reflects the literary heritage – as we can see from a glance at what the tradition had to say about nymphs and their trees. According to the *Homeric Hymn to Aphrodite,* an early and detailed source, when the nymphs are born

---

the manuscripts, favors our retaining οὐκέτι in the text while letting μηκέτι appear in the app. crit.

[64] In Fränkel's terminology, the most "harmonious" caesura, cf. "Der homerische und kallimacheische Hexameter", *Wege und Formen frühgriechischen Denkens* (Munich 1968) 128 #21 and 141 ad v. 2.

[65] For a similar analysis cf. L. Koenen, "Die Adaption ägyptischer Königsideologie am Ptolemäerhof", in *Egypt and the Hellenistic World, Proceedings of the International Colloquium Leuven – 24–26 May 1982* (Leuven 1983) 177 n. 95.

[66] Cf. *KG* II 345 for asyndeton with maxims following a question. This is also the interpretation of Körte-Händel, *Die Hellenistische Dichtung* (Stuttgart 1960) 36.

[67] There is a similar problem at Hymn 1.7–8 (πότεροι, πάτερ, ἐψεύσαντο; / "Κρῆτες ἀεὶ ψεῦσται"), where the quote may not represent the answer of Zeus, to whom the question is addressed (cf. McLennan ad v. 7 and ch. 2 p. 76 n. 42 below).

"pines or high topped oaks spring up with them…, but when the fate of death is near at hand, first those lovely trees wither where they stand, and the bark shrivels away about them, and the twigs fall down, and at last the life of the nymph and of the tree leave the light of the sun together" (v. 264-272):

τῇσι δ' ἅμ ἢ ἐλάται ἠὲ δρύες ὑψικάρηνοι
γεινομένῃσιν ἔφυσαν ἐπὶ χθονὶ βωτιανείρῃ… 265
ἀλλ' ὅτε κεν δὴ μοῖρα παρεστήκῃ θανάτοιο 269
ἀζάνεται μὲν πρῶτον ἐπὶ χθονὶ δένδρεα καλά,
φλοιὸς δ' ἀμφιπεριφθινύθει, πίπτουσι δ' ἀπ' ὄζοι,
τῶν δέ χ' ὁμοῦ ψυχὴ λείποι φάος ἠελίοιο.

This tradition is followed by Pindar, among others, who tells how Rhoikos saved a drooping tree by supporting it with a vine prop. The nymph subsequently admits to him that she would have died, "having been allotted a term as long as the years of a tree", ἰσοδένδρου τέκμαρ αἰῶνος θεόφραστον λαχοῖσα (fr. 165 Snell-Maehler).[68]

On the other hand, Plutarch (*de def. orac.* 415 c-d) quotes "Hesiod" (fr. 304 M-W), a source easily as venerable as the Homeric Hymn or Pindar (and a passage known to Callimachus, cf. fr. 260.42 and Pfeiffer's n.), as saying that Naiads outlive their trees, explicitly contrasting this fragment with that of Pindar mentioned above: "Nine generations long is the life of the crow and his cawing, / nine generations of vigorous men. Lives of four crows together / equal the life of a stag, and three stags the old age of a raven; / nine lives of the raven equal the life of the Phoenix; / ten of the Phoenix we fair-haired nymphs, daughters of Zeus of the aegis".

ἐννέα τοι ζώει γενεὰς λακέρυζα κορώνη
ἀνδρῶν ἡβώντων· ἔλαφος δέ τε τετρακόρωνος·
τρεῖς δ' ἐλάφους ὁ κόραξ γηράσκεται· αὐτὰρ ὁ φοῖνιξ
ἐννέα τοὺς κόρακας· δέκα δ' ἡμεῖς τοὺς φοίνικας
νύμφαι εὐπλόκαμοι, κοῦραι Διὸς αἰγιόχοιο.

Plutarch calculates that the nymph thus lives 9720 years!

Or again, contemporary with Callimachus, there is the strange scene in Apollonios of Rhodes' *Argonautica*, where the nymphs known as Hesperides turn into dust and earth in fear at the Argonauts' coming,

---

[68] There is a similar story in Eumelos fr. 15 Kinkel. And in the scholia to *Il.* 6.22 we hear that nymphs συναύξεσθαι μὲν αὐτοῖς τοῖς δένδρεσι, αὐαινομένων δὲ αὐτῶν καὶ ξηραινομένων συναποθνῄσκειν. Likewise, in Ovid's version of the Erysichthon myth (*Met.* 8.738 ff.) the nymph and her tree are indistinguishable (cf. esp. 762 *fluxit discusso cortice sanguis*, and her dying words, v. 771-773, *Nympha sub hoc ego sum Cereri gratissima ligno, / quae tibi factorum poenas instare tuorum / vaticinor moriens, nostri solacia leti*).

but then, pitying their plight, grow back into trees, miraculously completing the entire natural development of a tree in a moment (4.1423-30): "First grass sprang up from the ground; then long shoots appeared above the grass; and in a moment three saplings, tall, straight and in full leaf, were growing there, Hespere became a poplar; Erytheis an elm; Aegle a sacred willow. Yet they were still themselves; the trees could not conceal their former shapes – and that was the greatest wonder of all".

> ... καὶ δὴ χθονὸς ἐξανέτειλαν
> ποίην πάμπρωτον, ποίης γε μὲν ὑψόθι μακροί
> βλάστεον ὄρπηκες, μετὰ δ' ἔρνεα τηλεθάοντα
> πολλὸν ὑπὲρ γαίης ὀρθοσταδὸν ἠέξοντο·
> Ἑσπέρη αἴγειρος, πτελέη δ' Ἐρυθηὶς ἔγεντο,
> Αἴγλη δ' ἰτείης ἱερὸν στύπος. ἐκ δέ νυ κείνων
> δενδρέων, οἷαι ἔσαν, τοῖαι πάλιν ἔμπεδον αὕτως
> ἐξέφανεν, θάμβος περιώσιον...

Here, the trees and their nymphs are clearly not coeval.[69]

We see, then, that the literary tradition itself had no consistent answer. Callimachus, of course, was often set before conflicting traditions and would have to choose between them (thus, for example, the disputed location of Zeus' birth in Hymn 1.5f., ἐν δοιῇ μάλα θυμός, ἐπεὶ γένος ἀμφήριστον..., where he picks Arcadia over Crete). But here it is as though he takes the Muses' raw material and, because it suits his purpose in this Hymn, decides to skip the choice.[70] The Muses respond ambiguously, or fail to respond at all, because they embody the tradition and give it voice. For Callimachus, working in Egypt, this means that they are virtually synonymous with the library of Alexandria.

In reaching such a conclusion, I do not mean to imply that they had become a hollow convention – though one may have doubts later on, when Muses and books become indistinguishable (thus, in the 1st cent. B.C./A.D. epigram by Euenus, cf. p.19 above, a bookworm is told φεῦγ' ἀπὸ Μουσάων, i.e. keep away from the books; and a 4th cent.

---

[69] On the relationship of nymphs and trees generally cf. A. Henrichs, "Thou shalt not kill a tree", *Bull. Amer. Soc. of Papyr.* 16 (1979) esp. 85-87.

[70] Most scholars insist that the couplet represents a clear-cut choice. But the even split in opinions for and against coeval lives just goes to show the inherent ambiguity. Among those arguing for, see K. Kuiper, *Studia Callimachea* I (Leiden 1896) 130 and L. Koenen, op. cit. (n.66 above) 177 n.95; against, see Wilamowitz, *HD* II p.67, E. Howald and E. Staiger, op. cit. (n.63 above) 101, 109 n. ad 79f., and Mineur ad v.82. So far as I can see, only K.J. McKay, *Erysichthon, A Callimachean Comedy*, Mnem. Suppl. 7 (Leiden 1962) 177 and Reinsch-Werner, op. cit. (n.63 above) 188, 192, take the position that the ambiguity is deliberate and functional in the poem.

A. D. worm in Symphosius, XVI Buecheler, boasts "Littera me pavit ...exedi Musas"). In the 3rd cent. B. C., however, the Muses' sphere of action had simply moved to that same microcosm where the poet now functioned, namely in his books. There, they were very much alive and, like the books themselves, exerted a strong fascination on the poet. The shift in the Muses' domain and the open acknowledgement of the book in the poet's self-image were the final steps in a long process through which the "written" word had come to ever greater prominence (in the early parts of this chapter we traced its progress up through the philosophical schools). But the crucial push, in my view, that propelled those final steps, at last dislodging performance as the primary reality of verse (cf. p. 16 f. above), was the establishment of the great Hellenistic libraries, in particular that of Alexandria. It was only then that that "little world" of books became sufficiently ample not just to contain the collected tradition of the Greeks, but to assert itself as *the* essential fact in the poet's life - a fact that, tradition notwithstanding, he could no longer ignore.

From the new perspective of this microcosm, the poets (as appeared in the breakdown of regional distinctions) reinterpreted the world outside. And perhaps even Alexandria was recast in terms of this "lettered" aesthetic: The city, it seems, was divided into sectors called γράμματα, after the five initial letters of the alphabet.[71] This was not in itself an unusual practice. It seems to have become customary in Ptolemaic Egypt to call a city district γράμμα (cf. Preisigke s. v. and *Suppl*. Abschn. 22 s. v.). And even in the 5th century B. C. we find similar phenomena. Each Athenian tribe, for instance, was divided into ten μέρη, α through κ, and the courts were designated by letters starting with λ.[72] The original significance of the Alexandrian example was doubtless no different, the letters merely forming a recognizable set in a standard order. But a late source, pseudo-Callisthenes (I 32), thought otherwise, and in thinking so expressed something essential about this quintessentially bookish city.

For him, the letters conveyed a message: Ἐκέλευσεν (scil. Alexander) οὖν κτίζεσθαι τὴν πόλιν. θεμελιώσας δὲ τὸ πλεῖστον μέρος τῆς πόλεως Ἀλέξανδρος καὶ χωρογραφήσας ἐπέγραψε γράμματα πέντε· Α Β Γ Δ Ε· τὸ μὲν Α Ἀλέξανδρος, τὸ δὲ βῆτα βασιλεύς, τὸ δὲ γάμμα γένος, τὸ δὲ

---

[71] Cf. Philo of Alexandria, *In Flacc.* 55: πέντε μοῖραι τῆς πόλεώς εἰσιν, ἐπώνυμοι τῶν πρώτων στοιχείων τῆς ἐγγραμμάτου φωνῆς, and Ps. Call. I 32, which I discuss below. On the division generally cf. A. Calderini, *Dizionario dei Nomi Geografici e Topografici dell' Egitto Greco-Romano* I, 1 (Cairo 1935) 79 f.

[72] Cf. Aristot. *Ath. Pol.* 63.2-4 with the comments of P. J. Rhodes, *A Commentary on the Aristotelian Athenaion Politeia* (Oxford 1981) 702 and 704, and Aristoph. *Eccl.* 683 f.

δέλτα Διός, τὸ δὲ Ε ἔκτισεν πόλιν ἀμίητον (Alexander ordered the city to be founded. And after having laid the foundations for most of the city and plotted it out, he wrote on them five letters: Α Β Γ Δ Ε. The Α 'Alexander', the beta 'king' [βασιλεύς], the gamma 'offspring' [γένος], the delta 'of Zeus' [Διός], the epsilon 'founded' [ἔκτισεν] an inimitable city). The message with which pseudo-Callisthenes invests the letters of Alexandria gives them a meaning independent of and transcending their significance simply as members of a set. That is to say, he makes them function specifically as letters qua letters, (not just as ciphers), activating them as vehicles of communication. To be sure, in an era inclined to view letters as significant, i.e. the Hellenistic and its aftermath, the Alexandrian letters invited interpretation. But it is peculiarly apt that this city, that did more than any other to institutionalize the use of letters – as written objects – for communication, should be singled out in such a way that the letters representing its constituent parts and collectively symbolizing its totality are made to communicate a message; in other words, that the city itself is made a text.

The rise of the book with the establishment of the great libraries seemed to offer a fresh start and countless poetic paths upon which to set out. To paraphrase Pfeiffer (*Hist.* p. 88), if poetry was to be rescued from the dangerous situation in which it lay by the end of the 5th and in the 4th century, the means to do so were now at hand.

The aesthetic theory which came to guide the attempt was, I believe, well suited to the revolution brought on by the full acknowledgment and use of writing by the Hellenistic poets. Whereas an oral culture promotes expression that is fluent, voluble and fulsome,[73] its poetry marked by redundancy and great length, the technology of writing fosters a spare and finely etched style. Once again, the most prominent spokesman of the new Age is Callimachus. "A big book is a big evil", he says in a famous fragment (fr. 465). Callimachus championed the "small" poetic form (cf. fr. 1.5 ἔπος δ' ἐπὶ τυτθὸν ἑλ[ίσσω and the ὀλίγη λιβὰς ἄκρον ἄωτον, H. 2.112), rejecting comprehensive poems like those in the old Epic Cycle (Ep. 28). The latter were "fat" (fr. 1.23-4, cf. fr. 398) and "blustering" (fr. 1.19 μέγα ψοφέουσαν ἀοιδήν). Thundering might become Zeus, but not the poet (fr. 1.20 βροντᾶν οὐκ ἐμόν, ἀλλὰ Διός). A poem should be "slender" (fr. 1.24) and "child-like" (παῖς ἅτε, fr. 1.6). It should be judged in terms of "art" (τέχνη, fr. 1.17), not size.

There is yet a further contrast between oral and literate styles that is of relevance here. Oral poetry favors "heavy", that is to say "heroic" characters whose deeds are monumental (Ong *op. cit.*, p. 70), and hence

---

[73] Cf. W.J. Ong *op. cit.*, n. 1 above, p. 40-41.

easily memorable. This is the style of the old Greek epic. Callimachus and his contemporaries, however, focus on marginal figures deliberately set against an heroic backdrop so as to heighten the contrast.[74] Thus, for instance, in a recently discovered poem about Herakles and the Nemean lion (*SH* 254-269), Callimachus apparently has the hero hunt down and dispatch the beast in a few short verses while lingering on the homely details of Herakles' visit to the otherwise obscure farmer Molorchus and on the latter's successful hunt of bothersome household rodents through the invention of a new sort of mousetrap.[75] Perhaps we may view the sudden emergence of pastoral poetry now in this light as well. Although retaining the meter and diction of heroic epic, Theocritus and the other pastoral poets fix upon the most unheroic part of the epic tradition, namely the rustic world of the Homeric simile with its shepherds and hunters, wildlife, vegetation, etc.[76] Although the Hellenistic Greeks were unaware that their early poetry was the product of an oral culture, and it would never have occurred to them to consider the developments of their Age in terms of "orality-literacy contrasts", it is striking how their aesthetic conforms, albeit unconsciously, to this pattern. For us, it may be an indication of the depth of the change that occurred between the Classical and Hellenistic Eras.

In another Age, faced with a similarly changing world, the poet Tennyson longed for the time "when song was great", when a poet like the mythical Amphion could cause rocks and trees to move through the power of his song. Tennyson wished that he could populate his own garden with the mightiest oaks and most delicate beech-trees, making them run obediently into place just by strumming his lyre. But such things are no longer possible. Try as he may, "Tis vain," he says, "in such a brassy age

>   I could not move a thistle;
> The very sparrows in the hedge
>   Scarce answer to my whistle; ...
>
> But what is that I hear? a sound
>   Like sleepy counsel pleading;
> O Lord! - 'tis in my neighbor's ground,
>   The modern Muses reading.
>
> They read Botanic Treatises,
>   And Works on Gardening thro' there,

---

[74] It is interesting that Euripides, a forerunner in this regard, was reputed in antiquity to have had a large private library (Athen. I 3 a-b).

[75] Cf. especially P. J. Parsons, "Callimachus: Victoria Berenices", *ZPE* 25 (1977) 1 f. and E. Livrea, "Der Killer Kallimachos und die Mausefallen", *ZPE* 34 (1979) 37 f.

[76] For a perceptive, though somewhat different, explanation of the same phenomenon cf. F. T. Griffiths, *Theocritus at Court*, Mnemosyne Suppl. 55 (Leiden 1979) 40.

> And Methods of transplanting trees
>   To look as if they grew there.
>
> The wither'd Misses! how they prose
>   O'er books of travell'd seamen,
> And show you slips of all that grows
>   From England to Van Diemen...
>
> Better to me the meanest weed
>   That blows upon its mountain,
> The vilest herb that runs to seed
>   Beside its native fountain.

The attitude of the Hellenistic poets would have been quite different. Upon hearing of Muses who read botanical treatises, their ears would have pricked up. Their openness to innovation and readiness to experiment would have made them tolerant of most poetic ideas with which another culture could confront them. Perhaps, if they had had them, they would be listening to radios too, like Cocteau's Orpheus.

"Callimachi Manes et Coi sacra Philetae,
in vestrum, quaeso, me sinite ire nemus."

Propertius III 1.1-2

Rupture and Revival. The Poet's Link to the Literary Past

"Who would listen to another?" asks a stingy prospective patron in Theocritus, "Homer is enough for all" ("τίς δέ κεν ἄλλου ἀκούσαι; ἅλις πάντεσσιν Ὅμηρος." 16.20), and though his rejection of a new work is prompted by miserliness, it is also probably a fair gauge of the conservatism which contemporary poets had to face, a scepticism towards innovation, a preference for the familiar. For Alexandrian verse as we know it from Theocritus, Callimachus, Aratus etc., proves rather to have been the exception in the Hellenistic Age, and lengthy, traditional epics prevailed as the norm.[1] Callimachus condemns them programmatically as "hollow-thundering" songs on heroes and kings (fr. 1.19, 4-5). And a later poet, Pollianos, would characterize their authors as τοὺς "αὐτὰρ ἔπειτα" λέγοντας / ... λωποδύτας ἀλλοτρίων ἐπέων, i.e. "those who say 'αὐτὰρ ἔπειτα' (the trite epic formula denoting the next step in a poem), ... pilferers of other's epic verse" (*AP* XI 130.1-2 cf. Aristotle's critique of poets who depict things as happening not διὰ τάδε but μετὰ τάδε, *Poet.* 10, 1452a 21). In keeping with this view, few modern critics have complained that this thieving throng should, by an odd chance, have disappeared almost completely from our tradition, leaving us with little more than their names, some titles, a few pathetic fragments, and – most influentially – the polemics of the Alexandrian avantgarde against them. Yet their works are the backdrop against which we must assess the artistic developments of the Hellenistic élite, and this is especially so of the manner in which both groups approach their poetic past and put it to work.

In the absence of a longer piece by one of these so-called "pilferers", some critics have sought elsewhere for evidence from which to characterize their style. They have looked, for instance, to the monumental art of the Age – such as the frieze on the Pergamene Altar. And doubtless, the time-honored themes of heroic epic are there, majestically conceived and massive in execution, a valid aid in attempting to catch something of the spirit of the Hellenistic epics.[2] Yet if we rely exclusively on analogies and polemics, the result will be a distortion at best.

---

[1] Cf. ch. 1 n. 14 and 59.
[2] Cf. K. Ziegler, *Das hellenistische Epos* (Leipzig 1966) 43-52, J. Onians, *Art and Thought in the Hellenistic Age: the Greek World View 350-50 B.C.* (London 1979) 140 and G. Zanker, *A & A* 29 (1983) 136.

Better, I think, to see what can be gleaned from the surviving fragments, pathetic though they may be. And if the resultant picture of Hellenistic epic is not so relentlessly black and white as the polemics suggest, perhaps it will be the more realistic for the additional shades of uncertainty. Two anonymous epic fragments preserved among the Oxyrhynchus papyri (P. Oxy. 2883 = *SH* 946-947) will serve our purposes:

SH 946

τῆς προτέρης κραδ[
σ]τήμεναι ὡς τὸ πάροιθε[
ἀλλὰ τάδ' ἄμμιν ἔπειτα θεῶ[ν ἰότ]ητι μελήσει.
σὺν Διὶ δ' ἠώιους τάχα κεν φεύγοντας ἴδοιμεν
προτροπάδην, βελέεσσιν ὑφ' ἡμετέροισι δαμέν[τας,
ὄφρα τις ἐν Σπάρτηι βεβαρημ[έ]νος ἕλκεϊ λυγρῶι
μνήσεται ἡμείων μηδ' ἀσκηθὴς ὑπαλύξηι.
....]α μὲν ὡς ἐπέοικε τελευτήσειε Κρονίων
.....]ε φυλακτῆρες πυρὰ κείατε καὶ μεμαῶτες
......] ἔκτοσθεν φιλίην ῥύεσθε πόληα.
......]ν οὐδὲ καὶ αὐτός, ἐπεὶ τόδε κάλλιόν ἐστιν,
ἐν μ]εγάροις μενέω, φύλακας δὲ μετείσομαι ὦκα,
.... δυ]σμενέων ἐμπαζόμεθ' ἀλλ' ἐπέοικεν
......]πάντα τελεῖν φρονέειν δ' ἐπαρηρότα θυμῶι.
           ]ε καὶ ἴαχε λαὸς ὁμαρτῆι

your former courage (?)[
to stand as before[
but these things will concern us hereafter by the will of the gods.
With Zeus' aid perhaps we may see them running away in the
                                                              morning
in headlong flight, overcome by our arrows,
so that one in Sparta disabled by a grievous wound
will remember us, nor would he escape unscathed.
These things], as is fitting, may the son of Kronos accomplish.
But now], watchmen, light the watch-fires and with fervent eagerness
           ] outside, protect your city.
        ] nor shall I, since it is more fitting thus,
remain at home, but I shall swiftly visit the sentinels,
not that] I give a damn about the enemy, but it is proper
              ] to carry out all things and to plan things that suit the
                                                                    heart.
        ] and at once the people raised a shout

SH 947

ὣς [εἰπὼν ἀ]πέπαυσε μάχην, ἐπίθοντο δὲ λαοί
νυ[......] νίκηι γὰρ ἀγαλλόμενοι ποθέεσκον
κα[ί]περ κ[ε]κμηῶτες ἀνὰ κνέφας ἀντιάασθαι.
ἀσπασίη δὲ Λάκωσιν ἐπήλυθε νυκτὸς ὀμίχλη.

thus [speaking], he broke off the battle, and the men yielded [to the swift night.] for revelling in the victory they yearned, even though worn out, to engage (the enemy) all through the night.
But the mist of night came welcome to the Lakonians.

In his *editio princeps*, Edgar Lobel suggested that these two hexameter fragments derive from the *Messeniaka*, a local epic in at least 6 books by Rhianos of Bene, the 3rd cent. B.C. contemporary of Eratosthenes.[3] And indeed, the depiction of a Spartan foe (τις ἐν Σπάρτηι *SH* 946.6, δυ]σμενέων v. 13, Λάκωσιν *SH* 947.4) attacking a city (*SH* 947.10), and evidently having the worst of it (*SH* 946.4ff., 13; *SH* 947.2ff.), squares well with Pausanias' account of the 11 year Spartan siege of Eira in the 2nd Messenian War. As Pausanias himself tells us (IV 6.1-3), Rhianos was his primary source for this part of the war. The speaker of the first fragment, and perhaps also of the speech that preceded the second (ὣς [εἰπὼν v. 1), may well have been the Messenian hero (and Spartan nemesis) Aristomenes.[4] His portrayal by Rhianos evidently aimed at matching those of earlier epic heroes – or at least it prompted Pausanias to make such a comparison: "In Rhianos' epic, Aristomenes is no less glorious than Achilles in Homer's *Iliad*", (IV 6.3 'Ριανῷ δὲ ἐν τοῖς ἔπεσιν οὐδὲν Ἀριστομένης ἐστὶν ἀφανέστερος ἢ Ἀχιλλεὺς ἐν Ἰλιάδι Ὁμήρῳ).

Our fragments are indeed cast in the traditional mold of heroic epic both as regards diction and content. And, at least on a thematic level, they may have a specific epic model. For not only does the general theme of the city beleagered for years by a hostile power recall the cir-

---

[3] On the identification cf. also E. Livrea, *Gnomon* 57 (1985) 600-601. Given the echoes of *Iliad* 8 in both fragments (cf. below), I think it likely that Lobel was correct when he suggested (*ad finem* fr. 2) that "if [the two fragments] were contiguous (or even close neighbors), it would be reasonable to suppose that the night referred to in fr. 2 was that preceding the daybreak envisaged in fr. 1.4, and that the order of the two should be reversed."
Rhianos also wrote several other long epic poems on local history: Θεσσαλικά in at least 16 books, Ἀχαϊκά in at least 4 books, Ἠλιακά in at least 3 books.
[4] It seems probable that the siege of Eira comprised the bulk of the epic, though the fate of the Messenians after their ultimate defeat there and the death of Aristomenes in Rhodes were also described. Cf. W. R. Misgeld, *Rhianos von Bene und das historische Epos im Hellenismus* (Diss. Köln 1968) 77-99.

cumstances of Troy,[5] the situation resembles quite specifically that in the eighth book of the *Iliad* where, after the day's combat, night falls on the defenders of the city. For these, the coming of night is unwanted, since it halts their advance; for their frustrated attackers, however, it is the answer to their prayers (Τρωσὶν μέν ῥ' ἀέκουσιν ἔδυ φάος, αὐτὰρ Ἀχαιοῖς / ἀσπασίη τρίλλιστος ἐπήλυθε νὺξ ἐρεβεννή v. 487–488). Similarly in *SH* 947, the victorious defenders wish to extend the battle through the night, while the defeated Lakonians are grateful for the advent of darkness (...νίκηι γὰρ ἀγαλλόμενοι ποθέεσκον / κα[ί]περ κ[ε]κμηῶτες ἀνὰ κνέφας ἀντιάασθαι. / ἀσπασίη δὲ Λάκωσιν ἐπήλυθε νυκτὸς ὀμίχλη. v. 2–4). In *Iliad* 8 again, Hector exhorts his troops to keep pressuring the Achaeans so that "at least not without a struggle, unmolested, may they board their ships, but in such a way that some one of them will nurse his wound even back home, struck with an arrow or a sharp spear springing to his ship" (μὴ μὰν ἀσπουδί γε νεῶν ἐπιβαῖεν ἕκηλοι, / ἀλλ' ὥς τις τούτων γε βέλος καὶ οἴκοθι πέσσῃ, / βλήμενος ἢ ἰῷ ἢ ἔγχει ὀξυόεντι / νηὸς ἐπιθρῴσκων v. 512–515). Likewise, the speaker in our hexameter fragment hopes that "we may see them running away in the morning in headlong flight, overcome by our arrows, so that one in Sparta disabled by a grievous wound will remember us, nor would he escape unscathed" (σὺν Διὶ δ' ἠώιους τάχα κεν φεύγοντας ἴδοιμεν / προτροπάδην, βελέεσσιν ὑφ' ἡμετέροισι δαμέν[τας, / ὄφρα τις ἐν Σπάρτηι βεβαρημ[έ]νος ἕλκεϊ λυγρῶι / μνήσεται ἡμείων μηδ' ἀσκηθὴς ὑπαλύξηι. v. 4–7). Finally, both Hector and the speaker of *SH* 946 order fires to be lit (*Il.* 8.509 καίωμεν πυρὰ πολλά – πυρὰ κείατε *SH* 946.9). These echoes may add a melancholy undercurrent to the ostensible Messenian success, for these and their champion, like the Trojans and theirs, were doomed to fail in the long run. Pausanias (IV 20.5) explicitly compares the fall of Eira to that of Troy.

But while these elements hew quite closely to the final part of *Iliad* 8 (and so resemble the pointed allusions of the Alexandrian élite), others derive from altogether different scenes. And yet others show that our poet conceived of this passage as largely conventional – a "typical scene" as Homerists would call it –, the nocturnal assembley with paraenetic speech.[6] The concern with the night-watch, for instance, is typical (*Il.* 8.529, but also cf. 7.371, 18.299). Sentinels are described as keeping watch by a fire elsewhere too (*Il.* 9.88 πῦρ κήαντο on the Achaean

---

[5] Cf. A. Couat's discussion of Homeric echoes in the *Messeniaka* in *Alexandrian Poetry under the first three Ptolemies* (transl. J. Loeb, New York 1931) Bk. 3 ch. 2, esp. pp. 366–370.

[6] For a listing of paraenetic speeches generally cf. J. Latacz, *Kampfparänese, Kampfdarstellung und Kampfwirklichkeit in der Ilias, bei Kallinos und Tyrtaios* (Munich 1977) 246–250.

side; 10.418-420). The theme of leaders going among the sentinels appears in *Il.* 10.97f. (δεῦρ' ἐς τοὺς φύλακας καταβήομεν cf. also 10.180f.). The verb ῥύομαι used, as at *SH* 946.10, of the night-watch protecting its side is found at *Iliad* 10.416-417 (φυλακὰς δ' ἅς εἴρεαι, ἥρως, / οὔ τις κεκριμένη ῥύεται στρατὸν οὐδὲ φυλάσσει; used in connection with a city cf. "Hes." *Scut.* 105 ῥύεται τε πόληα). The sentiment with which our fragment begins, namely of "standing firm, as before" (*SH* 946.2), is familiar e.g. from Aias' words to Menelaos in *Iliad* 17.719-721: "we two shall fight.../... who previously / stood firm against bitter Ares" (νῶι μαχησόμεθα.../...οἳ τὸ πάρος περ / μίμνομεν ὀξὺν Ἄρηα). The desire to see the enemy overwhelmed by one's arrows at v.4-5 of our fragment most closely approximates the wording of *Iliad* 4.98-99 where Pandaros is told how Paris would rejoice "if he were to see Menelaos... overwhelmed by your arrow" (αἴ κεν ἴδῃ Μενέλαον.../ σῷ βέλεϊ δμηθέντα). Finally, what more conventional conclusion could our poet have given this speech than the people's shout of approval?

The conventional character of the passage stands out even more clearly in its diction. The first thing to observe in this regard is that this poet does *not* favor epic rarities, that is he does not seek out the Homeric *hapax legomena* or disputed words that are so characteristic of the Hellenistic avant garde. One is always left with the impression (after having sweated blood to trace the unusual words or forms by means of lexica and concordances) that the Alexandrian poets wrote with their "glossai" close at hand. Judging from what is left of this poem, its poet did not need them.

His style, moreover, is frequently clumsy.[7] I refer, for instance, to the redundancy of μηδ' ἀσκηθὴς ὑπαλύξηι (v.7), "nor would he escape unscathed", after the wish that, overcome by arrows, the wounded enemy should remember his adversary even back home; or to the almost mechanical recourse to divine assistance – θεῶ[ν ἰότητι (v.3), σὺν Διὶ (v.4), τελευτήσειε Κρονίων (v.8) – as well as to the peculiar harping on what is "proper" – ὡς ἐπέοικε (v.8), ἐπεὶ τόδε κάλλιόν ἐστιν (v.11), ἀλλ' ἐπέοικεν / ......]πάντα τελεῖν φρονέειν δ' ἐπαρηρότα θυμῶι (v.13-14).

Such clumsiness is compounded by another feature of our poet's diction – namely the numerous epic locutions adduced by Lobel, and now rehearsed and augmented by Parsons and Lloyd-Jones in their commentary to the fragments. For after examining the many parallels, exact or near, for such expressions as ὡς τὸ πάροιθε (*Od.* 2.312), θεῶν ἰότητι (*Il.* 19.9, *Od.* 7.214, etc.; cf. the whole phrase ἔπειτα θεῶν ἰότητι at *H.*

---

[7] "stilus inconcinnus", say Lloyd-Jones and Parsons.

H.Aphr. 166), σὺν Διὶ (*Od.* 16.260, *H.H.* 24.5, both unnoted by the editors), ἕλκεϊ λυγρῶι (*Il.* 15.393, 19.49), τελευτήσειε Κρονίων (*Od.* 20.236 etc.), ἐπεὶ τόδε κάλλιόν ἐστιν (*Od.* 3.70, 8.543, 7.159), ἴαχε λαός (*Il.* 13.822, 834, 17.723, etc.,[8] a reader comes away with the overwhelming impression that this author employs epicism in a "non-allusive" way – that is, his vocabulary is generally not intended to recall particular characters, descriptions or turns of phrase in specific scenes of the *Iliad* or *Odyssey*.[9] Rather, it is sprinkled indiscriminately throughout so as to lend the narrative a broad epic coloring, an elevated, venerable tone. Paradoxically, the very frequency of these ultimately gratuitous epicisms contributes to the awkwardness of the style.

Given the dominant impression of broad Homerizing, it can hardly be just coincidental that no critic has noted the larger resemblance in situation, discussed above, between our passage and *Iliad* 8 – though they duly cite the individual echoes.[10] Rather such non-allusive epicism tends, precisely because of its emphatically reproductive and vaguely evocative quality, to obscure specific similarities. The many conventional, non-specific epic elements effectively muddy the waters – or, in the programmatic "Bildersprache" of Callimachus' second hymn (v. 108 f.), we can say that our fragments are as far from their Homeric origins as the immense but filthy Assyrian stream (an image of the stale contemporary epic) from its pure (Homeric) source.[11]

---

[8] Cf. even such phrases as v. 11 καὶ αὐτός, ἐπεὶ = *Od.* 17.573 same *sedes;* and while οὐδὲ καὶ αὐτός does not exist in Homer, we *do* find οἶδα καὶ αὐτός in the same position (*Il.* 19.421).

[9] This seems to be what Lobel meant when, in his introductory remarks to the fragments, he said that "the language has a vaguely Homeric tincture without being in detail particularly imitative". If these fragments are indeed by Rhianos, one should note how dissimilar they are to his epigrams, for these exhibit a playfully elegant style entirely in keeping with Alexandrian practice. This is likewise true of the self-conscious allusiveness of his longest fragment (21 verses, p. 9 Powell, fr. 1; cf. G. Zanker's evaluation, *Realism in Alexandrian Poetry* [Kent 1986] 110-111 n. 151.). We note, moreover, that like many Alexandrian poets he was an active scholar, producing an edition of Homer which was frequently cited in the Scholia (cf. Pfeiffer, *Hist.* pp. 122, 148-149). Our fragments, by contrast, while clearly drawing on the style of old epic, are awkward and repetitive. Should we assume that Rhianos adopted different styles for different projects?.

[10] I refer to Lobel (*op. cit.*), Parsons and Lloyd-Jones (*op. cit.*), Livrea (*op. cit.*), and W. Luppe in his review of Lobel, *Gnomon* 46 (1974) 647-648.

[11] I follow here the interpretation of F. Williams, *Callimachus, Hymn to Apollo* (Oxford 1978) 85-89, who argues that when Phthonos stealthily whispers into Apollo's ear, criticizing the poet whose song is not as great as the sea (οὐκ ἄγαμαι τὸν ἀοιδὸν ὃς οὐδ' ὅσα πόντος ἀείδει v. 106), he is playing on a topical comparison of the sea (Pontos/ Okeanos) with Homer. Tacitly accepting the sea, i.e. Homer, as a positive standard, Apollo parries with different images for various kinds of song: the huge but muddy Assyrian river (traditionalist epic); the pristine droplets from the unsullied spring (refined, diminutive Callimachean verse). Both waters, in the old conception (cf. *Il.*

A final point remains to be made, namely that such mechanical use of epic conventions seems strongly to affirm the continued functioning of a *living* tradition. We find no perception whatsoever of the genre's anemia. Rhianos can devise an epic hero who is "no less glorious" than Homer's Achilles. And among the general populace there is evidently still an audience eager for such latter-day Achilleses. Old-fashioned epic is here alive and familiar, a taste passed on from generation to generation – unmindful of the rift which Alexander's conquests had produced in society and culture. And though the pointed allusions to *Iliad* 8 prevent us from describing the fragments as merely "das gedankenlose 'kyklische' Nachplappern" of old epic style (Christ-Schmid, *Geschichte der griechischen Literatur* II, 1 p. 116), their conventional quality is unmistakable, probably desired by, and pleasing to the public. Perhaps – if they possessed some awareness of the rift – it was even comforting.

Our fragments, then, – with their non-allusive epicism, familiar epic vocabulary, "typical" actions taken over intact, above all the sense they convey that traditional epic language and content remain not just viable but undiminished by any rupture between the old world and the new – probably provide us with a fair example of those traits that characterized the bulk of epic produced at this time.

Yet there were poets in whom the altered circumstances of the Hellenistic world produced an acute sense of discontinuity and isolation. This was especially true of those who left their native lands to come to Alexandria – a city not just geographically remote from the rest of the Greek world but lacking even those ties enjoyed by colonial Greek foundations, i.e. the institutional connection to a mother city with which it could share political, cultural and religious traditions.[12]

The rupture with the literary past, which these poets so keenly felt, is manifested in a variety of ways. Theocritus, for instance, writes four epigrams that pose as inscriptions for the statues of ancient poets (XVII Anacreon, XVIII Epicharmus, XXI Archilochus, XXII Peisander).[12a] We may, on the one hand, construe these poems as simple tributes to the greats of the past, as a setting of memorials – fictitious though they may be. Yet they also express Theocritus' remoteness from his prede-

---

21.195-197, Xenophanes fr. 30 *DK*), derived from the sea; just as all subsequent poetry was thought to have its fountain-head in Homer. But while the droplets of the spring communicate unimpeded with their source, the river's streams become sluggish and polluted, estranged from their origin. In literary terms, Callimachean song, though small in scale, is truer to its Homeric source than are those epics that resemble Homer in externals. For criticism of Williams' interpretation cf. A. Koehnken, *AJPh* 102 (1981) 411-422.

[12] Cf. G. Zanker, *A&A* 29 (1983) 137f.

[12a] I hope to treat these epigrams in detail in a future article.

cessors inasmuch as he explicitly consigns them to another age: Anacreon is "pre-eminent, if anything is, among poets of yore" (τῶν πρόσθ' εἴ τι περισσὸν ᾠδοποιῶν XVII.4); Archilochus is τὸν πάλαι ποιητάν (XXI.1); Peisander, πρᾶτος τῶν ἐπάνωθε μουσοποιῶν (XXII.3); Epicharmus, ὁ τὰν κωμῳδίαν / εὑρών (XVIII.1-2). Of course, this identifies the author of the epigrams, as well as his readers, as "modern" even as it sets Anacreon, Epicharmus, Archilochus and Peisander apart in the past. There is, however, another aspect of these poems that is even more important in this regard. I mean the fact that Theocritus is here casting the heritage in a very suggestive form – as a monument of stone or bronze, a literary fossil, envisioned by the poet and his reader. Contrary to what one may have heard, in this instance at least the mute stones do not speak. One could hardly imagine a more eloquent image for the radical otherness of the poetic past.

Yet such an image did in fact exist, and it rises now to sudden prominence: the image of ultimate rupture, death. The poetry of this age contains numerous expressions of mourning for the literary heritage. In his programmatic elegy, for instance (*SH* 705.18-20, discussed in the previous ch. p. 15, 37 f.), Poseidippus bids his readers to pay tribute to the great Parian poet Archilochus as follows: "but to the Parian nightingale give a mournful / flood, shedding empty tears from the eyes and groaning in lamentation" (ἀλλ' ἐπὶ μὲν Παρ(ί)ηι δὸς ἀηδόνι λυγρὸν ἐφ.[/ νᾶμα κατὰ γληνέων δάκρυα κεινὰ χέῳ[ν / καὶ στενάχων). To appreciate the full force of this gesture of mourning, one must recall that Archilochus had not died yesterday: Poseidippus is calling attention to the death of a poet who had flourished some 300 years before! Yet, for the Hellenistic author the painful sense of separation, normally marking only the initial period of bereavement, has once again become acute. In the 3rd cent. B.C., they are weeping – again – for Archilochus.

This same persistent grief appears in the *Lament for Bion* (late 2nd, early 1st cent. B.C.), where sorrow at the death of this contemporary bucolic author is likened to that felt for the poets of the past. Homer's death comes first, of course (v. 70 ff.), with a detailed description of how his father, the river-god Meles, filled his streams with tears and the sea with his cries of lamentation. A catalogue of further famous poets follows after (v. 87 ff.):

Ἄσκρα μὲν γοάει σε (scil. Bion) πολὺ πλέον Ἡσιόδοιο·
Πίνδαρον οὐ ποθέοντι τόσον Βοιωτίδες ὗλαι·
οὐ τόσον Ἀλκαίῳ περιμύρατο Λέσβος ἐραννά,
οὐδὲ τόσον τὸν ἀοιδὸν ὀδύρατο Τήιον ἄστυ·
σὲ πλέον Ἀρχιλόχοιο ποθεῖ Πάρος, ἀντὶ δὲ Σαπφοῦς
εἰσέτι σεῦ τὸ μέλισμα κινύρεται ἁ Μιτυλήνα.

Askra bewails you (scil. Bion) more by far than it does Hesiod.
The Boeotian woods do not yearn as much for Pindar.
Not so much did lovely Lesbos lament Alcaeus,
nor so much d:d the city of Teos mourn its singer (scil. Anacreon);
Paros misses you more than it does Archilochus, and not still for
Sappho's song, for yours Mitylene now laments.

With this extravagant enumeration, the grief at Bion's death is depicted as exceeding even that for the greatest poets of the past. Yet for our purposes the point of interest is the underlying assumption through which that grief is magnified all the more: namely that Askra is *still* bewailing Hesiod, the Boeotian woods *still* yearn for Pindar, Paros *still* misses Archilochus. A contemporary sense of loss for the poets of the past is simply taken for granted.[13]

The sentiment that we find reflected in these poems, however, receives its most striking embodiment elsewhere, namely in the development and proliferation of a specifically literary, purely fictitious version of the traditional epitaph (cf. ch. 1 p. 39 f.), among which those for the great poetic personalities of the past become especially common.[14] Homer, Hesiod, Archilochus, Pindar, etc. are recipients of funereal honors accorded to them across a gulf of space and time by an extraordinary range of Hellenistic poets. Antipater of Sidon (mid 2nd cent. B.

---

[13] With the Hellenistic Age, the death of poets becomes itself a poetic theme. Thus Euphorion of Chalkis (2nd half of the 3rd cent. B.C.?) wrote a poem called "Hesiod" (fr. 22, 22b p. 34 Powell) in which the only event we can identify with some certainty is the poet's death. And in a poem transmitted under the name of the early 3rd cent. B.C. author Sotades (15 p. 243 Powell) we encounter a straightforward list of great poetic dead:

…πάντες ὅσοι περισσὸν ἠθέλησαν εὑρεῖν   5
ἢ μηχανικὸν ποίημ᾽ ἢ σοφὸν μάθημα,
οὗτοι κακὸν εἰς τὸν θάνατον τέλος ἐποίησαν….
Αἰσχύλῳ γράφοντί ⟨τι⟩ ἐπιπέπτωκε χελώνη.   13
Σοφοκλῆς ῥᾶγα φαγὼν σταφυλῆς πνιγεὶς τέθνηκε.
Κύνες οἱ κατὰ Θρᾴκην Εὐριπίδην ἔτρωγον.
Τὸν θεῖον Ὅμηρον λιμὸς κατεδαπάνησεν.

All those who exceedingly wished to discover
either an artful product or subtle knowledge,
these made a bad end in death….
A tortoise fell on Aeschylus as he was writing something.
Sophocles choked while eating a grape from a bunch and died.
Dogs in Thrace devoured Euripides.
Hunger consumed the god-like Homer.

At a later time (3rd cent. A.D.) we think of Diogenes Laertius' *Pammetros,* a book of epigrams on the deaths of famous figures from the Greek tradition (cf. Diog. Laert. I 63).

[14] These form a large proportion of the Hellenistic epigrams on poets collected by M. Gabathuler, *Hellenistische Epigramme auf Dichter,* (Basel 1937).

C.) wrote no less than five sepulchral poems *on Anacreon alone* (*AP* VII 23 = *G-P* XIII, *AP* VII 26 = *G-P* XIV, *AP* VII 27 = *G-P* XV, *AP* VII 29 = *G-P* XVI, *AP* VII 30 = *G-P* XVII). Perhaps this shows a fondness of "variations on the same theme", as Gow and Page remark (vol. II p. 33), but it also reflects a significant, if bizarre, preoccupation with Anacreon dead! For Antipater, as for many of the more self-conscious poets of the Age, such fictitious epitaphs may have fulfilled a need to deal with the fact that the old poetic world (and its movers) in some fundamental sense no longer existed.

An epitaph by Simias of Rhodes (flor. ca. 300 B.C.) for the tragedian Sophocles provides an early example (*AP* VII 21 = *G-P* 4):

Τόν σε χοροῖς μέλψαντα Σοφοκλέα, παῖδα Σοφίλλου,
  τὸν τραγικῆς Μούσης ἀστέρα Κεκρόπιον,
πολλάκις ὃν θυμέλῃσι καὶ ἐν σκηνῇσι τεθηλώς
  βλαισὸς Ἀχαρνίτης κισσὸς ἔρεψε κόμην,
τύμβος ἔχει καὶ γῆς ὀλίγον μέρος· ἀλλ' ὁ περισσός
  αἰὼν ἀθανάτοις δέρκεται ἐν σελίσιν.

You who sang in the choruses, Sophocles, son of Sophillos,
  Kekropian (i.e. Athenian) star of the tragic Muse,
whose hair the twisting Acharnian ivy, blossom-bedecked,
  often crowned by the orchestra's altar and on the stage,
a tomb and a little plot of earth now holds you; but the rest of time
  beholds you in the deathless columns of your writing.

The poem contains all the earmarks of a traditional sepulchral epigram. The dead man is named, his ancestry and homeland established, his profession characterized and his achievements praised. The glory of his life, we are told, stands in sharpest contrast to the pitiful fact of death: a little plot of earth suffices to hold even so great a man as Sophocles. There could be no plainer statement of discontinuity and, with it, of the gulf that Simias felt between himself and the poet of the past. The irreparable rift is mirrored even in the simple opposition of tenses (aorist, v. 1-4, fixing the dramatist's accomplishments in time gone by; present, v. 5, asserting the continuing fact of his death). And although the conventional consolation that the dead man's works live on appears to secure a kind of continuity (v. 5-6), it in fact conceals another kind of gulf, namely that contained in the pointed contrast of ἐν σκηνῇσι (v. 3) and ἐν σελίσιν (v. 6) – the old norm of performance; the new importance of reading. δέρκεται (v. 6) describes not the action of the Athenian spectator who might have heard Sophocles singing (μέλψαντα v. 1) in the Theatre of Dionysus, but that of the 3rd cent. B.C. reader "seeing" the play in his mind. "The rest of time", ὁ περισσός / αἰών (v. 5-6) seems also to set that action apart as "modern" and distinct from the previous age. Not only is Sophocles dead, then, his medium of communication has become (for the learned Simias, at least) remote.

It is instructive to compare a very different (somewhat earlier) response to the literary heritage, in which past poets, far from resting in their graves, compete actively with their successors. Such a situation appears in an epigram which the tragedian Astydamas wrote for a statue of himself erected by the Athenians in the theatre of Dionysus to commemorate his victory in the dramatic competition of 340 B.C. (Page *FGE* p. 33-34 = Snell *TrGF* 1, 60 T 2 a). Astydamas here refers to the practice, introduced in 386 B.C., of reviving one fifth-century tragedy prior to the performance of the three new trilogies.[15]

εἴθ' ἐγὼ ἐν κείνοις γενόμην ἢ κεῖνοι ἅμ' ἡμῖν
οἳ γλώσσης τερπνῆς πρῶτα δοκοῦσι φέρειν,
ὡς ἐπ' ἀληθείας ἐκρίθην ἀφεθεὶς παράμιλλος·
νῦν δὲ χρόνῳ προέχουσ', οἷς φθόνος οὐχ ἕπεται.

Would that I had been born with them, or they with me,
who are esteemed for taking the prize in the pleasing word,
so that I, as befits the truth, would have been judged an equal
 competitor, starting level with the rest.
But now they are ahead in time, pursued no more by envy.

Though this epigram is so boastful that the Athenians would not allow it to be incised on the statue-base (Suda s.v. σαυτὴν ἐπαινεῖς), it still betrays a keen awareness of the situation's underlying oppressiveness. For although the older tragedies were performed outside the actual competition, they nevertheless shared the same stage and general time-frame, so that the audience would inevitably and easily compare and debate the relative merits of the two.[16] The poet thus sees himself as a competitor (παράμιλλος v. 3) in a race in which his opponent enjoys a perpetual edge,[17] unchecked by the handicap of envy. While Aristophanes in the *Frogs* had imagined a contest between deceased tragedians in the underworld, this poem – and the 4th cent. situation it reflects

---

[15] Cf. *IG* ii² 2338 = Snell, *TrGF* 1, DID A1 201 reprinted in Pickard-Cambridge, *The Dramatic Festivals of Athens*² (Oxford 1968) 104f. whose comments (p. 72) are apposite. Later, by the mid 3rd cent. B.C., several old tragedies would be performed in competition with each other, cf. Pickard-Cambridge, *op. cit.* p. 123-124 = Snell, *op. cit.* DID A4b.

[16] Thus also G.A. Seeck, *Das griechische Drama* (Darmstadt 1979) 185-186, who speaks of "Das 5.Jh. als Konkurrent". Cf. G. Xanthakis-Karamanos, *Studies in Fourth Century Tragedy* (Athens 1980) 22-24.

[17] χρόνῳ προέχουσ' playing cleverly on the custom that the performance of the revival preceded that of the trilogies. The epigram elaborates a comparison in the well-known lament of Choirilos of Samos (*SH* 317, cited in the previous chapter p. 13), where the poet complained that, in literary terms, he had been "left behind like the last in a race", ὕστατοι ὥστε δρόμου καταλειπόμεθ' (v. 4).

– take us a macabre step beyond: here the living must compete with the dead.[18]

The situation of the Alexandrian poets was altogether different. For their works and those of their predecessors were not required to appear in potentially embarrassing proximity to one another on the same stage. On the contrary, the simple act of reading which, as we have seen, now came to dominate production and reception of verse, kept them palpably apart. The distinction could not be more tellingly enunciated than in the two poems we have just examined. For Simias, a dramatic work existed not as it had for Astydamas in "live" performance, but in "deathless columns of writing" (ἀθανάτοις... ἐν σελίσιν v. 6). The genre which more than any other had been addressed to the community and experienced in public was now received in a qualitatively different way, in the largely private act of reading, where it was up to the individual to decide whether to compare a given play with any other, or even to terminate his own experience of the same simply by putting down the scroll. Poetic works thus remained discrete not only from each other, but, in a new and significant way, from their readers as well; for they were now communicated not by one human being to another, but by an object – the scroll – which could be viewed as "living" only in the metaphorical sense implied by the quotation marks with which I have set off the word. It is not least of all the new role of reading, and with it the fundamental difference in existential mode between reader and poem, that opens the door to that sense of rupture expressed in the recurrent image of death.

The more conventional 3rd cent. poets, of course, (purveyors of traditional epic) could regard themselves as vying with their great forerunner, Homer. Indeed, precisely this is implied in a famous passage from Theocritus' *Thalysia* (Idyll 7) where the goatherd-poet Lycidas avows that he hates those "cocks of the Muses who lose their toil with crowing against the Chian bard" (v. 47–48). But for those with some sense of the rift it was vain to compete with the past. So far as I can tell, the Hellenistic avant-garde is of a piece in never expressing its relationship towards the literary heritage in agonistic terms. Far more characteristic (and perhaps a deliberate contrast to the attitude described above) is Lycidas' wish somewhat later in the *Thalysia* that his illustrious precursor in bucolic song, Komatas, could be alive to sing to him today (v. 86–89):

---

[18] Later, the idea of living authors in competition with their predecessors entered the literature of critical theory. Pseudo-Longinus, for instance, describes Plato's relationship to Homer as follows (13.4): ὡς ἀνταγωνιστὴς νέος πρὸς ἤδη τεθαυμασμένον, ἴσως μὲν φιλονεικότερον καὶ οἱονεὶ διαδορατιζόμενος, οὐκ ἀνωφελῶς δ' ὅμως διηριστεύετο· θεοφοροῦνται πνεύματι τὸν αὐτὸν τρόπον, ὃν καὶ τὴν Πυθίαν λόγος ἔχει.

αἴθ' ἐπ' ἐμεῦ ζωοῖς ἐναρίθμιος ὤφελες ἦμεν
ὥς τοι ἐγὼν ἐνόμευον ἀν' ὤρεα τὰς καλὰς αἶγας
φωνᾶς εἰσαΐων, τὺ δ' ὑπὸ δρυσὶν ἢ ὑπὸ πεύκαις
ἁδὺ μελισδόμενος κατεκέκλισο, θεῖε Κομᾶτα.

> If only you had been numbered among the living in my day
> that I might have pastured your lovely goats in the mountains
> listening to your voice, while you reclined beneath oaks or pines
> sweetly singing, O sacred Komatas.

The similarity to Astydamas' wish, examined above, is striking. Yet it only underlines the great difference in tone. Like Lycidas, Astydamas wants to commune with the poets of the past, but whereas the dramatist's desire stems from a frustration at being confronted with a living past with which in effect he had to compete, Lycidas' wish is nostalgic in its awareness that Komatas belongs irrevocably to another age.

Yet we must not think that, though entombed, the literary past was moribund or without effect on the present. Our fictitious epitaphs do not attempt to nail down the coffin lid. On the contrary, they reveal that *rigor mortis* could be perceived in varying degrees and that despite their awareness of being "epigonoi", i.e. of having been born after the fact, the Hellenistic poets saw no cause for despair.

Their response is not one of frozen grief. Rather they found in this situation a source of empowerment. In Simias' epigram for Sophocles we saw that, while the dramatist might be dead, his written legacy lived on, an artifact open to critical scrutiny and appreciation. In one of Antipater's sepulchral epigrams for Anacreon, mentioned above, we are taken a step further (*AP* VII 26.1-4 = *G-P* XIV 1-4):

Ξεῖνε, τάφον πάρα λιτὸν Ἀνακρείοντος ἀμείβων,
   εἴ τί τοι ἐκ βίβλων ἦλθεν ἐμῶν ὄφελος,
σπεῖσον ἐμῇ σποδιῇ, σπεῖσον γάνος, ὄφρα κεν οἴνῳ
   ὀστέα γηθήσῃ τἀμὰ νοτιζόμενα....

> Stranger, you who pass by Anacreon's humble grave,
>   if ever any advantage came to you through my scrolls,
> pour on my ashes, pour the delicious libation, so that my bones
>   may rejoice, being sprinkled with wine....

Here again the effect of the author's books endures beyond his death. Yet we note two interesting differences. First, the contemporary passerby can, through a sympathetic act, a libation, in some sense reactivate Anacreon's boisterous ways – if only in the underworld. Second, Antipater effectively does just that by letting the dead man speak for himself and evoke those ways. That the departed should speak is, of course, a common feature of sepulchral verse. The use of this technique here, however, in a poem merely posing as an epitaph some 300 years after

Anacreon's demise, may be said to embrace also the desire of the Hellenistic poet to reanimate the spirit of his literary ancestor, to capture his voice.

Antipater is not, however, like the modern medium who, submerging his consciousness, subordinates his personality to that of the deceased.[19] He rather transforms the voice of his subject, making it unmistakably his own: the public's "advantage" (ὄφελος v. 2) was not an aim of Anacreon's verse as we know it; what is more, the 6th cent. B. C. poet would hardly have talked of "my books". That reference prompts us to reconsider our initial response to that traditional figure of sepulchral epigram, the passerby: while this character is unique within Greek literary genres as having always embodied the "reader" (for he was conventionally assumed to respond to the grave-stele as "text"), the reader of *this* poem remains a passerby only figuratively. For he encounters Anacreon's epitaph as he makes his way through the scroll. Here, as in other comparable epigrams, this contemporary nuance is part of the poem's point and charm.[20] And hence, as in the case of the fictitious book inscriptions discussed in the previous chapter (p. 29 f.), the poem's modernity was never in doubt.

Antipater's Anacreon speaks and is viewed as acting entirely from the confines of the underworld. Yet there were cases in which a poet's personality was depicted as retaining such a high degree of potency that, even in death, it might encroach on the realm of the living. Such was the conceit applied by a number of Hellenistic poets to that ferocious author of invective, Hipponax. In these poems, the reader is typically warned to tread softly in passing by the tomb of the iambographer lest he arouse his slumbering ire – since even in the perpetual night of death he is apparently a very light sleeper. Thus Leonidas of Tarentum (mid 3rd cent. B. C.) cautions the passerby not to "wake the angry wasp who has paused from his anger in sleep" (*AP* VII 408.1–2 = *G-P* LVIII 1–2), and the epigrammatist Alcaeus (early 2nd cent. B. C.) advises him to "pray that the corpse sleep in good will" (*AP* VII 536.6 = *G-P* XIII

---

[19] We note that Pseudo-Longinus would later describe the relationship between a poet and his literary antecedent in just this way, namely by depicting the former as possessed by the latter, like the Delphic Pythia by her god (13.2): πολλοὶ γὰρ [scil. poets] ἀλλοτρίῳ θεοφοροῦνται πνεύματι τὸν αὐτὸν τρόπον, ὃν καὶ τὴν Πυθίαν λόγος ἔχει.

[20] If, as H. White has proposed (*New Essays in Hellenistic Poetry* [Amsterdam 1985] 60–64), we retain the MS reading of line five (ὡς ὁ Διωνύσου μεμελημένος οὔασι κῶμος) rather than the emended text printed by Gow and Page (ὡς ὁ Διωνύσου μεμελημένος εὐάσι κώμοις), there may once more be a deliberate contrast between Anacreon's former performative mode of communication and the present reception of his work through books (cf. Simias' epitaph for Sophocles, above p. 59 f.). For White defends the MS tradition by arguing that κῶμος should appear with a capital K, and that Antipater's Anacreon describes himself as "I, Komos personified, who am dear to the ears of Dionysus".

6). Particularly interesting for our purposes is the variation with which Theocritus provides us (*AP* XIII 3 = *G-P* XIII = Gow XIX).

> Ὁ μουσοποιὸς ἐνθάδ' Ἱππῶναξ κεῖται.
> εἰ μὲν πονηρός, μὴ προσέρχευ τῷ τύμβῳ·
> εἰ δ' ἐσσὶ κρήγυός τε καὶ παρὰ χρηστῶν,
> θαρσέων καθίζευ, κἢν θέλῃς ἀπόβριξον.
>
> Here lies Hipponax, maker of verses.
> If you are wicked, do not approach this tomb;
> but if you are honest and a child of good parents,
> fear not, have a seat and, if you want, take a nap.

As in Antipater's sepulchral poem for Anacreon, the verses may be viewed as the utterance of the deceased,[21] and here again the poet transforms the dead man's voice to make it his own. Yet we note an important difference which, on the one hand, draws Theocritus significantly closer than Antipater to his archaic model, while simultaneously shifting him away from conventional (if fictitious) epitaph. For the poem is written not in any meter typical of epitaphs – indeed, it is to my knowledge unprecedented –, but in "scazons" (or limping iambs), the characteristic cadence of Hipponax' verse. Moreover, it is generally thought that Theocritus even appropriates Hipponactean vocabulary (cf. Gow and Dover *ad* κρήγυος v. 3), and it seems to me that there is also an attempt to capture some of that poet's humor, though in a very mild form, in the unexpected offer of a tombside nap (the which one might regard, whether one was honest or not, with a certain justifiable apprehension). In all, then, we see not just the critical appreciation present in Simias' poem on Sophocles, nor the somewhat more specific attempt of Antipater to "catch the spirit" of Anacreon, but rather an engaged exploration and adaptation of Hipponax – an author so vivid as virtually to leap out of his grave –, down to the details of diction, meter and style.

Reflected, then, in varying degrees of intensity in these fictitious epitaphs is precisely the tension which characterized the relationship of the Alexandrian authors with their poetic past: on the one hand the awareness of rupture so evident in this preoccupation with the literary dead; on the other, the ardent desire to bridge the gulf and establish a link – though one commensurate to the needs and expectations of the age. For the peculiar blend of tradition and innovation which distinguishes Hellenistic verse stands in direct proportion to the intensity with which the rift is felt; and if, as Harold Bloom has said, "disconti-

---

[21] Cf. Gow *ad* v. 1 κεῖται and note Hipponax' fondness for naming himself fr. 32.4; 36.2; 37; 117.4 West.

nuity is freedom",[22] then the linkage which these poets sought contains, I think, a healthy dose of that freedom.

The Alexandrian attempt to bridge the gulf – while still acknowledging it – yielded striking contrivances, the most obvious of which was simply to bring the dead back to life.[23] Thus Callimachus, building on the idea of Hipponax' posthumous virulence, actually resuscitates the poet in his first *Iambos* (fr. 191), having him scold the contentious *philologoi* at the Sarapeion (Dieg. VI 1.3-4) of his own Alexandria.

> Ἀκούσαθ' Ἱππώνακτος· οὐ γὰρ ἀλλ' ἥκω
> ἐκ τῶν ὅκου βοῦν κολλύβου πιπρήσκουσιν,
> φέρων ἴαμβον οὐ μάχην ἀείδοντα
> τὴν Βουπάλειον...
>
> Listen to Hipponax. For indeed I have come
> from the place where they sell an ox for a penny [i.e. Hades],
> bearing an iamb which does not sing
> the Boupaleian battle...

The meter here is the Hipponactean scazon, the dialect Ionic, both of which we encountered in Theocritus; likewise Hipponactean is the poet's naming of himself (cf. fr. 32.4; 36.2; 37; 117.4 West), his poor man's interest in cheap beef[24] and the tart, bantering style with which the fragment continues.[25] The content, however, is trimmed entirely to

---

[22] *The Anxiety of Influence* (Oxford 1973) 39.

[23] The basic thought is caught by D.A. Russell, "De imitatione" in *Creative Imitation and Latin Literature,* ed. D. West & T. Woodman (Cambridge 1979) 2, though apparently without thinking of such a striking manifestation: "The Hellenistic period..., with its blend of changing ideas and archaic forms, gave quite a new perspective to the use of models and tradition. It turned it into a matter not so much of continuity as of revival." Aristophanes had, of course, already paved the way for this Hellenistic fashion with the planned resurrection of either Aeschylus or Euripides in the *Frogs*. Significantly, however, both tragedians had died within recent memory; that is, they did not yet possess that patina of antiquity that the poets of archaic and classical Greece held for the Hellenistic Age. Cf. the case of Timon of Phlius (below p. 71f.).

I assume that Old Comedies with titles such as Ἀρχίλοχοι (Cratinus) or Ἡσίοδοι (Telekleides frs. 14-21 Kock I p. 213-215) referred exclusively to "followers" of these poets rather than to a resurrected Archilochus and Hesiod together with their followers, or to multiple resurrected Archilochuses and Hesiods. There is simply no evidence in the texts for either of the latter two suppositions. This is a question, however, about which there has been much speculation and little agreement. Cf. Kassel-Austin's preface to Cratinus' Ἀρχίλοχοι *PCG* IV p. 121. Cf. also the *Demoi,* where Eupolis brings back dead statesmen.

[24] Cf. F. Jung, *Hipponax redivivus* (Bonn 1929) 39.

[25] Cf. The analysis of D.L.Clayman, *Callimachus' Iambi* (Leiden 1980) 11-16. For the character of Callimachus' "revival" of Hipponax here, and generally in the *Iambi* cf. E. Degani, "Note sulla fortuna di Archiloco e di Ipponatte in epoca Ellenistica", in *Poeti greci giambici ed elegiaci* (ed. Degani, Milan 1977) 106-108, 113 ff.

the Hellenistic present: no barbs fly at Boupalos, Hipponax' quondam target (cf. fr. 1; 12.2; 15; 84.18; 95.3-4, 15; 95a; 120 West). The poet rather summons the Alexandrian literati to the temple of Sarapis, whither they run in droves, anxious (as any modern scholar would be) to view the wondrous apparition of a poet long dead, to whose works they would probably have devoted considerable study. The defunct iambographer in turn marvels at the multitude of the living who swarm about him "like flies around a goatherd" (v. 26), an ironic inversion of Odysseus' amazed fear at the multitude of dead that gather around him in the underworld at *Odyssey* 11.36-43. Commanding the scholars to be silent, Hipponax orders them to write down – could his words impress them any other way? – the tale which he is going to tell (σωπὴ γενέσθω καὶ γράφεσθε τὴν ῥῆσιν v. 31). He then dictates to them a surprisingly benevolent fable intended to make them put aside their jealous rivalries, their literary disputes, and live in concord (Dieg. VI 1.5-6, 19-21). Perhaps fr. 216, "they coughed as though drinking vinegar", represented the scholars' revulsion at such a disgusting thought (thus, apparently, Pfeiffer *ad loc.*). If so, the entire scene might reflect the ambiguous attitude of the Alexandrians to the past: on the one hand keen to encounter it, on the other distrustful of its authority.

In any case, Hipponax is not long for this world.[26] "Not even I have much time to spare," he says, "for I must whirl about, alas, in the midst of Acheron" (v. 33-35).[27] And consequently, upon finishing his tale, he states "the time has come to sail away... (in the boat) of Charon" (v. 96-97) – a significant reassertion of distance, since Callimachus, while starting from Hipponax, proceeds in his remaining twelve *Iamboi* to stretch the limits of the genre, producing poems in various uncharacteristic meters, atypical dialects, with bold thematic innovations (an "epinician" iambos in VIII, a birthday song in XII, etc.).[28] In the final poem of the series (XIII) he asserts that distance on a geographical level as well, stating that he sings *Iamboi* without having gone to Ephesus (home of Hipponax) or having mingled with Ionians (v. 63-64). The "revival" of iambic verse, as dramatized by Callimachus through the figure of Hipponax, is thus a conditional revival, one qualified by a

---

[26] He is Callimachus' temporary spokesman and not, as Clayman has argued (*op. cit.* p. 56-57), reincarnated *in* Callimachus.

[27] Incidentally, this is an unnoticed parallel to the troublesome Theocr. 1.140 where Daphnis "went to the stream and the whirlpool washed over" him. Hipponax' words seem to show that, while strictly speaking "the souls of the dead were not submerged in Acheron, but waited at the water's edge to be ferried across" (thus Dover *ad* Theocr. 1.140; cf. R. M. Ogilvie, *JHS* 82 [1962] 108-109 = *WdF* p. 173-174), one could nevertheless speak in this way of passing to the Underworld.

[28] Thus also Clayman, *op. cit.* p. 48.

strong awareness of difference in tastes and aims, of fracture in time and place.

It may be appropriate at this point to discuss a problematic fragment from Callimachus' *Aetia* (fr. 64) that falls mid way between the fictitious epitaphs which we examined and the full-scale resurrection of *Iambos* 1. Pfeiffer called it "Sepulcrum Simonidis", "The Tomb of Simonides".

> Οὐδ' ἄ]ν τοι Καμάρινα τόσον κακὸν ὀκκόσον ἀ[ν]δρός
> κινη]θεὶς ὁσίου τύμβος ἐπικρεμάσαι·
> καὶ γ]ὰρ ἐμόν κοτε σῆμα, τό μοι πρὸ πόληος ἔχ[ευ]αν
> Ζῆν'] Ἀκραγαντῖνοι Ξείν[ο]ν ἁζόμενοι,
> ...κ]ατ' οὖν ἤρειψεν ἀνὴρ κακός, εἴ τιν' ἀκούει[ς   5
> Φοίνικ]α πτόλιος σχέτλιον ἡγεμόνα·
> πύργῳ] δ' ἐγκατέλεξεν ἐμὴν λίθον οὐδὲ τὸ γράμμα
> ᾐδέσθη τὸ λέγον· τόν [μ]ε Λεωπρέπεος
> κεῖσθαι Κήιον ἄνδρα τὸν ἱερόν, ὃς τὰ περισσά
> ..καὶ] μνήμην πρῶτος ὃς ἐφρασάμην,   10
> οὐδ' ὑμέας, Πολύδευκες, ὑπέτρεσεν, οἵ με μελάθρου
> μέλλοντος πίπτειν ἐκτὸς ἔθεσθέ κοτε
> δαιτυμόνων ἄπο μοῦνον, ὅτε Κραννώνιος αἰαῖ
> ὤλισθεν μεγάλους οἶκος ἐπὶ Σκοπάδας.
> ὦνακες, ἀλ..[ι..]. γὰρ ἔτ' ἦν[15
> .....

Not even Kamarina could threaten so great an evil as the
   removal of a sacred man's tomb.
For my sepulcher, which before their city the Akragantians
   threw up for me in awe of Zeus Hospitable –
that sepulcher an evil man tore down, if you have heard of
   Phoinix, wicked commander of the city.
And he embedded my tombstone in the rampart tower, nor did he
   reverence the inscription which says that I, son of Leoprepes,
lie here, the sacred man of Keos, who devised the extra
   ...and first contrived the skill of memory;
nor did he tremble before you both, Polydeukes, who once removed
                                                                me
   alone of all banqueters from the hall,
which was about to fall, when the Krannonian palace, alas,
   crashed down upon the mighty Skopadae.
O lords,....

Here, as in *Iambos* 1 and the epitaphs for Anacreon and Hipponax, a dead poet speaks. Yet it is tantalizingly unclear from whence his voice is thought to emanate and to whom it is addressed (cf. v. 5-6). Simonides does not appear to have risen from the dead, yet neither does he speak through the medium of his tombstone. The medium seems rather to be Callimachus who impersonates the dead man, allowing him to borrow his voice in order to speak not from, but about his tombstone which, as we learn, has been desecrated and removed from its proper place. And just as the source of the voice is so disposed as to be traceable to no one but Callimachus, so the addressee can be none but the reader of the poem: for the Akragantines would not need to be told that they had built Simonides a tomb (v. 3-4), or asked if they had heard of Phoinix (v. 5-6).

The first couplet alludes to an oracle given the inhabitants of Kamarina when they asked if they should drain an eponymous lake. "Do not move Kamarina, for unmoved is better", they were told. But they ignored the oracle and their city suffered a catastrophe. It is even worse, however, to move a sacred man's tomb, asserts Simonides (Οὐδ' ἄ]ν τοι Καμάρινα τόσον κακὸν ὀκκόσον... v. 1); and the Suda (s.v. Simonides) reports that Akragas was indeed taken in war by Syracuse as a consequence of Phoinix' wicked deed.[29] No other source refers to this Phoinix.

This otherwise unattested figure, however, was clearly of interest to Callimachus. For his rash indifference encompasses not just the desecration of a tomb, but that of a very special tomb, namely a great poet's. But this means nothing to Phoinix, for the commander is a philistine. Not only does he ignore Zeus' guest-right, which Simonides enjoyed in Akragas (v. 4), he is utterly without regard for the literary dead or reverence for the authority of the written word (as embodied in the epitaph, οὐδὲ τὸ γράμμα / ἡδέσθη v. 7-8).[30] Nor does he know his literary history, as is clear from Simonides' allusion to the story of his rescue by the Dioskouroi when they brought the house down on the impious Skopadai (v. 11-14). But more, Phoinix' act may be viewed as peculiarly insulting to the character of Simonides' œuvre since that poet was especially famous for his poems on the dead (on those fallen at Thermopylae cf. *PMG* 531, Hdt. VII 228; at Marathon (?) cf. *Vita Aesch.*;

---

[29] Pfeiffer *ad* 6 ff. suggests that the war was one mentioned by Diod. XIX 3.70 during the reign of the Syracusan tyrant Agathokles (last quarter of the 4th cent.). It seems likely that the fragmentary 3-4 verses at the end of the poem referred to this defeat, since the Suda twice cites Callimachus' poem (v. 7-9 and 11-14) and may well depend on it for its information.

[30] This latter point will be even more emphatic if, as Lobel thought likely (*ad* P. Oxy.2211 vv. 9-10), the lacuna at the beginning of v. 10 contained a reference to Simonides' invention of the letters η, ω, ξ, ψ, cf. *ad loc.* P.Oxy. 1800, fr. 1.45 f. and Suda s.v. Simonides. This seems to me preferable to Maas and Pfeiffer's suggestion (*ad loc.*) that τὰ περισσά referred to Simonides' "sapientia": the coordinate relatives ὅς.../... ὅς in vv. 9-10 speak for two equally weighted statements, not for one which was very general, the other very specific. In either case, however, a suitable supplement for the lacuna has yet to be found.

see also Catull. 38.8; Horace II 1.38; Quint. X 1.64; Dionysius *de imit.* p. 205, 7 Usener; Aristid. XXXI 2 p. 212 Keil; cf. also H. Fränkel, *Dicht. u. Phil.* p. 346). Simonides thus defends *from the grave* the very tradition of funerary verse of which he was so prominent a representative.

Finally, Phoinix did not recall that Simonides was renowned for his invention of mnemotechnics, the system of memory (v. 10); and Simonides confirms his reputation in this regard by forgetting nothing. Through Callimachus' commemorative mediation, the memory of Phoinix lives on: an "evil man" (ἀνὴρ κακός v. 5), a "wicked commander" (σχέτλιος ἡγεμών v. 6), disdainful of epitaphs (v. 7-8), unawed by the gods (v. 10) – damned, in short, by the very μνήμη he sought to destroy.

Learned Hellenistic recollection thus comes to the aid of its archaic counterpart and kin. And Callimachus' love of *arcana* could find no more appropriate conduit. It is significant that this poem is full of first attestations: the story about Kamarina, Phoinix himself, the memory system, Simonides' deliverance from the destruction of the Skopadai – all these first appear here. While one could hardly suggest that Callimachus really was the first to relate these things (as Slater, *Phoenix* 26 [1972] 233, and others have pointed out, he probably had access to Chamaileon's περὶ Σιμωνίδου), I believe we *can* call this a learned poem; the full force of Simonides' indignation (so memorably expressed by his repeated use of possessive and personal pronouns: ἐμὸν...σῆμα, μοι v. 3, ἐμὴν λίθον v. 7, με Λεωπρέπεος v. 8, με v. 11) will have been shared only by the learned audience to which it is addressed. To the Alexandrian, Simonides *qua* dead man is evidently meaningful, his memorial worth preserving.

Yet the very form which Callimachus gives to his poem underscores the complexity of the relationship between commemorator and the thing commemorated. In this regard, the placing of the text of Simonides' tombstone in indirect discourse (v. 7-9) is significant. On the one hand, this may reflect at a syntactic level the inclusion of the original memorialization within Simonides' present discourse – itself a result of the epitaph's displacement from its proper site on the tomb and the fact that it has been embedded elsewhere (in a place unworthy of it). More importantly, however, it mirrors the overall obliqueness of the present context where Callimachus commemorates Simonides' epitaph or, more precisely, Simonides recalling and thereby repairing the loss of his memorial. The poem is thus a commemoration of a commemoration of a commemoration. And at each stage we see a process of incorporation: at the level of imagery, the tombstone embedded in the tower; at the level of syntax *oratio obliqua*; and at the level of poetic tradition, one poet's voice inscribed in that of another. For our previous difficulty in locating the source of Simonides' voice may now be viewed as another instance of what occurs when the archaic poet reformulates his epitaph in indirect discourse. It points up the mediated, oblique quality of the relationship between Callimachus and his remote predecessor. But - and here again we confront this paradoxical aspect of Hellenistic poetry - it does so even as the modern poet self-consciously aligns himself with the deceased and contributes to an act of retribution indeed perhaps more terrible than that which attended Kamarina. Akrages may in reality have been captured, but the poem itself is an act of reprisal.

A more radical contrivance to bridge the gulf was that employed by Ennius in the proem to his *Annals* (early 2nd cent. B.C.). Probably following a Hellenistic model,[31] the Latin poet claimed that Homer had appeared to him in a dream and told him that his soul had been reborn in Ennius' body.[32] We see at once how such an idea compels a poet to declare his literary allegiance and indebtedness in a far more consequent and, ultimately, restrictive way than had Callimachus in *Iambos* 1 or in the poem on Simonides: it would not be easy for Ennius to wriggle out of such a claim and profess a very different poetic orientation. Yet even this device would leave sufficient room for manoeuvering. Ennius could at once acknowledge discontinuity while asserting that it was not absolute: though Homer was deceased, his spirit could re-emerge in new circumstances and with a new shape - writing Latin hexameter, on Roman themes. It was up to Ennius to interpret what it meant to be an *alter Homerus* (Lucilius fr. 1189 Marx, Horace *Ep.* II 1.50), another Homer.

The dream of the dead Homer points us to yet a further way - not in itself imbued with the image of death yet closely related to it - in which Hellenistic poets could express their distance from the literary past and their desire to overcome their isolation. In the prologue to the *Aetia* (fr. 2), Callimachus describes a dream in which he was translated to Mt. Helikon and, like Hesiod, encountered the Muses, who forthwith initiated him into the mysteries of song and related to him the stories which form the first two books of the *Aetia*. What is of particular interest to us is that Callimachus no longer has an unmediated encounter with the Muses on Mt. Helikon as Hesiod had had. In order to recapture the Hesiodic experience, he puts himself into the state of consciousness which, to the Greek mind, most nearly approximated death, i.e. sleep - the brother of death, in mythological terms. The prologue to the *Aetia* thus reverses the procedure which we saw in Callimachus' first *Iambos* and in Ennius' proem. There the dead encroached on the

---

[31] Cf. C.O. Brink, *AJPh* 93 (1972) 559-560.
[32] For sources and discussion cf. O. Skutsch, *The Annals of Q. Ennius* (Oxford 1985) 147-153.

world of the living, thus forging a link between past and present; here a living poet assumes a death-like state and thus has access to the experience of the past.[33] It is only appropriate that Callimachus presents the material of the first two books of his *Aetia* as having been received in this state. For this, Callimachus' central work, is itself a most telling monument to the sense of rupture: a compendium of tales attempting to explain the peculiarities of the present by reference to their "causes" in the distant past, the very need for which bespeaks at once an awareness of the enormous gulf separating past and present, and the desire to bridge it.[34]

One final route to the poetic past was that taken by Timon of Phlius, the 3rd cent. B.C. Cynic poet, and with it we arrive at the opposite pole from the full-scale resurrection of *Iambos* 1. In a part of his *Silloi*, or "squint-eyed verses", Timon appears to have journied to the under-

---

[33] We note the strong possibility that Herodas (in his 8th *Iambos*, the "Dream") likewise used the medium of sleep in order to describe an encounter with a literary antecedent, i.e. Hipponax, whom the poet claims in the last lines of his poem to have emulated. It has often been assumed that the angry old man who upbraids him in his dream is none other than the archaic iambographer. And indeed, such abusive behavior, even towards an admirer, is precisely what we would expect from a notorious practitioner of invective. When the old man threatens the dreamer (καίπερ ὢν πρέσβυς / οὔλη κατιθὺ τῇ βατηρίῃ κόψω v. 59-60), he virtually quotes a line of Hipponax (δοκέων ἐκεῖνον τῆι βα{κ}τηρίηι κόψαι fr. 8 Degani = 20 West). κόπτειν, moreover, seems to be one of Hipponax' characteristic words (cf. fr. 120 and 121). And lastly we note that Alcaeus of Messene (*AP* VII 536 = 13 G-P) refers to Hipponax simply as ὁ πρέσβυς for the first four lines of a six line poem before finally mentioning his name. Unfortunately, given the state of Herodas' poem, we cannot be sure of the identification, cf. I.C.Cunningham, *Herodas' Mimiambi* (Oxford 1971) 194 with bibliography.

We should also note the scene of poetic initiation that occurs as a dream encounter with Anacreon in the opening poem of the Anacreontea (fr. 1 West). This poem may, as West has said (*Greek Metre* p. 152 and in the preface to his edition p. XVI-XVII), be as early as the 2nd or 1st cent. B.C.

[34] This point has been forcefully made by Zanker (*Realism* p. 120 f.), who points to the frequency of formulae such as εἰσέτι νῦν περ and ἔνθεν in Hellenistic poetry to denote continuity (cf. esp. p. 121 n. 32). One could establish a scale of aetiological interest between Homer, at the one extreme, and Callimachus at the other. Homer has remarkably few *aetia*, the only one of real prominence being that of Achilles' tomb (*Od.* 24.80-84; cf. *Il.* 7.84-91 and 23.245-248). As Nagy has pointed out (*The Best of the Achaeans* [Baltimore 1979] 342; cf. 159-161), the only other example is in the narrative of the Achaean wall (*Il.* 12.2-33), where - significantly - we learn why there is no trace of that wall in the present: "It is almost as if all the 'props' that mark an Achaean expedition against Troy are to be obliterated once the expedition is over and the attention of epic switches to other places, other stories" (Nagy p. 160). There is, then, little attempt to link the heroic world to the poet's present. The Age of Heroes stays remote: that is part of its affect. While *aetia* are certainly present in pre-Hellenistic verse (e. g. at the end of many tragedies), they are not nearly as all pervasive as they are in Hellenistic verse. There, the interest in forging a link between present and past seems to reach its height.

world – in self-conscious emulation of Odysseus – to question his great predecessor in Sillography, the inventor of the genre, Xenophanes.[35] As A. A. Long has written, "Xenophanes played a role in the *Silloi* comparable to that of Virgil in Dante's *Inferno*."[36] He served as Timon's guide, and answered his queries about the shades of the philosophers. While it remains unclear how much of the *Silloi* assumed this dramatic form (cf. A. A. Long, *op. cit.* p. 81), a statement in Diogenes Laertius IX 111 suggests that it comprised at least the last two of three books: "The second and third books take the form of a dialogue. [Timon] appears asking Xenophanes of Colophon about every philosopher, and Xenophanes describes them to him; the older philosophers in the second book; the later ones in the third." To my knowledge, no one has noted the suggestive similarity between (the last two books of) Timon's *Silloi* and the first two books of *Aetia* by his contemporary, and possible acquaintance, Callimachus.[37] Both poets avail themselves of the dialogue form set – in either case – in a supernatural encounter with authoritative figures of the literary tradition and conceived as a strategy for gaining access to themes from the distant past.

We see then that images of death abound. Yet they are only one expression of discontinuity. Another, which will concern us in the remainder of this chapter – in a pair of heterogeneous examples drawn from Callimachus' Hymns – , is literary allusion: perhaps the single most characteristic mark of Hellenistic verse.

We observed in discussing the anonymous epic fragments at the start of this chapter that literary antecedents could be cited in a non-allusive manner. The language was for the most part familiar, the actions typical, limited attempt was made to evoke identifiable events, personages or turns of phrase. It is well to stress, however, that non-allusive citation could equally draw on poetic rarities; that is, it could use precisely

---

[35] This "katabasis" was first proposed by A. Meineke, *Philologicarum Exercitationum in Athenaei Deipnosophistas* (1843) 6–7, and has since been generally accepted. It is based 1) on the report in Diog. Laert. IX 111 (quoted below) that Timon held a conversation with Xenophanes in this work and 2) on the evidence of repeated formulae, such as οἷον and verbs of seeing and recognition, recalling the first *Nekyia* of the *Odyssey* (cf. the prefatory comments of Lloyd-Jones and Parsons on *SH* 775–840). While I subscribe to the *communis opinio*, it is prudent to recall that Timon's colloquy with Xenophanes, and his viewing of the dead philosophers, are equally conceivable when set in a dream of a katabasis, or even simply in a dream. For the parallel with the format of the first two books of Callimachus' *Aetia* cf. below.

[36] *Proc. Cambr. Philol. Soc.* 204 (1978) 78.

[37] According to Diog. Laert. IX 110, Timon knew and wrote of Ptolemy Philadelphus. His verses on the disputatious grammarians in the Alexandrian Museum (*SH* 786) are perennial favorites in the scholarly literature on the period. Cf. also the anecdotes concerning his acquaintance with Aratus (Pfeiffer, *Hist.* p. 98).

the *hapax legomena* or disputed words which were the meat of Alexandrian allusive play – without intending allusion. This is brought home to us in the grotesque, but amusing story of how Alexarchos, brother of Cassander (one of Alexander's successors), intended to found the city of Ouranopolis on the Athos peninsula, desiring to introduce there a new language composed entirely of glosses, i.e. poetic rarities (Athen. III 98 c, cf. Schmid-Staehlin II 1 p. 116 with n. 3 and 4). As soon as such glosses become everyday speech, however, they relinquish *eo ipso* all allusive potential for their speakers and, by consequence, for those who hear them (representing, for the less learned among the latter, an entirely new language). The words become merely a new set of signs which, as in any other language, have no meaning apart from that assigned to them by usage in a given culture, being thought rare, unintelligible or (as would now be the case in Ouranopolis) common because of that usage.

The self-conscious literary allusion of the Hellenistic poets was of an altogether different order. Specific scenes, characters, details of narrative, diction and style were evoked with unremitting precision – the fruit of the most intimate knowledge of antecedent texts. And though such a technique was nothing new,[38] the authors of this time pushed it further than ever before and assigned to it a position of unexampled pre-eminence. This learned predilection has long been seen – and, for the most part, censured – by Classical scholars. "It is their imitativeness and their allusiveness which more than anything else have tended to discredit Hellenistic poets", said Pfeiffer in "The Future of Studies in the Field of Hellenistic Poetry" (*JHS* 75 [1955] 71 = *Ausg. Schr.* [Munich 1960] 154). To be sure, the critical climate, since Pfeiffer wrote these words, has changed: it is now widely acknowledged that allusion was no mere stylistic device known from occasional use in earlier verse and now just grown more prominent, but rather that it was central and formative, a generative nucleus, for the poetry of the Age.[39] Yet for all the ingenuity

---

[38] Cf. for instance L. Rissman's book on Homeric allusion in Sappho, *Love and War, Homeric Allusion in the Poetry of Sappho*, (Meisenheim 1984). Cf. also M. Kumpf, *The Homeric Hapax Legomena and their Literary Use by Later Authors, Especially Euripides and Apollonius of Rhodes*, (Diss. Ohio State Univ. 1974). On archaic use of allusion generally cf. J. A. Davison, "Quotations and allusions in Early Greek Literature", *Eranos* 53 (1955) 125–140 = *From Archilochus to Pindar* (New York 1968) 70–85, and A. E. Harvey, CQ 7 (1957) 207.

[39] A forerunner in this regard was Wilamowitz (cf. e.g. *HD* I 181–182: "Wir merken hier, daß die Hörer für gelehrte Dichtung Verständnis mitbringen. Nicht nur homerische und hesiodische Verse müssen ihnen gegenwärtig sein... Überhaupt lebt der Dichter von fremden Gedanken..."), but – as E. R. Schwinge has shown in "Wilamowitz' Verständnis der hellenistischen Poesie" (*Wilamowitz nach 50 Jahren*, Darmstadt 1985, 151–177, esp.

and effort that recent scholars have expended on unearthing allusions, they have largely ignored the question of why allusion became so essential, so indispensible a feature of Hellenistic verse.

No one explanation, of course, could account for a phenomenon of such variety. Nevertheless I would like to suggest one factor which may have moved the poets to favor this mode of expression. I mean their sense of rift. Theirs was a passionate, relentless endeavor - an obsessive endeavor - to permeate their works with the literature of the past, to acquire and exhibit encyclopaedic grasp, as though to insist that they knew it after all, that despite historical-geographical impediments and isolation they were as familiar now with the cultural heritage as a cultivated person might have been in the time when it was being produced -

---

167-171) - for all his efforts to judge Hellenistic poetry on its own terms, Wilamowitz remained bound to the "klassizistische Perspektive" (167).

The decisive contribution towards understanding the central role of allusion in Hellenistic poetry was made by Hans Herter in his essay "Kallimachos und Homer" (*Xenia Bonnensia. Festschrift zum 75jährigen Bestehen des Philologischen Vereins und Bonner Kreises* [Bonn 1929] 50-105 = *Kleine Schriften* [Munich 1975] 371-416), where Callimachus' *Hymn to Artemis* was subjected to a sensitive and penetrating interpretation in light of the Homeric tradition. It was here that Herter formulated the memorable statement that it was the goal of the Hellenistic poets "in den Bahnen Homers so unhomerisch zu sein wie möglich" (p. 50 = 371).

A whole school of Classicists has since proclaimed Hellenistic poetry to be "arte allusiva" (though the term was coined by G. Pasquali in his 1942 essay "Arte allusiva", *Italia che scrive* 25 [1942] 185f. = *Stravaganze quarte e supreme* [Venice 1951] 11-20 = *Pagine stravaganti* vol. 2 [Florence 1968] 275-283, I refer here to G. Giangrande [cf. *CQ* 17, 1967, 85 f. = *Scripta Minora Alexandrina* I, Amsterdam 1980, 11 f.] and his circle at the Classics Research Center of Birkbeck College, London.). Unfortunately, this school has also magnified the importance which Herter attached to discovering the Homeric backdrop of a given poem, making this the single guiding principal of their work: "the orthodox framework of interpretation as practised by specialists in Hellenistic poetry", as Giangrande declares on page 1 of an essay which stands programmatically at the start of his *Scripta Minora Alexandrina* I (Amsterdam 1980 = *QUCC* 15, 1973, 73 ff.). Worse still, with few exceptions the work of this school does not equal that of Herter, its avowed master (cf. *CQ* op. cit. p. 85 = p. 11 with n. 2; and Giangrande's suggestion that one vilified Classicist go "to Bonn to study under Herter for a while", *Scripta Minora op. cit.* p. 5). The result has been a new cottage-industry, devoted to discovering allusions - one-sidedly Homeric - wherever they exist and occasionally (as some might admonish) where they do not. We must credit this school with recognizing the fundamental role of allusion for Hellenistic poets, and with placing it in the limelight as never before. Yet its application of that "orthodox framework" is often almost mechanical - perhaps made the more grimly determined because of the particularly belligerent reaction of this school to criticism (cf. the pages of their journal, *Museum Philologum Londoniense*) - ; its scholarly output accordingly suffers from those defects that usually appear when a method is pushed to extremes.

With regard to allusion in Latin poetry, important contributions have been made by G. B. Conte, *The Rhetoric of Imitation* (Ithaca 1986), and R. Thomas, "Virgil's Georgics and the Art of Reference", *HSCP* 90 (1986) 171-198.

perhaps even more so! The allusiveness of these poets was, I submit, not merely fashionable erudition. Rather it reflects the profound desire to compensate for a perceived epigonality and artistic disjunction. Social and geographical isolation in Alexdandria could only have intensified this desire, for the burden of asserting one's cultural identity in such an old and alien civilization would have been especially onerous.[40] In part, then, the avid, at times extravagant cultivation and preservation of the heritage is like that familiar to us from immigrant communities throughout the ages: a desire to be more Greek than the Greeks.[41] Put somewhat differently, the underlying hope of these poets' allusiveness is meaningful continuity. And a readership that desired to appreciate the allusions, that found them pleasurable, would naturally have had to share this obsessive bent and the deep-seated need from which it arose. Consequently the very mastery that the Hellenistic poets are so zealous to establish and display is itself a sign of rupture.

The distance of which this impassioned allusiveness is both a symptom and a redress determines the nature of the Hellenistic relationship to the literary past. To be sure, the assertion of that relationship could sometimes turn fanatical and end in barren pedantry, in a poetry overwhelmed by the past. More frequently, however, the search for meaningful continuity was tempered by the very sense of rift from which it had itself arisen. That is, while an awareness of the gulf might on the one hand be a cause for lamentation, it could at the same time engender the sense of freedom evident in the unfettered and inventive use to which the Hellenistic poets put the past. Perhaps we owe the last great flowering of Greek culture at Alexandria to this fructifying rupture.

---

[40] In a similar vein, though not explicitly with regard to allusion, cf. A. W. Bulloch, *Cambr. Hist. of Class. Lit.* I (Cambridge 1985) 543: "the enormous political upheavals and subsequent reshaping and expansion of the Hellenic world in the 4th century gave many Greeks a sense of separation from their roots and their past, and a weakening of their identity as Greeks: their reaction was often to intensify and reaffirm traditional values, both social and cultural – and for the Alexandrian writers, of course, this coincided with their immediate scholarly concerns, to acquire and put on a sound basis the texts of the great writers of the past."

[41] The assertion of Greek identity is particularly evident in the great social importance which the gymnasium acquired in the Hellenistic era. The significance of this institution has been impressively described by M. P. Nilsson, *Die Hellenistische Schule* (Munich 1955), who calls it "der Herd und die Hochburg der griechischen Kultur, das Wahrzeichen des Griechentums, das die Griechen von den Eingeborenen unterschied" (p. 84), "dort fühlten sie ihr Griechentum" (p. 92); cf. also L. Koenen, *Eine agonistische Inschrift aus Ägypten und frühptolemäische Königsfeste* (Meisenheim 1977) 1, 17. On the purposeful preservation and cultivation of Greek institutions (such as the pan-hellenic agon, theatrical performances, visual arts, etc.) cf. C. Préaux, *Le Monde Hellénistique* II (Paris 1978) 550–565 and N. Lewis, *Greeks in Ptolemaic Egypt* (Oxford 1986) 26–27.

The strange case of Ouranopolis showed us that non-allusive citation could extend even to the rarest poetic glosses. Correspondingly, deliberate, pointed reference to the literary past, born of the certainty that one was irrevocably fixed on the further side of a divide, is evident even down to the most elementary and obvious use of a famous quotation. By "quotation" I mean a syntactically self-contained utterance which, within the work of a given poet, preserves intact the words of another. Such a quotation provides the simplest means for bridging the gulf with the past since it creates a juncture, a visible seam between present and past on the scroll. Yet while imbedded in new surroundings, the quotation remains fundamentally alien, perceived as a foreign body within its adoptive text, set off as it were by quotation marks (although, of course, these did not exist in the ancient world).

A particularly famous quotation in Callimachus' *Hymn to Zeus* may help to show what role this device could play in connection with rupture and revival.[42] Let us call to mind the context in the hymn: After

---

[42] Actually, we encounter two such quotations in Callimachus' *Hymn to Zeus*. The first (v. 8) has lost its original context, however, so that we cannot say what Callimachus did with his source. Nevertheless, its setting in the *Hymn to Zeus* suggests an amusing play between ostensible adherence to traditional authority and witty irreverence toward the same:

The poet, after an opening invocation, raises the vexed question of where the father of gods and men was born: some say Crete, others Arcadia (v. 4-7). To find an answer Callimachus avails himself of a waggish stroke. He turns with his query to the very subject of the poem, that is to Zeus himself: "which of these, father, lied?" (πότεροι, πάτερ, ἐφεύσαντο; v. 7). The god's reply (I take it to be such, though there are no introductory or closing formulae. Cf. McLennan *ad* v. 7; N. Hopkinson, CQ 34 [1984] 140; S. Goldhill, *Proc. Cambr. Philol. Soc.* 212 [1986] 27-28; and the Muses "reply", *H.* 4.84-85, ch. 1 p. 42 above) is as radical as it is humorous, for he responds with a quotation, a verse from the 6th/5th century poet Epimenides of Crete: "Κρῆτες ἀεὶ ψεῦσται", "Cretans are always liars" (for conjecture as to the original context, cf. E. Maass, *Aratea* [Berlin 1892] 343-346 and M. West, *The Orphic Poems* [Oxford 1983] 47). To our astonishment, the ruler of the universe is depicted as a man (?!) of letters citing literary antecedents to adjudicate a scholarly dispute – a cosmic model for standard Alexandrian practice.

A literary quotation such as this must be distinguished from a proverb, παροιμία, which characteristically becomes detached from its inventor and assumes a life of its own within the popular oral tradition. While "Cretans are always liars" has a certain proverbial quality, it is unattested before Callimachus (thereafter cf. Paul's *Letter to Titus* 1.12; Clem. *Strom.* I 59), never entered the paroemiographic tradition and, as we shall see, acquires its full force not as a bit of folk wisdom, but only in connection with its author, the Cretan Epimenides.

For while the quotation Κρῆτες ἀεὶ ψεῦσται permits Callimachus to proceed as though sanctioned by the heritage with the variant of Zeus' birth which is nearer to his heart and poetic programme, i.e. the lesser known Arcadian version (first found here!), the educated reader would not have overlooked that the quotation itself derives from a Cretan, Epimenides, and that by its own standards it is thus fundamentally untrustworthy (thus far also Goldhill, *op. cit.* above). Worse still, if Zeus was born in Crete after all (as was

establishing the fact of Zeus' sovereignty on Olympus, the poet turns to the god's relationship with men. To start, he lists in the form of a priamel the sorts of men not chosen by Zeus for special patronage (v. 70-71): "not those experienced / with ships, not the shield-bearing man, not even the singer" (...οὐ σύ γε νηῶν / ἐμπεράμους, οὐκ ἄνδρα σακέσπαλον, οὐ μὲν ἀοιδόν·). With "not even" (οὐ μὲν, cf. Denn. *GP* 362), the poet communicates his pride in his high position on the list. Yet such areas of human endeavor are relegated by the god to other, lesser divinities. For his part Zeus selects "the rulers of cities themselves" (v. 73-74).

A second list (v. 74-75), reversing the hierarchy of the first with careful variations, now depicts those who are under a ruler's way: the landholder (γεωμόρος), the skilled with the spear (ἴδρις αἰχμῆς), the oarsman (ἐρέτης), all things, for what is not in a ruler's power? The rhetorical question is, of course, not meant to be answered. Far more, it brushes any response aside. Yet we are left wondering whether the absence of the singer from this second list might not be a pointed, significant omission.

This suspicion grows when, in a third and culminating preambular catalogue, he appears as prominently positioned as in the first. Here the poet names those "inferior" divinities and their human charges to whom he alluded before: to Hephaestus, for instance, belong the smiths, warriors to Ares, hunters to Artemis of the Chiton, to Phoebus those well skilled in the paths of the lyre, "but from Zeus come kings", "ἐκ δὲ Διὸς βασιλῆες" (v. 76-79). This, the crowning entry in the list, is a quotation: the celebrated hemistich from the section on kings in Hesiod's *Theogony* (v. 96), and it comes like a response to the naming of the poet in the previous line, as though to confirm that he is indeed one skilled in the ways of song (εὖ εἰδότας οἴμους v. 78). What an altogether different sort of poetic σοφία this is from that which one might

---

commonly thought ever since Hesiod *Th.* 468ff.), the idea of this verse coming from his mouth is even more troubling: Could it be that the king of the gods himself is leading us astray? Later in the poem (v. 60f.) Callimachus himself remarks "may I tell lies which can persuade the listener's ears" (ψευδοίμην ἀίοντος ἅ κεν πεπίθοιεν ἀκουήν v. 64). Perhaps he is doing just that with his quotation, exploiting its capacity to persuade, even adding a "compelling" reason of his own: "And indeed, O lord, the Cretans forged your tomb. But you didn't die, for you are forever" (v. 8-9). This justification notwithstanding, it is clear that Callimachus intends us to sense (and enjoy!) the underlying dubiousness of the argumentation. We see then that the quotation is a device by which the poet invokes and ostensibly binds himself to a past authority, yet that authority, even as it commands respect for its own success and stature within the tradition, turns out itself to be inherently open to doubt and interpretation.

have found before: it is a Hesiodic quotation that establishes an author's credentials![43]

The quotation is clearly intended to muster the full weight of Hesiodic authority behind the poet's cause (a common function of quotation). And it is the more weighty when one considers how exceptional such a sentiment as "ἐκ δὲ Διὸς βασιλῆες", "but from Zeus come kings", would have been within a poetic tradition engendered largely under very different conditions, namely those of the democratic or aristocratic polis. Because the Ptolemaic rulers, however, were keenly interested in bolstering their particular conception of absolute (soon to be divine-) monarchy by reference to venerable Hellenic precedent, their poets were constrained to return again and again to the very beginnings of Greek literature in order to find material suitable to their needs. Consequently, the Hesiodic vision of ideal similarity and a special bond between earthly and heavenly kingship was bound to strike an especially resonant chord. Callimachus could hardly have enlisted a bigger gun in the service of royal praise. And that he himself is entirely devoted to the sentiment appears to be demonstrated in his having reproduced even the immediate Hesiodic context where, as in our hymn, the half-line follows directly upon a statement of the poet's ties to Apollo (v. 94 f.). Thus, as Ziegler has said (*RhM* 68, 1913, p. 338), "mit diesem Zitat erweckt er den Anschein, als ob er nichts anderes gesagt habe als Hesiod."

Yet the very impressiveness of the quotation distracts from a subtext of which we become aware only upon recalling the larger context of the Hesiodic line. At v. 79 of the *Theogony* Hesiod brings to a close his catalogue of the Muses with Kalliope who, he says, "is the most excellent of all, for she..." (v. 79-80 ἣ δὲ προφερεστάτη ἐστὶν ἁπασέων / ἣ γὰρ...) – and here we expect the poet to turn to his own profession and explain that this Muse has a special rapport with the singer. Instead, startlingly, we hear that she *also* attends (n. b. καί) on kings: ἣ γὰρ καὶ βασιλεῦσιν ἅμ' αἰδοίοισιν ὀπηδεῖ. Whomever of these the Muses honor from birth, upon his tongue they pour sweet dew, and from his mouth flow soothing words (τῷ μὲν ἐπὶ γλώσσῃ γλυκερὴν χείουσιν ἐέρσην, / τοῦ δ' ἔπε' ἐκ στόματος ῥεῖ μείλιχα· v. 83-84).

Homer had described the eloquence of king Nestor in similar terms (*Iliad* 1.249 τοῦ καὶ ἀπὸ γλώσσης μέλιτος γλυκίων ῥέεν αὐδή, "from his

---

[43] This is not to say that earlier authors do not avail themselves of quotations. They do. But, unlike in our example, quotations in archaic lyric are generally identified as such by the poets using them: e. g. Solon 20 W, Sim. 8 West, Sim. *PMG* 581, Pind. *I* 6.66-67, *P* 4.277-278, *P* 6.20f., *O* 6.16-17, Bacch. 5.91-93, etc. Such a practice may be a response to the greater fluidity, i. e. uncertainty, of the tradition at this time; that is, to the lack of a canon as existed in Hellenistic times.

tongue the sound of his voice flowed sweeter than honey", cf. Hesiod's v. 97), yet for him there had been no hint that this ability was due to the Muse.[44] Kings, as Martin West observes (*ad* v. 80 ff.) "are not usually regarded by the Greeks as being dependent on the Muses". That rhetoric is a gift of these goddesses appears to be Hesiod's innovation – as the explanatory καί in ἢ γὰρ καὶ βασιλεῦσιν... (v. 80) suggests.

The poet goes on to detail how the divinely favored monarch is revered by all since he practices his art in the public assemblies so as to assuage disputes and to guide the community wisely, persuasively. "Such is the sacred gift of the Muses to mankind" (τοίη Μουσάων ἱερὴ δόσις ἀνθρώποισιν v. 93, i. e. all men profit from that gift which a king receives from the Muses since it provides them with the conditions necessary for a better life) "for..." – and now comes the interpretatory crux, the logical "salto mortale", as Kurt von Fritz has described it:[45] "for, you see (τοι Denn. *GP* p. 537), it is through the Muses and fardarting Apollo that there are singers upon the earth and players of lyre, but from Zeus come kings" (ἐκ γάρ τοι Μουσέων καὶ ἑκηβόλου Ἀπόλλωνος / ἄνδρες ἀοιδοὶ ἔασιν ἐπὶ χθόνα καὶ κιθαρισταί, / ἐκ δὲ Διὸς βασιλῆες).

The question is what does γάρ τοι in ἐκ γάρ τοι Μουσέων... explain? It explains, in my view, the latent and expected antithesis between singers and kings that underlies the whole passage from v. 80 f. The singers are the unspoken foil for the kings in the καί of v. 80: that is, while it goes without saying that Kalliope attends the singer, she also attends the king. But of course, as the following verses show, the Muses' involvement with kings, significant though it is, is selective, a "Wahlverwandtschaft" or elective affinity with those that they choose to honor from birth (v. 81–82). *For*, you see, singers are from the Muses (i. e. "naturverwandt"), but kings come from Zeus.[46] γάρ τοι thus explains the implied adversative phrase which we have made explicit with "but of course... etc." above.[47]

---

[44] In a passage from the *Odyssey* (8.166-177), which has striking parallels to that in Hesiod, eloquence is given by indeterminate gods (οὕτως οὐ πάντεσσι θεοὶ χαρίεντα διδοῦσιν / ἀνδράσιν, οὔτε φυὴν οὔτ' ἂρ φρένας οὔτ' ἀγορητύν v. 167-168). On the connection between the Homeric and Hesiodic passages cf. R. P. Martin, *TAPhA* 114 (1984) 29-48.

[45] *Festschr. Snell,* (Munich 1956) 42 = WdF *Hesiod* p. 311.

[46] Or, as von Fritz has put it (*op. cit.,* n. 45 above, p. 313), "ihr Amt haben die Könige nicht von den Musen oder von Apollon, sondern von Zeus. Sie sind immer noch Könige ohne die Musengabe. Damit steht es anders bei den Sängern. Sie haben ihr Amt, ihr ganzes Sein als Sänger, von Apollon und den Musen. Das ist der Unterschied."

[47] For γάρ explaining what is only implicitly, and not actually, present in the context cf. Denn. *GP* 61 f. and Barrett *ad* Eur. *Hipp.* 181-182: "γάρ... seems to introduce an explanation not of any particular words... just uttered, but of the underlying idea."

The words that follow further differentiate the singers from kings: ὃ δ' ὄλβιος, ὅντινα Μοῦσαι / φίλωνται· γλυκερή οἱ ἀπὸ στόματος ῥέει αὐδή ("but blessed is he, whomever the Muses love as their own: the voice pours sweet from his mouth" v. 96-97). Though generally construed as referring to the kings, the lines thereby yield a tortured train of thought, for the subsequent verses (98 f.) exemplify the "voice" that "pours sweet" by reference to the *singer*, not the king (cf. West *ad* v. 94-97). I would argue, therefore, that we must take ὃ δ' ὄλβιος, ὅντινα Μοῦσαι / φίλωνται· etc. as already referring to the singer,[48] and that this is apparent in the contrast with the corresponding lines about the king in v. 81 f.: ὅντινα τιμήσουσι Διὸς κοῦραι.../ (83) τῷ μὲν ἐπὶ γλώσσῃ γλυκερὴν χείουσιν ἐέρσην, / τοῦ δ' ἔπε' ἐκ στόματος ῥεῖ μείλιχα· ("whomever [*scil.* of kings] the daughters of Zeus honor.../ (83) upon his tongue they pour sweet dew, and from his mouth flow soothing words."). For all the similarity between these passages, one difference at once leaps out, namely that in v. 81 the Muses "honor" (τιμήσουσι) someone, in v. 96-97 they "love" (φίλωνται) him. φιλεῖν at this time retains a good measure of its root meaning, i.e. "jemanden als einen der Seinen betrachten bzw. behandeln".[49] Having just heard that poets come from the Muse, but that kings belong to Zeus, it makes sense that φίλωνται refer to the poet: the Muses might sometimes honor a king, but the poet is one of their own.

We cannot accept von Fritz' apparent interpretation of τοίη Μουσάων ἱερὴ δόσις ἀνθρώποισιν in v. 93 as a generalizing transition from kings (via mankind) to poets, and hence as the antecedent of γάρ τοι in v. 94: "eine Musengabe, die nicht nur Königen gegeben wird..., sondern auch anderen Menschen. Darauf folgt endlich 'denn von den Musen und von dem fernhintreffenden Apollon sind die Sänger...'." (*op. cit.*, n. 45 above, p. 43 = 312-313) τοίη must refer to the preceding discussion of the Muses' gift to kings, the fruit of which mankind enjoys in the form of good government while not itself receiving a comparable gift.

According to Friedlaender (*Hermes* 49, 1914, 10 = WdF 287) - followed by West (*ad* v. 94-97) - we should read verses 94-96 as though they were concessive, i. e. "Denn wenn auch die Sänger von Apoll und den Musen stammen und die 'Könige' (nicht von ihnen, sondern) von Zeus, so verleihen doch die Musen (allen, also auch den von Zeus stammenden 'Königen') die Macht der Rede." Yet this enfeebles the distinction between singers and kings expressed with such memorable and (surely) deliberate bluntness in v. 94-96, a distinction virtually provoked by the bold, unprecedented linking of the king with the Muse.

[48] Thus already von Fritz, *op. cit.*, and P. Pucci, *Hesiod and the Language of Poetry* (Baltimore 1977) 18-19.

[49] Thus H. B. Rosen, "Die Ausdrucksform für 'veräußerlichen' und 'unveräußerlichen Besitz' im Frühgriechischen. Das Funktionsfeld von homerischen φίλος", *Lingua* 8 (1959) 291, followed by M. Landfester, *Das griechische Nomen "philos" und seine Ableitungen* (Hildesheim 1966) 109. Cf. generally E. Benveniste, *Le vocabulaire des institutions indoeuropéennes* (Paris 1969) 335-353.

There can, then, on occasion be significant common ground between monarch and bard. Indeed, it is Hesiod's evident and emphatic interest in elaborating the advantages of this potential participation in the Muse on the part of the ruler – to wit, that the latter can fully realize his civic function only with her help – that (at first sight) renders harsh his equally emphatic insistence on the fundamental distinction between poet and king. Yet that distinction is primary. The potential conjunction is colored *a limine* by a strong awareness of its limitation: poets and kings remain in their essence apart.[50]

Returning to Callimachus' hymn, we find the conjunction of singer and sovereign is gone; only the difference remains: "From Phoebus come those well-versed in the ways of the lyre; 'but from Zeus come kings'" ("ἐκ δὲ Διὸς βασιλῆες" v. 77-78). Though keeping the half-line whole, Callimachus alters – or simply discards – its original context and thereby exposes the gulf between the Hesiodic poem and his own, between the world of the early archaic state and the realities of the Ptolemaic court. For in his *Hymn to Zeus* the king is pointedly aloof from an active use of the Muse.[51] In fact, the public arena for such use – the political institutions of the city-state – had become obsolete. The monarch now reigned omnipotent, as sublime and distant from his subjects as was his patron deity Zeus.[52] We need only think of the humble setting of the hymn as a symposium (v. 1, cf. McLennan *ad* v. 1), i. e. a festive gathering of friends, to sense the remoteness from Zeus' kings – "than which there is nothing more god-like" upon the earth (Διὸς οὐδὲν ἀνάκτων / θειότερον, v. 79-80) and among whom Callimachus' sovereign is supreme (περιπρὸ γὰρ εὐρὺ βέβηκεν v. 86):

---

[50] Thus also von Fritz (*op. cit.* p. 313): "Von einem Anspruch, daß der Sänger mit dem König gehen solle, ist hier schlechterdings nichts zu finden. Könige und Sänger werden im Gegenteil deutlich voneinander abgesetzt".

[51] This is also the case in a passage of Theocritus' *Encomium to Ptolemy* (17.73-75): Διὶ Κρονίωνι μέλοντι / αἰδοῖοι βασιλῆες, ὃ δ' ἔξοχος ὅν κε φιλήσῃ / γεινόμενον τὰ πρῶτα. Here Theocritus combines an allusion to *Theogony* 96 (ἐκ δὲ Διὸς βασιλῆες) with one to another passage from the same section on kings (v. 80-82): ἢ (scil. the Muse) γὰρ καὶ βασιλεῦσιν ἅμ' αἰδοίοισιν ὀπηδεῖ· / ὅντινα τιμήσουσι Διὸς κοῦραι μεγάλοιο / γεινόμενόν τ' ἐσίδωσι διοτρεφέων βασιλήων, / τῷ μὲν ἐπὶ γλώσσῃ γλυκερὴν χείουσιν ἐέρσην. The Hellenistic poet lets Zeus assume the function which the Muses perform in Hesiod: Zeus, not the Muse, looks upon the king at birth and subsequently cares for him. The king may support his poets (v. 112-116), but he himself has no active part in the Muse.

[52] Thus also Ziegler, *op. cit.* p. 338: "König und Untertanen sind auf Erden getrennte Welten". And correspondingly, p. 337: "Erst an den hellenistischen Höfen konnte Zeus nicht nur zum besonderen Gott und Schützer der Könige werden, sondern sogar, wie es im kallimacheischen Hymnus geschieht, gleichsam dem Volk entzogen und für den Hof reserviert werden".

ἑσπέριος κεῖνός γε τελεῖ τά κεν ἦρι νοήσῃ·
ἑσπέριος τὰ μέγιστα, τὰ μείονα δ', εὖτε νοήσῃ.

by evening he achieves those things that he thought of that morning;
by evening the greatest, the lesser the moment he thinks them.
(v. 87-88)

Ruling was no longer even the partial domain of the Muse. But neither did the poet sway large audiences in a public forum any more through the skillful use of words: perfomance, as mentioned above (p. 16-17, 61), had given way to the private act of reading. That kinship in the Muse, to which Hesiod could still appeal, and which had played out its role on the civic stage, was thus a thing of the past. For both government and literature had undergone a process of progessive isolation – from the populace and from each other. Poet and sovereign had withdrawn into separate spheres.

In the gap between poetic and political spheres, the poet acquired the freedom of a marginal figure.[53] He could afford an occasionally ironic or witty stance towards matters of royal interest because his domain was so circumscribed.[54] He could exempt himself – in a very gentle gesture of independence – from the list (v. 74-75) of those explicitly under the king's control (cf. above). And I would suggest that we see a quiet assertiveness even in his choice of a location previously unattested as the birthplace of his ruler's patron god, that is Parrhasia: "freedom of speech" (v. 10).

We have seen, then, that even as he affects continuity by quoting Hesiod's ἐκ δὲ Διὸς βασιλῆες, even as he aligns himself with the tradition so as to enlist its authority in support of his encomiastic intent, Callimachus obliquely but unmistakably asserts that that alignment is conditional, that the continuity conceals a break. Hesiod speaks; his words remain his own (set firmly apart within the hymn by our mental quotation marks). Yet while accurately resuscitated into the contemporary poem, these words acquire there a different shade of meaning, tinged by the personality of the Hellenistic author who invoked them and by the alien environment created for them in which to appear. The quotation thus does not differ substantially in function from the device of resurrecting an archaic author such as Hipponax into 3rd cent. B.C. Alexandria. Both respond to that aforementioned need for meaningful

---

[53] A phenomenon productively analyzed by N. Austin, *TAPhA* 98 (1967) 1f. esp. 18-21 with reference to Theocritus 16, and more generally by F. T. Griffiths, *op. cit.* ch. 1 n. 76 above, p. 42-43, 50.

[54] He had the licence, for instance, to link royal praise in an epinician (the *Victoria Berenices*) with a myth about the invention of the mousetrap! or to eulogize his queen through the persona of a lock of her hair (the *Coma Berenices*).

continuity (cf. p. 75 above), establishing a bridge to the past and allowing that past to speak in the here and now - albeit with a voice transformed by the filter of its new surroundings. Indeed, after the necromantic fiction of raising the poetic dead, a quotation is the closest we come to hearing the voice of an ancestral bard as "participant" in the literary present.

Such famous quotations are rare in Hellenistic verse, however. Far more typical, indeed all-pervasive, are complex and subtle forms of allusion where the poets attempt with obsessive persistence to penetrate the most minute particulars of the tradition. The unheard-of lengths to which they went in this attempt is itself, as mentioned before, an eloquent sign of their sense of rift. Conversely, it may (as in the case of the quotation) also reflect the necromantic urge, that desire to reanimate the past so as to establish a significant - albeit conditional - colloquy with it. I say conditional since, in the resultant dialogue with the dead, the living interlocutor characteristically reasserts the distance between himself and his antecedent text. At least that is what usually happens among the Hellenistic avant-garde.

An intricate, multi-layered allusion in Callimachus' *Hymn to Artemis*, which plays simultaneously upon two, perhaps three, passages from other poems, exhibits these opposing tendencies with a special and provocative twist: the poet establishes his link with the past not just in matters of detail; rather in a sweeping, programmatic sense he appears to proclaim allegiance to, and to espouse the style of, a specific antecedent poet. Yet even then, as we shall see, the precursor's authority is revealed to be far from absolute. "A diachronic gulf", as G. W. Most has put it (*Hermes* 109 [1981] 188)," - the centuries separating the various traditions of archaic and classical Greece from the Oikoumene of Alexander and his successors - is reinscribed" on the text. The passage from the hymn runs as follows:[55]

ἡνίκα δ' αἱ νύμφαι σε χορῷ ἔνι κυκλώσονται	170
ἀγχόθι πηγάων Αἰγυπτίου Ἰνωποῖο	
ἢ Πιτάνῃ (καὶ γὰρ Πιτάνη σέθεν) ἢ ἐνὶ Λίμναις,	
ἢ ἵνα, δαῖμον, Ἀλὰς Ἀραφηνίδας οἰκήσουσα	
ἦλθες ἀπὸ Σκυθίης, ἀπὸ δ' εἴπαο τέθμια Ταύρων,	174
μὴ νειὸν τημοῦτος ἐμαὶ βόες εἵνεκα μισθοῦ	
τετράγυον τέμνοιεν ὑπ' ἀλλοτρίῳ ἀροτῆρι·	
ἦ γάρ κεν γυιαί τε καὶ αὐχένα κεκμηυῖαι	
κόπρον ἔπι προγένοιντο, καὶ εἰ Στυμφαιίδες εἶεν	178

---

[55] For a somewhat fuller discussion of these verses cf. *ZPE* 54 (1984) 1-8 and 56 (1984) 16.

> εἰναετιζόμεναι κεραελκέες, αἳ μέγ' ἄρισται
> τέμνειν ὦλκα βαθεῖαν· ἐπεὶ θεὸς οὔποτ' ἐκεῖνον
> ἦλθε παρ' Ἥλιος καλὸν χορόν, ἀλλὰ θεῆται
> δίφρον ἐπιστήσας, τὰ δὲ φάεα μηκύνονται. 182

> But when your nymphs encircle you (sc. Artemis) in the dance
> near the springs of Egyptian Inopos,
> or at Pitane (for Pitane is yours as well), or at Limnai,
> or Halai Araphenides, deity, where you came to live
> from Scythia, and renounced the customs of the Taurians,
> then may my cows not plow a field for a wage,
> a field of four γύαι under another's plowman,
> for surely lame and with their necks worn out
> would they return to the dung, even if they were Stymphaian,
> nine years old, and drawing by the horns, which are far the best cows
> for plowing the deep furrow; since the god Helios never
> passes by that lovely dance, but he gazes at it,
> his chariot stopped, and the lights of day stretch on.

This passage has long drawn critical comment. For although it begins uneventfully enough with a learned catalogue of the places where Artemis' nymphs encircle her in the dance, verses 175 f. seem deliberately confusing. When those nymphs are dancing, says Callimachus, "may my cows not plow a field of four γύαι..., for they would surely return to the dung lame and with their necks worn out (175-178)." To find the sophisticated urban poet posing as a calculating farmer is unexpected, to say the least.[56] The reader's puzzlement is compounded, moreover, by the poet's fear for his cows if Artemis' chorus were dancing. What link could there be between these ostensibly unconnected occurrences? That is, what is there about this dance that could warrant such rustic anxiety? The answer is withheld until the second half of v. 180 and following: "the god Helios never passes that lovely chorus by, but rather halting his chariot he gazes at it, and the days grow long."

Yet while these verses explain the farmer's cares, they in no way explain why the poet would care to assume this guise in the first place. In this regard, the prominent allusions contained in this passage may help us further. The first, as has long been recognized, refers to a famous scene in the *Odyssey* (18.356 ff.).[57] Here, the suitor Eurymachus

---

[56] One initially feels that the βόες of v. 175 may be motivated by nothing more than the Ταύρων of v. 174.

[57] For this allusion cf. K. Kuiper, *Studia Callimachea* I (Leiden 1896) 91-92; H. Herter, "Kallimachos und Homer", *Kleine Schriften* (Munich 1975) 415 and n. 173; E. Cahen, *Les Hymnes de Callimaque* (Paris 1930) 129; F. Bornmann, *Callimachi Hymnus in Dianam* (Florence 1968) ad v. 176.

offers Odysseus a menial job on his land for pay so as to taunt him, μισθὸς δέ τοι ἄρκιος ἔσται, "and the wage will indeed be sufficient" (v. 358, to which Callimachus apparently refers with εἵνεκα μισθοῦ, "for a wage" v. 175). But Odysseus, he says, will never do an honest day's work so long as he can beg. Odysseus replies in kind, challenging Eurymachus to a contest of mowing when the days are long, or plowing on a large field, or even doing battle (v. 366 ff.):

> Εὐρύμαχ᾽, εἰ γὰρ νῶιν ἔρις ἔργοιο γένοιτο
> ὥρῃ ἐν εἰαρινῇ, ὅτε τ᾽ ἤματα μακρὰ πέλονται,
> ἐν ποίῃ, δρέπανον μὲν ἐγὼν εὐκαμπὲς ἔχοιμι,
> καὶ δὲ σὺ τοῖον ἔχοις, ἵνα πειρησαίμεθα ἔργου
> νήστιες ἄχρι μάλα κνέφαος, ποίη δὲ παρείη.   370
> εἰ δ᾽ αὖ καὶ βόες εἶεν ἐλαυνέμεν, οἵ περ ἄριστοι,
> αἴθωνες μεγάλοι, ἄμφω κεκορηότε ποίης,
> ἥλικες ἰσοφόροι, τῶν τε σθένος οὐκ ἀλαπαδνόν,
> τετράγυον δ᾽ εἴη, εἴκοι δ᾽ ὑπὸ βῶλος ἀρότρῳ·
> τῷ κέ μ᾽ ἴδοις, εἰ ὦλκα διηνεκέα προταμοίμην.   375

Eurymachus, might there be a contest of farm work between us
in the Springtime, when the days are long,
in the grass, and that I might have a well-curved scythe,
and you one like it, so that we might make trial of our work,
fasting till it becomes quite dark, and the grass would be abundant.
Or would that there were oxen to drive, the best there are,
tawny and big, both well glutted with grass,
equal in age and in drive at the plow, with strength not feeble,
and that there were a field of four γύαι, and the earth should give way
                                                              to the plow;
then you would see me, whether I could cut a straight, continuous
                                                              furrow.

The echoes of this scene in our passage are numerous and striking. Both Homer and Callimachus mention the length of days (v. 367 ὅτε τ᾽ ἤματα μακρὰ πέλονται ~ τὰ δὲ φάεα μηκύνονται, v. 182), the best sort of cows (v. 371 βόες ..., οἵ περ ἄριστοι ~ Στυμφαιίδες .../, αἳ μέγ᾽ ἄρισται v. 178-179), the size of the field (τετράγυον v. 374 ~ v. 176 same *sedes*), the plow or plowman (v. 374 ὑπὸ ... ἀρότρῳ ~ ὑπ᾽ ... ἀροτῆρι v. 176) and the sort of furrow to be cut (v. 375 ὦλκα διηνεκέα προταμοίμην ~ τέμνειν ὦλκα βαθεῖαν v. 180).

But while many scholars have noted Callimachus' dependence on this episode, and even compared the diction of the two in detail, none has publicly drawn the obvious conclusion that Callimachus' wish and that of Odysseus are precisely contrary, that is, whereas Odysseus at his most typically boastful (cf. a similar boast at 15.317 f.) is eager to plow a field of four γύαι when the days are long, Callimachus rejects the hero's course of action, saying that even Stymphaian oxen would be useless if, in a single day, they had to plow a τετράγυον νειόν.

Even in antiquity, the precise meaning of the old epic word τετράγυος was in doubt.[58] But Callimachus, like Homer apparently, takes it to be an enormous expanse: if the sun stood still, i.e. with unlimited time, the best possible cows might plow it, but they would almost die of fatigue in the process. On a normal day, even they would never come near to accomplishing their task. Only a hero like Odysseus, living in an heroic age, could plow four γύαι in a single day.[59] By Callimachus' time, the τετράγυον νειόν had become, as A. W. Mair put it, "the typical heroic field",[60] a tract too vast for a modern, third century man to plow.

Far preferable, in Callimachus' view, to play the cautious, calculating farmer – a role entirely in keeping with his poetic principles since it is essentially that of Hesiod, whose poetry the Hellenistic author championed as a model for his own (cf. Reinsch-Werner, op. cit., 4-19). Nearly as prominent as the allusion to Homer in our passage is one to the *Works and Days*: to the section that deals with plowing and when it ought to be done (v. 414 f.). Hesiod begins with the temporal correlatives ἦμος... τῆμος... τῆμος (v. 414, 420, 422), Callimachus with ἡνίκα ... τημοῦτος (v. 170, 175). As one might expect in a work that is partially organized as a farming calendar, such correlatives are commonly used by Hesiod as introductory formulae (cf. also 486, 488; 582, 585; ἦμος ...τότε 679, 681; εὖτ' ἄν...δὴ τότ' 458, 459; 564, 565; 609, 611; 619, 621; etc.). Their appearance in Callimachus, similarly applied, is the first sign of Hesiodic coloring – an especially clear-cut sign, as the word τημοῦτος is a Hesiodic *unicum* (ἀλλ' ὁπότ'...τημοῦτος 571, 576) which does not reappear before Callimachus.[61] The Hellenistic poet knows better than to plow when the days are longest, for Hesiod expressly recommends the time: ἦμος δὴ λήγει μένος ὀξέος ἠελίοιο / καύματος ἰδαλίμου, "when the strength of the piercing sun leaves off / from its

---

[58] According to a late source (Eustathius), it was the amount of land that a strong man could plow in a day. The only other pre-Callimachean instance appears to be *Od.* 7.113 (same sedes), where it is used adjectivally, as in our passage. In *Od.* 18 it is substantive. Thus, as Reinsch-Werner points out (p. 91), "indem K. das Wort adjektivisch verwendet, weist er über die Szene, die er inhaltlich anklingen will, hinaus und hat damit dem Leser die beiden einzigen Fundstellen...ins Gedächtnis gerufen."

[59] Similarly Bornmann ad v. 176: "quattro γυῖαι, una misura che, in quanto allusiva alla sfida di Odisseo, ha del favoloso... È però evidente che si tratta di un' area grande." Cf. also Reinsch-Werner, 91.

[60] *Callimachus, Hymns and Epigrams* (Loeb Classical Library 1955) 75 n. g. This interpretation is apparently that of Apollonius of Rhodes as well, cf. *ZPE* 54 (1984) 7-8.

[61] For this and the rest of the paragraph cf. Reinsch-Werner, 88-93. Her discussion of the interconnection between the Hesiodic and Homeric passages to which Callimachus alludes (cf. 88-89 n. 1) is interesting but not relevant to our present discussion.

sultry heat" (v. 414-415), that is November. Further, Hesiod specifies, like Callimachus, that the cows should be nine years old (*WD* 436 βόε δ' ἐνναετήρω ~ εἰναετιζόμεναι v. 179), for such are the best (*WD* 438 τὼ ἐργάζεσθαι ἀρίστω ~ αἳ μέγ' ἄρισται / τέμνειν v. 179-180). The furrow in the *Works and Days* is straight (ἰθείην αὔλακ' v. 443), in the *Hymn to Artemis*, by a slight variation, it is deep (ὦλκα βαθεῖαν v. 180). Callimachus likewise shows himself a follower of Hesiod on the subject of lending cattle. *Works and Days* vv. 451-454 describe the plight of a man who does not own cows:

> ...κραδίην δ' ἔδακ' ἀνδρὸς ἀβούτεω·
> δὴ τότε χορτάζειν ἕλικας βόας ἔνδον ἐόντας·
> ῥηίδιον γὰρ ἔπος εἰπεῖν· "βόε δὸς καὶ ἄμαξαν·"
> ῥηίδιον δ' ἀπανήνασθαι· "πάρα ἔργα βόεσσιν."
>
> ...but it stings the heart of a man without oxen.
> Then is the time to fatten the horned oxen within the stalls.
> For it is easy to say: "loan me a pair of oxen and a wagon;"
> and it is easy to refuse: "but there is work for the oxen."

Callimachus' situation is just what Hesiod recommends. As an owner of cows, he is independent and can say to others "πάρα ἔργα βόεσσιν", "but there is work for the oxen", as in effect he does in our passage ("may my cows not plow a field...for a wage under another's plowman" v. 175-176). In short, he is his own man, knows when to plow his field and what sort of oxen are best for the job. He rejects the pompous posture of the epic hero for the cautious, wise and humbler style of the Hesiodic farmer.[62]

I have argued elsewhere (*ZPE* 54, 1984, 1-8) that, in adopting this wholly uncharacteristic rustic pose, the urban poet is playing upon the traditional motif of poetry as "plowing", the poet as "plowman" (cf. Pind. *N*. 6.32; *N*. 10.26; *P*. 6.2 cf. *Ol*. 9.27; Pratinas *PMG* 712 a; *PMG* 710; Anon. *PMG* 923.4), and that in favoring the Hesiodic stance rather than that of Homer's heroic epic he is making a programmatic statement concerning his poetic, not his agricultural, preferences. His greater affinity for the Hesiodic posture, however, deliberate and marked though it is, only goes so far. For there is hardly a word in either the Homeric or Hesiodic allusions that Callimachus does not alter. He appears in a comical way even to be practicing agricultural one-upmanship by asserting that the best animals for plowing are female (ἐμαὶ βόες v. 175, αἳ μέγ' ἄρισται v. 179) - in Homer and Hesiod

---

[62] This rejection may extend to 3rd cent. epic as well if, in addition to Homer and Hesiod, Callimachus is alluding to Ap. Rh. III 1340-1344, rather than the other way around. For a discussion of this extensive contemporary allusion cf. *ZPE* 54 (1984) 7-8.

they are male (βόες..., οἵ περ ἄριστοι *Od.* 18.371; βόε.../ ἄρσενε.../ τὼ ἐργάζεσθαι ἀρίστω *WD* 436-438) - and by specifying that they must be Stymphaian (v. 178).[63]

But beyond this, Callimachus transforms the context of both antecedent passages - the hero's boast, the farmer's almanac - into something unmistakably his own: a form particularly suited to current tastes, the riddle.[64] The section was recognized as "ein Rätselspiel" by Reinsch-Werner (*op. cit.* 87), and fits well the definition of αἴνιγμα given by Aristotle (*Poetics* 1458a 26f.): αἰνίγματός τε γὰρ ἰδέα αὕτη ἐστί, τὸ λέγοντα ὑπάρχοντα ἀδύνατα συνάψαι, i.e. the nature of a riddle is this: to attach impossible things to a given utterance. It can be classed a "cosmic riddle", using the category of K. Ohlert (*Rätsel und Rätselspiele der alten Griechen,* Berlin 1912, 83-105). Of those cited by Ohlert, our riddle is closest to the Homeric description of the Laistrygonian city of Lamos (*Od.* 10.82-86):

..........ὅθι ποιμένα ποιμὴν
ἠπύει εἰσελάων, ὁ δέ τ' ἐξελάων ὑπακούει.
ἔνθα κ' ἄυπνος ἀνὴρ δοιοὺς ἐξήρατο μισθούς,
τὸν μὲν βουκολέων, τὸν δ' ἄργυφα μῆλα νομεύων·
ἐγγὺς γὰρ νυκτός τε καὶ ἤματός εἰσι κέλευθοι

.....where herdsman calls to herdsman
as he drives in his flock, and the other answers as he drives his out.
There a sleepless man could have earned a double wage,
one by herding cattle, and one by putting white sheep out to graze.
For the paths of night and day are near to one another.

As already Krates saw (Schol. *Od.* 10.86), Homer seems to locate the Laistrygonians in the far north, playing upon the brevity of their summer nights, where, even when it is dark, daylight is never far off (v. 86).[65]

It may be, as Kuiper suspected (*op. cit.* p.91), that Callimachus had this very passage in mind when creating his own: both authors deal with farming for a wage under circumstances when the normal time scheme is out of joint. But, more importantly, both follow the same form: a situation is assumed (the dance of Artemis' nymphs / the care

---

[63] Thus also Reinsch-Werner p.92.

[64] For the Alexandrian love of riddles cf. Wilamowitz, *HD* II, 151-152, as also their taste for Technopaignia. Callimachus wrote a riddling work called "Athena" (Pfeiffer, Test. no. 23: καὶ τὴν Ἀθηνᾶν ὕστατον μέλπω πάλιν / γρίφῳ βαθίστῳ καὶ δυσευρέτοις λόγοις).

[65] Thus also K. Müllenhoff, *Deutsche Altertumskunde* vol.1 (Berlin 1870) 5ff. and Wilamowitz, *Homerische Untersuchungen* vol.7, Philol. Unters. (1884) 168. The long winter nights of the north - "Cimmerian nights" - became a favored motif in late Greek erotic epigram, cf. *AP* 5.223, 283.

of livestock among the Laistrygonians), which leads to a puzzling statement for which there is no apparent cause in the original situation (the poet's fear for his cows / the sleepless man's double wage) – cf. Aristotle's ἀδύνατα συνάψαι – and is finally resolved in a closing explanation (v. 180 ἐπεὶ θεός... / ἐγγὺς γὰρ... *Od.* 10.86) of cosmic proportions.

Thus, even as he declares himself a disciple of a poetic precursor, i.e. Hesiod, and goes to great lengths to follow in his footsteps, Callimachus radically alters the Hesiodic framework, turning the earnest teachings of his chosen master into an entertaining Hellenistic "Rätselspiel". In so doing, he suggests that for all his desire to connect with the tradition – to be Hesiodic –, a gulf both in aims and outlook persists. "Hesiodic" Callimachus, as he has recently been called,[66] is an apt designation only insofar as it embraces the possibility (or better, probability) of deviation from Hesiod.[67]

In this passage from the *Hymn to Artemis* we encounter precisely that sort of ubiquitous, obsessive allusion that is a hallmark of the Hellenistic *avant garde*, and which, in its very intricacy, bespeaks the epigone's desire to make up for his perceived belatedness. We have seen this impulse inspire a response so flamboyantly self-dramatizing as Hipponax' resurrection or Timon's underworld-journey to consult Xenophanes. Here, in a less spectacular – though essentially equivalent – approach, the poet fills his verse with his predecessors' presence, evoking the disembodied voices of the heritage through the medium of allusion.

Yet the very passion – or even vehemence – with which these poets assert their intimacy with the past serves only to underline how fundamentally alien it remains. This is not the easy familiarity of peers. Rather, by constant recourse to the tradition, to the ancient models, the poets effectively set those models apart, permanently, as authorities, suggesting thereby the existence of a canon (though none had as yet been fully established in Callimachus' time). Thus even as they engage in a process of insistent reanimation, the Alexandrian authors are setting memorials as definitive as, if less overt than, the fictitious epitaphs with which our discussion began. Paradoxically, the distance that remained, and that in the epitaphs provoked expressions of mourning, serves now to liberate the poets from any slavish adherence to the past, providing them rather with the necessary latitude for creativity and innovation. And it is precisely against the backdrop of an unprece-

---

[66] Cf. the title of the book "Callimachus Hesiodicus" by Reinsch-Werner.

[67] We recall the ambiguous reaction of the Alexandrian literati toward Hipponax in Callimachus' 1st *Iambos* (cf. p.66 below), with its mixture of intense interest and skepticism.

dented awareness of the tradition, that the original Hellenistic genius comes to the fore.

*

In chapter one we saw how the contemporary Hellenistic world, with its new awareness of writing and the book, was brought to bear upon age-old notions of inspiration and the poet's self image. In chapter two we reversed the process, tracking attempts to revive the past and to make it function in the literature of the present. In either case, though with differing emphases, our concern was with the relation of present and past, of innovation and tradition, and with their peculiar admixture in the Hellenistic Age. In the final chapter we will endeavor to synthesize the critical perspectives of the previous two by examining in detail a single exemplary poem: Callimachus' *Hymn to Delos*. This is a work that lends itself to such an analysis for a variety of reasons. First of all, it is the longest surviving poem (326 verses) by the most prominent literary representative of the day. Secondly, it deals with a traditional theme *par excellence* – that is, with the birth of the song-god, Apollo. More importantly, however, we are in the unique position of not only knowing of, but actually possessing the Classical works that serve as Callimachus' models – works that are acknowledged to be of the highest quality. The hymn may serve, therefore, as a kind of laboratory in which we can observe how the poet receives, and responds to, his models over the course of a lengthy sustained narrative. At the same time, however, this hymn contains extensive and prominent reference to important contemporary events, to wit the invasion of the Celts against Delphi in 279/8 B.C. and the subsequent mutiny of Celtic mercenaries against Ptolemy Philadelphus in Egypt. It even bears many specifically Egyptian traits. The remote literary past thus shares the stage with the preoccupations, both poetic and political, of modern-day Alexandria. The drama of this association and interpenetration will be our main concern in what follows.

Callimachus' Hymn to Delos

It is striking that this poem, which takes as its "constant source of inspiration" the *Homeric Hymn to Apollo*,[1] should be called a hymn to *Delos*. And it is of fundamental importance that an interpretation of the poem try to explain what so conspicuous a reallignment in topic might mean. We have often seen before that it is precisely there where the Hellenistic poet deviates from his chosen antecedent that one may grasp his intent: the meaning lies in the difference. What, then, did Callimachus find so appealing about Delos? Why, in contradistinction to his archaic model, did he make it his central theme? These questions provide our point of departure and form the constant backdrop for our reflections on the poem.

We may explain an interest in Delos in various ways. But for our purposes, a glance at 1) the historical cirumstances and 2) Callimachus' programmatic interests will prove most helpful.

Chronology

The *Hymn to Delos* is the only Callimachean hymn that can be located within a certain time-span in the poet's life. And, as we shall see, the historical circumstances of this particular period suggest a motive for the shift to *Delos*. The *terminus post quem* is supplied by references in Apollo's second prophecy (v. 162-195) to the mutiny of the four thousand Celtic mercenaries hired by Philadelphus to combat his half-brother Magas. This mutiny took place not long after the Celtic attack on Delphi (279/8 B.C.),[2] which is likewise referred to in the prophecy. The most probable date for the uprising seems to be ca. 275 B.C.[3]

---

[1] Thus Mineur p.4, and virtually all critics before him: Kuiper, *op. cit.* (ch.2 n.57 above) 111; Herter, *op. cit.* (ch.2 n.39 above) 379; Wilam. *HD* II 63; E. Howald and E. Staiger, *Die Dichtungen des Kallimachos: Griechisch und Deutsch* (Zürich 1955) 99-101; Reinsch-Werner, *op. cit.* p.292.

[2] The attack is dated on the basis of Polyb. II 20.6, Paus. X 23.9 and the Coan inscription, Syll.³ 398, cf. G. Nachtergael, *Les Galates en Grèce et les Sôteria de Delphe*, Academie Royale de Belgique, Memoires de la classe des Lettres, Collection in 2nd serie, T. LXIII, Fascicule I, 1977, 172-175.

[3] Cf. Nachtergael *op. cit.* 170-171 with n.204; E. Will, *Histoire Politique du Monde Hellénistique*² (Nancy 1979) 145-146. Besides our hymn, there are only two other sources

A *terminus ante quem* has generally been seen in the defeat of the Ptolemaic fleet in the battle of Cos (262/1) at the end of the Chremonidean war (ca. 266-261), after which time Ptolemaic power in the Cyclades declined sharply.[4] But, as recent scholars have pointed out, that does not in itself preclude a later date for our poem (as Wilamowitz believed, *HD* II 62), since the Ptolemies continued to compete for influence on Delos down through the reign of Ptolemy III Euergetes (i.e. 246-222 B.C.).[5] The island was too important to be ignored by a

---

for this mutiny: the scholia *ad* v. 175-187 and Paus. I 7.2, quoted in Pfeiffer's apparatus to the scholia.

Some scholars (e.g. Wilamowitz, *HD* II 62; P.M.Fraser, *Ptolemaic Alexandria* [Oxford 1972] 657-658 and n. 337) have thought that the reference to Ptolemy as θεός (v. 165) presupposes the existence of the cult of the Theoi Adelphoi, first attested in *P. Hibeh* 199: 11-17 which is probably datable to 272/1 (cf. L. Koenen, *Eine agonistische Inschrift aus Ägypten und frühptolemaische Königsfeste* [Meisenheim 1977] 45 n. 92, though cf. also Wörrle's doubts, *Chiron* 8 [1978] 215 n. 67). Some even assume that because there is no mention of his queen Arsinoe, the hymn must have been composed after her death on July ninth, 270 (cf. F.T.Griffiths, *Maia* 29-30 [1977-1978] 95 n. 3. For the date see W.H.Mineur, *Callimachus Hymn to Delos, Introduction and Commentary* [Leiden 1984] 16-18, Pfeiffer's *Kallimachos Studien* [Munich 1922] 8 and his prolegomena to vol. II of the Callimachus edition, p. XXXIX.).

As to the first supposition, the fact that someone is called "god" in a poem does not imply the existence of a dynastic cult (cf. Demetrius Poliorcetes in Hermocles 1.13 ff., Powell p. 174; or, much earlier, Rhesus in Euripides' tragedy of that name, whom the chorus addresses: σύ μοι Ζεὺς ὁ φαναῖος v. 355). Moreover, it should be recalled that Philadelphus received divine honors from the Egyptians upon acceding to the throne (cf. J. Quaegebeur, "Reines Ptolémaiques et Traditions Égyptiennes" in *Das Ptolemäische Ägypten,* ed. H.Maehler and V.M.Strocka [Mainz 1978] 246) and that, in marrying his sister Arsinoe sometime between 279 and 274, he took a significant and very public step towards adopting Egyptian kingship practices (cf. Fraser *op. cit.* p. 217; on the date cf. K.J.Beloch, *Griechische Geschichte* IV 2 [Berlin 1927] 182; H.Volkmann, "Ptolemaios" *RE* XXIII 2, 1658). What is more, he was revered as a god on a local basis by Greeks as early as 280 in Byzantium (cf. C.Habicht, *Gottmenschentum und die griechischen Städte,* Zetemata 14 [1956] 116-121) and, more importantly, in Delos probably by 274 (cf. *IG* XI 4, 1038 = Durrbach, *Choix* # 21, p. 30-31, v. 23-27 ὅπως δὲ καὶ τῶν ἱερῶν ὧν θύουσιν οἱ νησιῶται ἐν Δήλωι τοῖς τε ἄλλοις θεοῖς καὶ Σωτῆρι Πτολεμαίωι καὶ βασιλεῖ Πτολεμαίωι..., cf. P.Roussel, *BCH* 31 [1970] 342-343; P.Bruneau, *Recherches sur les cultes de Délos a l'époque hellénistique et a l'époque impériale* [Paris 1970] 532). Thus, inasmuch as Ptolemy's divinity is here simply prophesied within a mythological framework, a definite link to the cult of the Theoi Adelphoi need not be assumed. Further, Arsinoe's absence tells us no more than does the absence of the king in the Adonis song of Theocritus 15 (v. 100-144), where both Berenice and Arsinoe appear. The poem's theme, not its political context, determines its cast of players.

[4] Thus Herter, *RE* Suppl. XIII 238, Griffiths, *op. cit.* (n. 3 above) 95.

[5] Thus R.Bagnall, *The Administration of the Ptolemaic Possessions outside Egypt* (Leiden 1976) 156, cf. also Will, *op. cit.* (n. 3 above) 231-233.

The beginning of Ptolemaic dominance in the Aegean is dated to 286. An inscription of Ios (without date, *IG* XII 5, 1004 = *OGIS* 773) honors Zenon, a commander of ἄφρακτα πλοῖα, undecked ships, under the nesiarch Bacchon (*Prosop. Ptol.* VI # 15038),

kingdom with pretensions to power. Another dating criterion which until now has been overlooked may merit consideration, namely the reference - in a section dealing with the present-day situation - to Φοίνισσα Κύρνος (v. 19): Corsica could probably not have been called "Carthaginian" after being conquered by Cn. Cornelius Scipio in 259. That Callimachus' reference is informed is suggested by the general interest in the West during his era, e. g. in the historian Timaeus, whose influence on Callimachus is well known (cf. Pfeiffer's index s. v. Timaeus), and in Lycophron.[6]

A *terminus ante quem* of 259 would essentially confirm the drift of previous scholarly consensus, for the years 275-259 correspond to those in which Ptolemaic influence in the Aegean and especially on Delos was at its height (cf. Theocritus 17.90 where Ptolemy rules καὶ Κυκλάδεσσιν, ἐπεί οἱ νᾶες ἄρισται / πόντον ἐπιπλώοντι).[7] Since Delos was the administrative, economic and cultic hub of the Cyclades, and further, one of the foremost religious sites in all of Greece, the Ptolemies did their utmost to cultivate close ties to the island. There was considerable prestige at stake in such a connection. Indeed, a tribute to the island's centrality to Hellenic culture would effectively put Ptolemy on the map for possessing it. A hymn to Delos at this time would thus be a shrewdly chosen theme for a poet at the court in Alexandria.[8]

---

who was appointed by Ptolemy (Bagnall, *op. cit.*, 137). This same Zenon is honored in an Athenian decree of 286/5 (*Syll.*[3] 367) in which he is likewise commander of undecked ships. Together, the inscriptions show that by 286/5, Ptolemy could appoint whom he wished as nesiarch to the κοινὸν τῶν νησιωτῶν. From 285 to 260, the Ptolemies held a virtual monopoly on benefactions for, and honors from, Delos (Bagnall, *op. cit.,* 154 n. 139).

[6] For this interest generally, cf. A. Momigliano, *Terzo Contributo alla Storia Degli Studi Classici e dell Mondo Antico* (Rome 1966) 35-51. On pre-Roman Corsica, cf. J. and L. Jehasse, *La Nécropole Préromain d'Aléria,* Gallia Suppl. 25 (Paris 1973) 16-23.

[7] Critics have tried to narrow the date down further by establishing a relative chronology between our hymn and Theocritus 17, the *Encomium to Ptolemy* (written before Arsinoe's death in 270, cf. Gow's preface). Unfortunately, no convincing argument as to priority has yet appeared, though the two poems exhibit many noteworthy parallels (cf. F. T. Griffiths, *op. cit.* [n. 3 above] 97 ff.; cf. also W. Meincke, *Untersuchungen zu den enkomiastischen Gedichten Theokrits* [Diss. Kiel 1965] 116-124 and G. Schlatter, *Theokrit und Kallimachos* [Diss. Zürich 1941]).

[8] There have been many attempts to link the hymn to a specific occasion. A. Reinach, *REA* 13 (1911) 46 n. 1 suggested the Nesiotic Ptolemaia of 276/5 and is followed most recently by C. Meillier, *Callimaque et son Temps* (Lille 1979) 180-191. Both see the poem as commissioned by the islanders for performance during cult ceremonies. Less extreme is Cahen's view (*Callimaque,* 281-283) that the poem was recited at Delos, but separate from the actual ceremony, as a kind of primer for the subsequent ritual, or as reinforcement thereafter. It is unlikely, however, that a poem deriving much of its impact from recondite traditions and literary allusion, most of it unrelated to Delos, should be intended for an audience in a local festival (cf. H. Herter, *Gnomon* 12 [1936] 456-457). Rather, the address to Ptolemy at the very heart of the poem makes Alexandria with its

Callimachus' Programme

But while political considerations certainly made Delos an attractive theme, Callimachus also saw in it a potential vehicle for a programmatic statement.

As is well known, Callimachus rejected the stale tradition of continuous poems on a grand scale, like those of the *Epic Cycle* (*Ep.* 28), that dealt with heroes and kings (fr. 1.3). "Fat" (fr. 1.23-24; cf. fr. 398), and "bombastic" (fr. 1.19 μέγα ψοφέουσαν ἀοιδήν) are the words he selects to describe them. "Thunder is not for me", he says, "but for Zeus" (fr. 1.20 βροντᾶν οὐκ ἐμόν, ἀλλὰ Διός). His preference is rather the "small" poetic form, and he choses to unroll his verse only a little ways, like a child (fr. 1.5 ἔπος δ' ἐπὶ τυτθὸν ἑλ[ίσσω / παῖς ἅτε and cf. the ὀλίγη λιβὰς ἄκρον ἄωτον, *H.* 2.112). The critics should judge his poems by their "art" (τέχνῃ, fr. 1.17), not by their size. For Apollo bid him cultivate a "slender" Muse, and follow the narrow, untrodden path (fr. 1.25-28). Consequently, his poetry stands apart from all that is vulgar (*Ep.* 28), and "purity" is one of its distinguishing traits (*H.* 2.110-112).

In what follows, I shall suggest that Delos' characteristics (her diminutive size and slender, delicate stature; her purity and love of song; her freedom from violence and war) allowed Callimachus to see in her not only an island but a metaphor for those poetic principles. These characteristics are conspicuous here precisely because of their absence from the *Homeric Hymn*. For such distinguishing moments regularly acquire a significance as markers of the poet's design. It is here, as we saw in the previous chapter, that we grasp not just the relationship that an

---

highly sophisticated audience, both in the Museum and at the court, a far more likely location. Tarn's suggestion that Arsinoe commissioned the hymn as a gift for Philadelphus is mere speculation (*Antigonos Gonatas* [Oxford 1913] 211 n. 41, followed by Griffiths, *op. cit.* [n. 3 above] 95-96), as is the view put forward by Fraser (*op. cit.* [n. 3 above] 657) that it "commemorates" a festival following the first Syrian War in 271/270. The same can be said of Mineur's thesis that the Hymn was written as a birthday poem for Philadelphus and performed at a banquet in his honor on 7 March 274 (cf. my review of Mineur's commentary *AJPh* forthcoming).

Wilamowitz was surely correct in stressing the Hymn's purely literary character (*HD* II 15) and in arguing that the opening question (Τὴν ἱερήν, ὦ θυμέ, τίνα χρόνον ἢ πότ' ἀείσεις / Δῆλον v. 1-2) and its answer (νῦν v. 9) indicate an unspecified, imaginary occasion (ibid. 62, followed by Herter, *Gnomon* 12 (1936) 456-457 and *Bursian Jahresbericht* 255 (1937) 204-205). The numerous rites described in this hymn are given roughly equal emphasis: the Delphic Septerion v. 177 a-b (with Pfeiffer's n.); the yearly ἀπαρχαί v. 278 ff.; the marriage rites of the Deliades v. 269 ff.; the constant singing and dancing v. 300 ff.; the decoration of Aphrodite's statue v. 307-9; the yearly Athenian θεωρία and the Geranos dance 310 ff.; the sailor's dance around the altar and the biting of the olive tree v. 316 ff. These rites (cf. generally Bruneau *op. cit.* [n. 3 above] 16-52) convey a general picture suited to Callimachus' poetic purpose rather than to any specific event.

author attempts to establish with his poetic antecedent, but the distance that separates them both in terms of cultural/historical circumstances and in poetic aims. It will be our task, therefore, not only to note the distinctions, but to explain them.

For those who may question *a limine* the appropriateness of thus delving beneath the surface and attributing an apparently allegorical intent (ὑπόνοια) to Callimachus, it will be helpful first of all to recall that in the 3rd century B. C. such an approach would have been nothing startling. As is well known, this was the period in which allegorical criticism experienced its great blossoming, especially through the work of the Cynics and Stoics (cf. R. Pfeiffer, "The Image of the Delian Apollo and Apolline Ethics", *Journal of the Warburg and Courtauld Institutes* 25 [1952] 30 = *Ausg. Schr.* p. 68 and J. Onians, *op. cit.* ch. 2 n. 2 above, p. 95–105). In fact, there are some prominent examples of precisely such a practice in Callimachus – examples so familiar that we tend to overlook them:[8a] his Apollo, for instance, discusses poetry in transparently allegorical terms (the contaminated river, the pristine spring and bees) in the second Hymn; in the prologue to the *Aetia*, malignant mythical wizards, the Telchines, are made to stand for the poet's detractors; or again, allegorical techniques are used to interpret a statue of Apollo in fr. 114, as Rudolf Pfeiffer demonstrated in the article cited above. Things beneath the surface are, I shall argue, a prominent theme in the *Hymn to Delos* (cf. p. 141 below). It should not surprise us that the terms of comparison are not always explicit.

I shall further suggest that the hymn operates on two levels: the one concerned with the success of Callimachean song as embodied in the topic Delos; the other with the worldly success of Ptolemy Philadelphus and his counterpart, Apollo. In both cases, this success is cast as a victory over barbarism and chaos. Through the birth of Callimachus' patron, Apollo, Delos triumphs over the hackneyed heroic style which favors violence and noise.[8b] In the political sphere, Philadelphus and

---

[8a] The same could be said of Theocritus. Few scholars, for instance, would interpret Simichidas' journey in the *Thalysia*, and Lycidas' gift to him of a stick after their exchange of songs, as *merely* a country outing in which Simichidas acquires a useful rustic implement, a λαγωβόλον (v. 128). Most would see both journey and gift as connected in some way with poetic initiation – though beyond this very general consensus there is. notorious lack of agreement. Similarly, Theocritus seems to be dealing in hidden meanings when he apparently identifies Ptolemy Philadelphus with Herakles by carefully masking the king's birthday within astronomical and chronological data about the mythical hero at the start of his *Herakliskos* (*Idyll* 24, cf. Gow *ad* v. 11 f.). A related phenomenon originating in the Hellenistic Age is the use of acrostichs (such as was mentioned in ch. 1 p. 15) to add a hidden dimension to the surface meaning of a text.

[8b] Reinsch-Werner, p. 322 ff., likewise suggests a polemical stance against epic precedent, but that stance is specifically directed against the *Homeric Hymn to Apollo*. The

Apollo subdue the menace of the Gauls. These victories result in a harmonious world where the political order protects and fosters Delos (both as a place and as a poem); and Delos in turn brings glory to the political order.[8c] From both the political and programmatical perspective, then, the thematic appeal of Delos becomes manifest.

The Myth of Asteria

While keeping the Homeric Hymn as his most obvious and pervasive model, Callimachus turned to another narrative, of which he makes extensive use throughout his poem, in order to effect his shift from *Apollo* to *Delos*. Before turning to an analysis of the hymn itself, therefore, we must examine this other antecedent. I am referring to the story of Asteria, the nymph who fled the embrace of Zeus by leaping into the sea, there to become the floating-later immovable-island Delos, Apollo's birthplace.[9] Although this myth looms large in the hymn, critics have displayed only passing interest. This is due in part to the (justifiable) pre-eminence accorded the Homeric Hymn and scholarly preoccupation with epic "Sprachgebrauch";[10] in part also to the fragmentary state in which this myth appears in the pre-Callimachean tradition.

Hymn to Delos competes with, and actually defeats that hymn in a musical agon, she argues, and it does so (predictably enough) by programmatic recourse to Hesiod. That, according to Reinsch-Werner, is the significance of the phrase Δῆλος δ' ἐθέλει τὰ πρῶτα φέρεσθαι / ἐκ Μουσέων (v. 4-5). But as Mineur points out (*ad* v. 4 f.), "if that was Callimachus' intention in using the phrase, the audience certainly would not have noticed it ..., since nowhere do *Delos*' first four lines suggest any connection with *h. Ap.*"

[8c] A similar line of interpretation was advanced, as I discovered after having developed my own, by L.J. Bauer in his dissertation, *Callimachus, Hymn IV: An Exegesis* (Brown Univ. 1970) 31-32, 66-70. Bauer saw that the erratic wanderings of Leto and Asteria aptly characterized the chaos of the world before the advent of Apollo and Ptolemy, and that harmony and order subsequently reigned. His analysis, however, is problematic in its heavy psychologizing. Thus, Leto's and Asteria's behavior "displayed a psychological state akin to the neurotic" (p. 66, cf. p. 31); in the world of Ptolemy and Apollo, by contrast, "rationality is the ruling principle" (p. 70, cf. p. 83). Bauer, moreover, does not recognize the significance of Delos as an emblem for Callimachean song.

[9] For this myth cf. K. Wernicke, *RE* II s. v. p. 1780-1782; Roscher I, 1 s. v. p. 655-656; H. Papastavrou, *Lex. Icon. Myth. Class.* II, 1 p. 903-904.

[10] This preoccupation remains even more than 65 years after M.T. Smiley in "Callimachus' Debt to Pindar and Others", *Hermathena* 18 (1919) 46, complained that "epic reminiscences in Callimachus' poems are so prominent that, in discussing his sources,... critics have turned their attention almost exclusively to 'Homer', leaving well-nigh unnoticed the extensive Pindaric background of his poems." Smiley himself, however, devotes barely more than a page to the *Hymn to Delos,* and is content to let those echoes which he discovers stand uninterpreted. A notable exception to this general trend is M. Poliakoff's "Nectar, Springs and the Sea: Critical Terminology in Pindar and Callimachus", *ZPE* 39 (1980) 41-47.

Above all, however, it reflects the critics' failure to perceive as important the change in theme from *Apollo* to *Delos*-or to perceive it at all.[11] The earliest mention of Asteria is in Hesiod (*Th.* 409), where she appears as Leto's sister, the daughter of Koios and Phoibe. Callimachus' primary source, however, was almost certainly Pindar (*Pae.* 5, *Hymn* 1 fr. 33 c-33 d and *Pae.* 7 b Snell-Maehler), and this fact suggests why the allusions are more thematic than verbatim: the vocabulary of Pindaric lyric was not readily compatible with Callimachus' hexameter.

On the assumption that he was thoroughly familiar with these poems,[12] we turn to the texts themselves in which Asteria appears. The first is *Pae.* 5 - in its brevity and simple monostrophic structure in dactylo-epitrites (with ritual cry at the start of each strophe), an unusual poem among the otherwise elaborate aeolo-iambic Paeans:[13]

[Εὔ-]   35
βοιαν ἕλον καὶ ἄνασσαν·

Ζ΄ ἰήιε Δάλι' Ἄπολλον·
καὶ σποράδας φερεμήλους
ἔκτισαν νάσους ἐρικυδέα τ' ἔσχον
Δᾶλον, ἐπεί σφιν Ἀπόλλων   40
δῶκεν ὁ χρυσοκόμας
Ἀστερίας δέμας οἰκεῖν·

---
[11] Hopkinson, for instance, seems to forget that the hymn is dedicated to Delos. In describing the hymns (*Callimachus, Hymn to Demeter* [Cambridge 1984] 13) he calls "the first pair 'masculine', the second 'mixed' (twins)." In what way Artemis and Delos can be called twins, however, is not stated.

[12] A virtual certainty (as pointed out already by Smiley, *op. cit.* n. 10 above, p. 48) given the evidence of his work with the Pindaric corpus in compiling the *Pinakes* - the lists made for the library of Alexandria, in which the holdings were arranged both generically and by author (cf. generally Pfeiffer, *Hist.* p. 126-134; R. Blum, *Kallimachos und die Literaturverzeichnung bei den Griechen* [Frankfurt 1977] 169-244). Fragment 450, for instance, tells us that he situated the 2nd Pythian among the Nemean odes, thereby implying that the order of the Epinicians was established by him according to the location of victory. Such information, in turn, was usually derived from indications in the text itself. We may assume, therefore, that Callimachus made editorial decisions for the lists on the basis of his personal reading of the poems. First-hand knowledge is likewise attested in the scholia to Bacchylides' dithyramb "Cassandra" (fr. 23 Snell-Maehler). According to this source, Callimachus classified the poem as a paean because it included the ritual cry "Ie", which is especially - though not exclusively - characteristic of that genre (ἐν τοῖς π]αιᾶσι Καλλίμαχον / διὰ τὸ ἰή,] οὐ συνέντα ὅτι / τὸ ἐπίφθ]εγ{γ}μα κοινόν ἐ/στι καὶ δ]ιθυράμβου: 16-19). The 2nd cent. B.C. grammarian Aristarchus criticised the decision, arguing rather that it was a dithyramb, and it was his opinion which carried the day: the poem was subsequently transmitted among the dithyrambs. Again, however, we see Callimachus forming an editorial judgment by means of his own investigation of the text. His collection and classification of the Pindaric Paeans (as well as other genres) was doubtless undertaken in the same way.

[13] Perhaps a sign that it was quickly composed on short notice. The only other Paean certainly in dactylo-epitrites is *Pae.* 13.

Η΄ ἰήιε Δάλι᾿ Ἄπολλον·
Λατόος ἔνθα με παῖδες
εὐμενεῖ δέξασθε νόῳ θεράποντα 45
ὑμέτερον κϝλαδεννᾷ
σὺν μελιγάρυι παι-
ᾶνος ἀγακ'λέος ὀμφᾷ.

They took Euboea and inhabited it;

Ie-ie Delian Apollo;
and they peopled the scattered
islands rich in flocks, and they held glorious
Delos, for Apollo
of the golden hair gave them
the outward form of Asteria to inhabit.

Ie-ie Delian Apollo;
there, O children of Leto,
receive me with kindly disposition as your
servant to the melodious,
sweet-voiced strain
of the far-famed Paean.

As we see, the reference to Asteria is very compressed, occurring *en passant* within a description of the Dark-Age migration of the Ionians from Athens to the Aegean isles[14] – among which Delos, the performance site of the poem (v. 44), was especially prominent. The dating proposed by Snell, "(post annum 478?)", apparently refers to the situation of growing Athenian influence on Delos and in the Aegean after the Persian Wars with the establishment of the Delian League in 478/7 B.C. If this is correct, the account of the Ionian migration from Athens would have provided historical legitimacy for that confederation. More broadly, the poem sought to affirm the special bond between Athens and Delos: for it seems plausible that the speaker of the final strophe is the Athenian chorus, and that the wish for the good will of Apollo and Artemis is expressed not only on its own behalf, but for Athens itself, of which it was the representative. And Asteria? The reference to the nymph was apparently ornamental. Yet in the phrase Ἀστερίας δέμας, "the outward form of Asteria", the poet is not just using periphrasis (cf. LSJ s.v. δέμας). Rather, he succinctly suggests the whole myth: the

---

[14] Thus the scholion *ad* v. 35: οἱ ἀπ᾿ Ἀθηνῶν Ἴωνες, supported by the mention of "Pandoros, son of Erechtheus" in a marginal note at v. 45. On this basis, Snell suggested the superscription: "For the Athenians (?) to Delos". The migration is described by Hdt. I 143, 146; cf. also J. Boardman, *CAH* III 1 (Cambridge 1984) 770.

"outward form" is that which the nymph assumed as an island – Delos – after eluding Zeus with a plunge into the waves. Pindar, it seems, could assume that the story was known. And indeed, he relates it twice himself in detail.

The first of these more extended accounts occurs in the *Hymn to Zeus* (fr. 33 c–33 d).[15] Here, as part of a wedding song for Cadmus and Harmonia, the Muses sing a Theogony in which the birth of their leader, Apollo, on the island Asteria/Delos is one of the themes:

χαῖρ', ὦ θεοδ'μάτα, λιπαροπ'λοκάμου
παίδεσσι Λατοῦς ἱμεροέστατον ἔρνος,
πόντου θύγατερ, χθονὸς εὐρεί-
    ας ἀκίνητον τέρας, ἄν τε βροτοί
Δᾶλον κικλῄσκοισιν, μάκαρες δ' ἐν Ὀλύμπῳ   5
    τηλέφαντον κυανέας χθονὸς ἄστρον.

***

ἦν γὰρ τὸ πάροιθε φορητὰ
    κυμάτεσσιν παντοδαπῶν ἀνέμων
ῥιπαῖσιν· ἀλλ' ἁ Κοιογενὴς ὁπότ' ὠδί-
    νεσσι θυίοισ' ἀγχιτόκοις ἐπέβα
νιν, δὴ τότε τέσσαρες ὀρθαί   5
    πρέμνων ἀπώρουσαν χθονίων,
πέτ'ραν ἀδαμαντοπέδιλοι
κίονες, ἔνθα τεκοῖ-
    σ' εὐδαίμον' ἐπόψατο γένναν.   10
.]..ισ[
...

***

Hail, O god-built, sprout
most desirable to the children of Leto with the shining locks,
daughter of the sea, the broad earth's
    immovable wonder, whom mortals
call Delos, but the blessed ones on Olympos
the far-seen star of the dark earth.

***

for previously she was carried
on the waves by the gusts of every kind
of wind. But when the child of Koios (i.e. Leto), frantic
    with the pangs of imminent birth, set foot
on her, then four straight pillars

---

[15] A very conspicuous setting and doubtless well-known to Callimachus, for it was the opening poem in the first book of the ancient edition of Pindar, cf. Snell's discussion of the hymn in *Die Entdeckung des Geistes*[4] (Göttingen 1975) ch. 5.

> with adamantine bases
> shot up from the roots of the earth,
> and on their capitals they supported
> the rock. There she gave birth
> and gazed on her blessed children.

In the first of the two fragments (which, to judge from the meter and basic continuity of thought, belonged to strophe and antistrophe respectively) we encounter a series of paradoxical juxtapositions: The island is initially hailed as "god-built", θεοδμάτα, a word used of towers (*Il.* 8.519), halls (Alcm. *PMG* 2 iv. 5, cf. *PMG* 12.8), streets (Bacch. 11.58) and other massive constructions;[16] immediately thereafter, however, she is a "sprout", an entity growing in nature. The subsequent invocations invert this order: she is now a "daughter" of the sea, that is an animate being (which, as we learn in the antistrophe, at one time floated freely among the waves); then, however, the earth's "immovable wonder", a τέρας among islands because, according to the tradition (Hdt. VI 98; Thuc II 8.3), she was so firmly fixed in the earth that no earthquake ever shook her. Each of these contrasting pairs hints at the peculiar double life of this island without explaining it: that will be the function of the antistrophe.

Before that, however, Pindar introduces a further contrasting pair, the island's mortal and immortal names.[17] This is of particular interest for the Callimachean myth of Asteria in the *Hymn to Delos*, since the Hellenistic poet, like his archaic counterpart, subjects the name to an etymological interpretation.[18] These differ considerably, however, according to the poet's given needs. What matters for Pindar is the special quality of this "star-like" isle from an Olympian perspective (μάκαρες δ' ἐν Ὀλύμπῳ v. 5). It is, after all, "god-built" and for this reason (as the antistrophe shows) an "immovable wonder". As such – i. e. as a divine creation, not as the wind-swept drifter – it shines for the gods like a "far-seen star" amidst the earthly darkness.

Callimachus' interpretation reveals a markedly different conception (v. 36–38):

---

[16] A favorite word of both Pindar and Bacchylides, it was also employed metaphorically by the former, e. g. of ἀρετή *I.* 6.11, ἐλευθερία *P.* 1.61. The usage in our hymn, however, is evidently quite literal, as is shown by fr. 33 d.5 f. Was Pindar thinking of the four adamantine columns when he called Delos θεοδμάτη at *Ol.* 6.59?

[17] On this custom cf. West *ad* Hesiod *Th.* 831.

[18] The hesitation of some critics to see it as such ("perhaps a play on the earlier name of Delos", Slater s. v. ἄστρον c; "a possible allusion", Mineur *ad* v. 37) is unjustified. To be sure, Pindar describes Aegina, too, as a star (Διὸς Ἑλλανίου φαεννὸν ἄστρον *Pae.* 6.126). Yet the crucial difference in our case is that he explicitly calls attention to the "far-seen star" as a *name* (κικλήσκοισιν v. 5).

...οὔνομα δ' ἦν τοι
Ἀστερίη τὸ παλαιόν, ἐπεὶ βαθὺν ἥλαο τάφρον
οὐρανόθεν φεύγουσα Διὸς γάμον ἀστέρι ἴση.

...and your name was
Asteria of old, since you leaped into the deep pit (of the sea)
from the heavens, fleeing the lust of Zeus like a shooting star.

First, the Hellenistic author derives Asteria's name not from ἄστρον, as before, but ἀστήρ. This is an eye-catching change. ἀστήρ no doubt more satisfactorily approximates the form of the name (especially, as here, in the dative), and Callimachus accentuates the resemblance by setting that name and its etymological explanation as a conspicuous frame around the verses 36-37: Ἀστερίη.../...ἀστέρι ἴση. Is the Alexandrian scholar/poet correcting his archaic model?

More important, however, than the change in suffix is the semantic distinction between ἄστρον and ἀστήρ. Both may denote a star that is fixed. The former, however, can have only this meaning; the latter is used of a shooting star as well.[19] For Pindar, of course, the fixity of Delos, ἀκίνητον τέρας that it is, is of primary importance: ἄστρον is thus the appropriate word. Callimachus, by contrast, catches precisely that exuberant mobility that he wishes to highlight by using the word ἀστήρ. For him, far more than for Pindar, this is one of Asteria's crucial traits. For in fleeing from Zeus (*de facto* a κινητὸν τέρας, or "mobile" wonder, now sighted by sailors, now out of their sight v. 41-44) she keeps herself chaste and pure – and that, in Callimachus' view, appeals to Apollo: "being pure myself, may I be a care to the pure", the god declares (v. 98 εὐαγέων δὲ καὶ εὐαγέεσσι μελοίμην). Only such a place could be Apollo's birthplace. But as we shall see in the next section (p. 120), it is not just her one-time leap that makes her appealing, but her continuing mobility as well. For Apollo's choice is due at least in part to a perceived compatibility between his own pre-natal journeys in the womb of his mother Leto and the unfettered roamings of his sacred island.

This broader significance of the derivation from ἀστήρ is fully revealed through a further difference between the Hellenistic poet and his source. In Pindar, Asteria and Delos are contemporaneous names, the one immortal, the other mortal. Indeed, if τηλέφαντον ("far-seen" fr. 33 c.5) plays on δῆλος ("conspicuous"), the divine and human names are virtually glosses. Callimachus turns them into a sequence, reflecting an evolution from one form of existence to another.[20] The island was

---

[19] Thus already L.J. Bauer, *op. cit.* n. 8c above, p. 62.
[20] This is thus an example of the "changing of names", or μετονομασία, with respect to islands, in which we know Callimachus took a scholarly interest. Cf. his work entitled κτίσεις νήσων καὶ πόλεων καὶ μετονομασίαι and Pfeiffer *ad* fr. 601.

called Asteria as long as it floated freely, that is until Apollo was born; thereafter, the sailors renamed it Delos, since it no longer floated ἄδηλος ("obscurely") among the waves (v. 51-53). In making this change, Callimachus endows the period before Apollo's birth with a contour and definition not present in Pindar. For the name Asteria denotes an entire era in the island's existence, the chief characteristic of which is mobility. This era, in turn, is balanced against another, each thereby thrown into yet higher relief. For Callimachus creates a complementary etymology wherein the second period in the island's existence finds adequate expression, namely that of motionless stability. Each phase receives its proper weight, since the island's mobility is, according to Callimachus' conception, the *sine qua non* for its later fixity.[21]

Following a gap of several lines, the Pindaric hymn starts up again in the third verse of the antistrophe with a γάρ-clause. We infer that something said in the missing lines was here explained with the words ἦν γὰρ τὸ πάροιθε φορητὰ κυμάτεσσιν κ. τ. λ. ("for previously she was carried on the waves"), and, as τὸ πάροιθε ("previously") indicates, it probably had to do with the island's present condition as opposed to its free-floating status in the past: Delos/Asteria was not always the "god-built...immovable wonder" that she is now, but only became so after a certain point, "for previously she was carried..." – or something to that effect. But as soon as Leto alighted on her, she was fixed to the spot forever[22] unshakable as no other island: four mighty pillars, sprung from the roots of the earth, hold her fast on their capitals like the pediment of a temple. With the story of this drifting "daughter of the sea" conjoined to the earth in so unprecedented a way, Pindar evidently wished to offer an *aition,* an explanation of the τέρας that Delos alone of all the islands in the sea was never shaken by an earthquake.

In his *Hymn to Delos,* Callimachus does not mention this alleged imperviousness to earthquakes. He does, however, insist on Delos' steadfast character. She is the "hearth of the islands" (ἱστίη ὦ νήσων v. 325), an image which powerfully evokes her fixity since, as Plato mentions (*Phdr.* 247 a), a hearth is immovable, its goddess Hestia never a participant in the procession of the gods. And at the poem's start she

---

[21] From these considerations it will be clear why Callimachus ignores Delos' other early name, Ortygia, although Pindar uses it in *Pae.* 7 b, one of the sources of the *Hymn to Delos* (cf. below). It simply provides none of the rich and very relevant etymological possibilities to be found in Asteria and Delos. That this is a functional omission is further suggested by the fact that Callimachus elsewhere identifies Ortygia with Delos, cf. *H.* 2.59 (with Williams' n.).

[22] We are, however, apparently meant to imagine that she was already a rock when she was blown this way and that by the winds, since in *Pae.* 7 b.47 she is similarly described as a εὐαγέα πέτραν while clearly still floating (cf. v. 49).

is "firmly fixed in the sea" (πόντῳ ἐνεστήρικται v. 13) - στηρίζειν being, as Williams has shown (*ad H.* 2.23), the "*mot juste* for a god fixing·an object permanently and immovably". "By whom" Callimachus' island was fixed, however, i.e. the identity of the agent implicit in the passive verb ἐνεστήρικται, is disclosed only somewhat later, in verses 51-54: "but when you [*scil.* Asteria] held out your soil as a birthplace for Apollo,...no longer did you float obscurely (ἄδηλος), but amidst the waves of the Aegean sea you planted the roots of your feet" (ἡνίκα δ' Ἀπόλλωνι γενέθλιον οὖδας ὑπέσχες, / ...οὐκέτ' ἄδηλος ἐπέπλεες, ἀλλ' ἐνὶ πόντου / κύμασιν Αἰγαίοιο ποδῶν ἐνεθήκαο ῥίζας). Whereas Pindar, then, had four majestic columns rise up from the ocean floor at the moment of Leto's landing, Callimachus - in a stunning inversion of his predecessor's stately image - has Asteria send down the (appealingly humble) roots of her feet into the sea.[23] Moreover, whereas Pindar's island is exclusively on the receiving end, a divine foundation, θεοδμάτα and hence ἀκίνητον, Callimachus' Asteria gives herself to Leto of her own free will, intrepidly standing her ground even in the face of grave threats from Hera and her minions, who wish at all costs to prevent Apollo's birth. The fixing of the island thus assumes an utterly different hue, especially as all the other islands had been forcibly implanted in the sea by Poseidon (v. 30-35). Delos is "firmly fixed in the sea" (πόντῳ ἐνεστήρικται) as a result of Asteria's determination alone (hence the *passivum resultativum*).

Pindar explained the "immovable wonder" of Delos by reference to its unique genesis: the unparalleled mooring of the drifter, Asteria, in the brace of four miraculous pillars. Yet the idea of a free-floating island itself required an explanation, and this formed the theme of another poem "to Delos": Pindar's *Paean* 7b = fr. 52h (Snell-Maehler). The poem consists of one enormous triad, with a strophe of 20 verses (matched only by fr. 140b),[24] and an epode of 17 (the longest in Pindar).[25] The first nine verses are so fragmentary that we can say only that they contained an invocation of Apollo, and mentioned a "mother" - maybe Leto or Mnemosyne, mother of the Muses. Begin-

---

[23] Thus also Most, *op. cit.* p. 190.

[24] Among the epinicians, only four have strophes of more than 10 verses: *Ol.* 1; 14; *P.* 5; *I.* 8. - none of more than 12. The paeans and dithyrambs, by contrast, so far as we can tell given their fragmentary condition, were more frequently longer and more elaborate (*n. b.* the preponderance of iambo-aeolic rhythms among the paeans). Perhaps this difference reflects the weightier demands of writing for religious festivals.

[25] Among the epinicians, not one has even 10 verses. The epode of closest comparable length is that of *Pae.* 6 with 13, cf. however also fr. 169.

ning with verse 10, however, we are better informed. Here, Pindar makes a programmatic statement concerning his song:[26]

κελαδήσαθ᾽   ὕμνους   10
Ὁμήρου [δὲ μὴ τρι]πτὸν κατ᾽ ἀμαξιτόν
ἰόντες, μ[ὴδ᾽ ἀλ]λοτρίαις ἀν᾽ ἵπποις,
ἐπεὶ αὐ[τοὶ ἐς π]τανὸν ἅρμα
Μοισα[ῖον ἀνέβα]μεν.
ἐπεύχο[μαι] δ᾽ Οὐρανοῦ τ᾽ εὐπέπλῳ θυγατρὶ   15
Μναμ[ο]σύ[ν]ᾳ κόραισί τ᾽ εὐ-
μαχανίαν διδόμεν.
τ]υφλα[ὶ γὰ]ρ ἀνδρῶν φρένες,
ὅ]στις ἄνευθ᾽ Ἑλικωνιάδων
βαθεῖαν ε..[..].ων ἐρευνᾷ σοφίας ὁδόν.   20

ἐμοὶ δὲ τοῦτο[ν δ]μέδω-
κ.ν] ἀθάνατ[ο]ν πόνον
[   ]
[˻δέλτου˼   ]   24

let hymns   resound,
but not going in the well-worn wagon-tracks
of Homer, nor with others' horses,
for [we ourselves have mounted] the winged chariot
of the Muses.
But I pray to the beautifully robed daughter of Ouranos,
    Mnemosyne, and to her daughters,
    to grant me skill.
For blind are the wits of men
who, without the Heliconian maidens,
explore the lofty road of wisdom.

But to me they have given
    this immortal labor
[   ]
[of the writing tablet (?)]

It is to the insight of Max Treu[27] that we owe the elucidation of this extraordinarily emphatic assertion of originality and independence from Homer. Treu saw that in a song sung on Delos about the birth of Apollo, an injunction to avoid "the well-worn wagon-tracks of Homer" could hardly be prompted by the one mention of Delos in the Homeric epics (the praise of Nausikaa at *Od.* 6.162 f.). Pindar's polemical stance

---

[26] For the sake of clarity, I include Snell's *exempli gratia*-supplements except in v. 12 where I adopt Koenen's μ[ὴδ᾽ ἀλλοτρίαις cf. *ZPE* 54 (1984) 2 n. 5, cf. below.

[27] In his review of Bowra's *Pindar*, *Gymn.* 74 (1967) 151 and n. 11.

must rather refer to a poem in which both Delos and Apollo's birth receive extensive treatment. Viewed thus, his critique can only be aimed at the *Hymn to Apollo,* where precisely these themes appear and which Thucydides (III 102) still held to be a genuine Homeric composition. "Homer" is thus the author of that hymn.[28] But Pindar rejects not only the wagon-tracks of the epic bard. He also renounces "the horses of others", i.e. he distinguishes himself from other poets as well.[29] His declaration of originality is thus a very broad one, indeed it is absolute. The story which he is about to tell, and for which he prays for the special assistance of the Muses, is one that has never been told before – it is Pindar's own: the story of Asteria.[30] Nearly half the poem is devoted to laying the poetological groundwork for this innovative myth,[31] an eloquent sign of its importance to the poet.

Following a gap of 7 verses, the text resumes in an extremely fragmentary state.

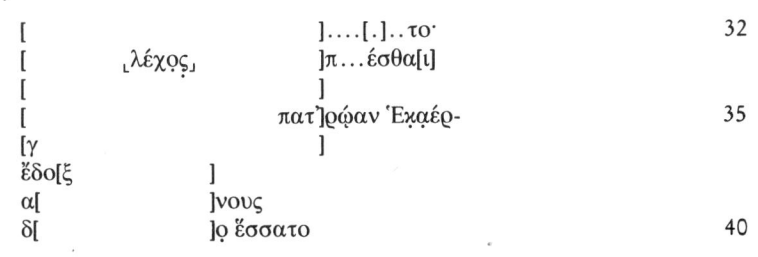

```
[                    ]....[.]..το·           32
[       ⌊λέχος⌋      ]π...ἐσθα[ι]
[                    ]
[                    πατ]ρῷαν Ἐχαερ-         35
[γ                   ]
ἔδο[ξ                ]
α[                   ]νους
δ[                   ]ρ ἔσσατο               40
```

---

[28] Treu proposed, moreover, that Pindar's subsequent statement, "blind are the wits of men who, without the Heliconian maidens, explore the lofty road of wisdom" (τυφλαὶ γὰρ ἀνδρῶν φρένες κ.τ.λ.), contains an attack against the τυφλὸς ἀνήρ, the blind singer of Chios, as the author of that Homeric Hymn describes himself (*H. H. Ap.* 172): "ein Übertrumpfen der Selbstaussage des Rhapsoden".

[29] Snell's supplement for v. 12, ἀ[λλ' ἀλ]λοτρίαις, must be rejected. He translates, "don't go in the beaten tracks of Homer, but with new horses..." (*Poetry and Society,* Bloomington 1961, p. 57). ἀλλότριος, however, does not have this meaning. Lobel (*ad* P. Oxy. 2442 v. 10 f.) saw the correct sense: "Here I should guess he promises a 'new' and 'original' song, 'off the beaten track', 'not riding in another's car', 'for I myself can drive the Muses' winged chariot' or the like". I therefore adopt the supplement proposed by Koenen, cf. n. 26 above.

[30] This sweeping claim to originality is an argument against Bowra's otherwise appealing suggestion (*Pindar* p. 33-4) that, in such proximity to a rejection of the Homeric path, the Ἑλικωνιάδες of v. 19 might not be just synonymous with Πιερίδες (as in *I.* 2.34; 8.57, cf. Bacch. fr. 65.14), but could refer to the Muses of Hesiod. We should note in Bowra's defense that Pindar subsequently calls Asteria Κοίου θυγάτηρ (v. 44), thus apparently following the Hesiodic genealogy (*Th.* 404 f.).

[31] I propose that v. 24 was still part of the introduction to the myth, since the "writing tablet" (δέλτου) of that verse (gleaned from the Σ) is most plausibly explained as belonging to the common 5th cent. metaphor for poetic recollection, the tablets of memory (cf. ch. 1 n. 5). If this is the case, the poet will have depicted his inner evocation of the myth as a preamble to telling it. The preamble may, of course, have extended beyond v. 24.

[......]α[
.]υνας· τί πείσομα[ι
ἦ Διὸς οὐκ ἐθέλο[ισα
Κοίου θυγάτηρ π[
ἄπιστά μ[ο]ι δέδο[ι]κ̣α̣ κ̣α̣μ̣[45
δέ μιν ἐν πέλ[α]γ[ο]ς
ῥιφθεῖσαν εὐαγέα πέτραν φανῆναι[
καλέοντί μιν Ὀρτυγίαν ναῦται πάλαι.
πεφόρητο δ' ἐπ' Αἰγαῖον θαμά·
τᾶς ὁ κράτιστος ἐράσσατο μιχθείς   50
τοξοφόρον τελέσαι γόνον

[   ]
[natal bed   ]
[   ]
[heredi]tary to the Far-dar-
[ter   ]
[   ]
seemed[   ]
[   ]
[   ] clothed him/herself (sat down?)

[   ]
           ] What will happen to me?"
She spoke. Not wishing [to mount the bed,
of Zeus, the daughter of Koios [fled into the sea.
That which is unbelievable to me I shrink [from telling.
But the story runs
that she, having hurled herself into the
sea, appeared as an undefiled rock.
The sailors of old called her Ortygia.
And frequently she was carried about upon the Aegean,
till the almighty (Zeus)
desired, after having coupled (with Leto),
to achieve the goal (of birth) for his bow-wielding son.

We can tell from the word λέχος, "natal bed" in v. 33 (supplied by Snell from Σ: λέχος ἐπὶ τὴν λοχείαν) that the myth of Apollo's birth had begun, and this is confirmed by the appearance of his epithet, "far-darter", in v. 35. According to the scholia to v. 38, somebody says that he/she is in a great quandary (Σ]ον λέγει ἀπ[ο]ρία[ν ἔχειν πολ]λήν). This could be the poet faced with an embarrassing myth to tell (thus Wilamowitz, *Pindaros* 328 cf. v. 45), but it seems to me more likely that this refers already to that innovative myth that Pindar had promised in the first half of his poem, i.e. the story of Asteria. Accordingly it would be that nymph who complains of having no way of escape (ἀπορία) from the advances of Zeus - before finding the one remaining path to safety: a leap into the sea (v. 47). With v. 42, we have Asteria's own words - "what will happen to me?" - at the moment before her flight.

In consequence of her leap, Asteria is able to maintain her purity, becoming a εὐαγέα πέτραν, "an undefiled rock" (cf. the simple πέτραν of fr. 33 d.8, where her flight from Zeus is not mentioned) - a motif which, as we saw above, will be crucial for Callimachus. Her courageous dive, moreover, provides the explanation for her singular freefloating status. Yet for Pindar, her independence only goes so far. She drifts until (τᾶς = τέως, cf. V. Schmidt, *Glotta* 53, 1975, 39) Zeus apparently makes her come to a halt (v. 50 f.). In just this way, the four pillars of fr. 33 d sprang up without Asteria's participation in order to fix her to the spot. The island is tied in another sense as well, however, for Pindar calls her the "daughter of Koios" (v. 44), i.e. he presents her as Leto's "Hesiodic" sister.[32] By playing upon this sibling bond, he explains the choice of Asteria as Apollo's birthplace: she is his aunt; the delivery is accomplished *en famille*.[33]

Callimachus evidently mined this narrative for his *Hymn to Delos*. Chief among the themes he adopted are 1) Asteria's purity (*Pae.* 7 b.47), maintained through 2) her courageous independence in refusing Zeus (*ibid.* v. 43 f.), which results in 3) her leap into the waves (*ibid.* v. 46 f.) and 4) her subsequent free-floating status until Apollo's birth (*ibid.* v. 49 f.; cf. also *H.* 1 fr. 33 d.1 f. and probably *Pae.*, 5.41). Callimachus pointedly drops the Hesiodic/Pindaric idea that Leto and Asteria are sisters,[34] and can thereby elaborate the island's independent temper by making Apollo's birth depend not on any familial bond, but on Asteria's free choice alone (v. 195 κείνην γὰρ ἐλεύσεαι εἰς ἐθέλουσαν); no external powers fix her to the spot: she willingly brings herself to a halt (v. 200 f. ὡς δ' ἴδες, [ὣς] ἔστης) and sends down her roots as an anchor (v. 53-54).[35]

---

[32] We deduce - contra Wilamowitz, *Pindaros* p. 328 n. 1 - that the poet means Asteria, not Leto, because she is described as *"not* wishing [something] of Zeus" (v. 43), and because the personal pronoun μιν in v. 46, referring to Κοίου θυγάτηρ, does not suit Leto in this context. The designation "daughter of Koios" makes it certain that Pindar, although not using the name Asteria in what survives of the text, was nonetheless thinking of that name as in Hesiod, rather than of some other from an alternate tradition.

[33] Is Zeus satisfying his grudge against the daughter of Koios who rejected him, by making her the place where his son is to be born by her sister?

[34] Indeed, while Leto is called Κοιηίς at v. 150, Apollo's detailed description of the island for his mother's benefit (v. 191-195) suggests that, patronymic notwithstanding, she did not even known who Asteria was (cf. Mineur *ad* v. 37)!

[35] As a complement to this very active Asteria, Callimachus added a correspondingly active Apollo. For this motif he could turn to another Pindaric source: the myth of the island Rhodes in *Olympian* 7. This island, like Callimachus' Asteria, had not always been

Yet the decisive factor in Callimachus' use of these individual motifs must be seen in the sweeping claim which colors them all: namely, in that radical originality (especially with regard to the Homeric Hymn) which Pindar so forcefully asserts for the story of Asteria. For Callimachus, too, as our analysis of the *Hymn to Delos* in the following section will show, the figure of Asteria embodied something new, and this

clearly visible in the sea - not, as in Callimachus, because it drifted this way and that, but because it was still submerged beneath the waves (v. 54-57):

φαντὶ δ' ἀνθρώπων παλαιαί
ῥήσιες, οὔπω, ὅτε χθό-
να δατέοντο Ζεύς τε καὶ ἀθάνατοι,
φανερὰν ἐν πελάγει Ῥόδον ἔμμεν ποντίῳ,
ἁλμυροῖς δ' ἐν βένθεσιν νᾶσον κεκρύφθαι.

Ancient stories of men report
that when Zeus and the immortal gods
were alloting the earth
Rhodes was not yet visible on the ocean main,
but lay hidden, an island in the briny depths.

One god, however, was not present during the allotment, namely Helios, who was therefore left without a place to call his own (v. 58-59 ἀπεόντος δ' οὔτις ἔνδειξεν λάχος Ἀελίου·/ καί ῥά νιν χώρας ἀκλάρωτον λίπον). The situation is parallel, then, with that of Apollo in Callimachus' hymn, since he too is absent (he has yet to be born) and has no place allotted to him as a birthplace. We should note, moreover, that Callimachus elsewhere seems to have identified Apollo with Helios (cf. Williams *ad H*. 2.9, 52, 93) - a fact which would have made it particularly appealing and easy for him to draw on *Olympian* 7. The parallels do not stop here, however. In response to Helios' complaint, Zeus decided to recast the votes. The sun-god, however, had something else in mind (v. 61 f.):

...ἀλλά νιν οὐκ εἴασεν· ἐπεὶ πολιᾶς
εἶπέ τιν' αὐτὸς ὁρᾶν ἔν-
δον θαλάσσας αὐξομέναν πεδόθεν
πολύβοσκον γαῖαν ἀνθρώποισι καὶ εὔφρονα μήλοις.

...But he would not permit him. For he said
that he himself had seen within the grey
waters, growing from the bed of the sea,
a land that would be fruitful for men and kindly
to their flocks.

Helios chooses Rhodes (which is still submerged), just as Callimachus' Apollo chooses Delos (which is still adrift); and as Helios stops Zeus from granting him someplace else, so the unborn Apollo stops his mother from choosing Kos (v. 162 ἀλλά ἑ παιδὸς ἔρυκεν ἔπος τόδε). Both gods, moreover, form their choice by *seeing* the place which they want (*Ol.* 7.62 εἶπέ τιν' αὐτὸς ὁρᾶν; *H*. 4.191 ἔστι διειδομένη τις ἐν ὕδατι νῆσος ἀραιή). Finally, in either case the choice results in the creation of a proper island, whose name is suggested by its peculiar genesis: Rhodos, "the rose", "blossomed forth from the watery sea" (v. 69-70 βλάστε μὲν ἐξ ἁλὸς ὑγρᾶς / νᾶσος); Asteria became Delos because she no longer floated obscurely (ἄδηλος v. 53) among the waves.

It is worth noting here that Callimachus may have drawn on further Paians by Pindar in composing the *Hymn to Delos*. In particular, Paian 12 contains a description of

would likewise set him apart from his Homeric antecedent. The Pindaric *novum* remained the Callimachean *novum*. Yet the continuity with his ancient model, the ostensible allegiance which Callimachus thereby established, was not absolute. Rather, as we shall see, by the

---

Apollo's birth on Delos during which Zeus sits atop Mt. Kynthos in order to guard Leto against Hera's wrath:

           ...ἔνθα [
κελαινεφέ᾽ ἀργιβρένταν λέγο[ντι
Ζῆνα καθεζόμενον   10
κορυφαῖσιν ὕπερθε φυλάξαι π[ρ]ονοί[ᾳ,
ἀνίκ᾽ ἀγανόφρων
Κοίου θυγάτηρ λύετο τερπνᾶς
ὠδῖνος·
           ...where
they say that shrouded in clouds, thunder-flashing
Zeus, sitting
upon the peaks, kept prescient watch,
when the gentle
daughter of Koios released herself of joyful
labor;

Callimachus evidently inverts this situation, having Hera set Ares and Iris atop Mts. Haimos and Mimas respectively in order to prevent Leto from giving birth to Apollo:

         ...εἶργε δὲ Λητώ   60
τειρομένην ὠδῖσι· δύω δέ οἱ εἴατο φρουροί
γαῖαν ἐποπτεύοντες, ὁ μὲν πέδον ἠπείροιο
ἥμενος ὑψηλῆς κορυφῆς ἔπι Θρήικος Αἵμου
θοῦρος Ἄρης ἐφύλασσε...
ἡ δ᾽ ἐπὶ νησάων ἑτέρη σκοπὸς αἰπειάων
ἧστο κόρη Θαύμαντος ἐπαΐξασα Μίμαντι.   66
        ...and she (scil. Hera) prevented Leto
afflicted with birth-pangs; and she had two lookouts set
to watch the earth, the one guarded the soil of the mainland
sitting atop the high peak of Thracian Haimos,
furious Ares...
the other set over the steep islands as watchman
sat, the daughter of Thaumas, having rushed atop Mimas.

A faint echo of Zeus' active role in protecting Leto at the moment of her birth – a motif not present in the *Homeric Hymn to Apollo* – may be present in Callimachus' hymn in the very compressed statement (v. 259) that "Hera did not begrudge it, since Zeus took away her anger". Finally we note that, unlike in the account from the Homeric Hymn, Callimachus has the Delian maidens sing at Apollo's birth. To my knowledge, the only precedent for this role is Paian 12.19 where, immediately following the birth, "the native woman (i.e. Delian maidens) sang" (ἐφθέγξαντο δ᾽ ἐγχώριαι).

A further Paian to keep in mind – should new fragments ever come to light – is the 10th (= fr. 521 Snell-Maehler), since this contains our earliest reference to the Delphic Septerion festival (cf. Snell, *Hermes* 73 [1938] 439), which plays an important part in the *Hymn to Delos* (cf. p. 130 f. below) as well as in other poems by Callimachus (cf. *Iambos* 4.34 f. with Pfeiffer's n. and *Aetia* IV fr. 86–89 with the Diegesis *ad* fr. 86 and Pfeiffer's n.).

very insistence with which he refers to his venerable antecedents (the *Homeric Hymn to Apollo* and the Pindaric poems discussed above), the Hellenistic poet calls attention to the altered circumstances of his Age. *His* Delos is set in a Ptolemaic sea and linked directly to Egypt underground. Indeed, as will be argued presently, it becomes the embodiment of Callimachean verse itself.

The Hymn to Delos: Delos and Callimachean Poetry

In the hymn's prooimion (v. 1-10), the island's chief characteristics are already plain to see. The poet asks himself when he will sing of sacred Delos. He calls her Ἀπόλλωνος κουροτρόφος (v. 2), thereby explaining the designation "sacred". Κουροτρόφος, however, as yet conceals the coming play with personification, which will be of great importance in this hymn. For the word is rarely used literally of someone rearing a child; rather, it often appears metaphorically of places (thus, for instance, Ithaka is ἀγαθὴ κουροτρόφος at *Od.* 9.27 cf. *LSJ* s. v.). All the Cyclades are sacred, says the poet, but Delos shall take the Muses' prize: Δῆλος δ' ἐθέλει τὰ πρῶτα φέρεσθαι / ἐκ Μουσέων (v. 4-5). We note that the poet again makes use of a word (ἐθέλει) that does not demand personification (cf. *LSJ* II 1), but can in retrospect be so construed (i.e. "wants to take" the Muses' prize). What gives Delos her preeminence? It was she who first cared for Apollo and praised him as a god. Here, in v. 6, the island's personification is made explicit. With the words λοῦσέ τε καὶ σπείρωσε, Delos assumes the role of nurse, which in the poem's model, the *Homeric Hymn to Apollo,* had been the function of several goddesses (cf. the similar wording: λόον...σπάρξαν δ' v. 120-121). Having established her credentials, the poet announces that he will sing of Delos now (νῦν v. 9), and by implication ensures the success of his poem. For as Delos praised Apollo, thus earning his love (ἤνεσε v. 6), Apollo will praise the poet (αἰνήσῃ v. 10) for celebrating Delos. That is, if anyone scorns this poem, he acts in defiance of the god himself.

The impression with which the prooimion leaves us is one of perfect reciprocity between the god and his island. Both are mentioned four times in the first ten lines (Delos, moreover, in all four case-endings; cf. also the vocative in v. 27), always in reciprocal relationships: Delos receives her epithet (Ἀπόλλωνος κουροτρόφος) from Apollo; she washes, swathes and praises the god. Apollo hates the singer who neglects to celebrate Delos; the god receives his epithet (Κύνθιος) from the island. This attachment culminates in the artful structuring of verses 9 and 10: the former framed by Delos and Apollo, the latter inversely by Apollo (Κύνθιος) and Delos (τιθήνης). Later in the poem, the reciprocity will be equally in evidence. At the crucial moment of self-characterization (v. 266 ff.), the island never proclaims itself Δῆλος; rather it states simply ἀλλ' ἀπ' ἐμεῖο / Δήλιος Ἀπόλλων κεκλήσεται.

Callimachus now sets forth (v. 11-27) the basic paradox of Delos, namely that in spite of its wretched physical state it is preeminent among islands because of Apollo's favor. The section is divided into three carefully balanced parts of five, seven and five lines each (cf. diagram p. 146). The first (11-15) deals with Delos' purely physical circumstances: an uninviting island set in a stormy sea; the second (16-22) with Delos leading the great isles to the home of Okeanos and Tethys, – her position in the assembly of islands at the house of Okeanos, before the poem shifts to the past with ἦ ὡς (v. 30), paralleling that of Apollo in the assembly of the gods on Olympus in the *Homeric Hymn to Apollo* before that poem likewise turns to the past with ἦ ὡς in v. 25 (cf. Wilamowitz, *Die Ilias und Homer* [Berlin 1916] 458); the third (23-27) with the stationary island once more: but now surrounded not by the hostile sea (cf. ἀμφί...ἑλίσσων v. 13) but by the sheltering power of Apollo (ἀμφιβέβηκεν v. 27). Her preeminence is thus explained by reference to Apollo's special love for her. The first and third sections supplement, and correspond to, each other. The one begins with κείνη, the other with κεῖναι; in the one Delos is ἠνεμόεσσα, in the other she is unaffected ὑπὸ ῥιπῆς βορέαο; and as she is ἄτροπος (immovable) in the one, her protector-god is unshakable (ἀστυφέλικτος) in the other.[36] These complementary aspects (profane and sacred) of the stationary island frame the central tableau of the islands on their journeys. Together, they prime the reader for the bizarre flight of the islands and other localities later in the poem.

To explain how Delos came to be foremost among islands, i.e. to provide the *aition* for why she enjoys Apollo's special favor, Callimachus turns to what Wilamowitz (*HD* II 63) aptly called the γοναὶ Δήλου (cf. diagram p. 146). Here he pointedly reminds us of his departure from the *Homeric Hymn to Apollo,* and of his conspicuous realignment from Apollo to Delos, by recalling the antecedent hymn's preamble – not to *Delos'* birth as here, but to that of *Apollo* (cf. W. H. Race, *op. cit.* ch. 1 n. 35 above, p. 7 n. 8). Where, in the older hymn, Apollo's birth had been preceded by the poet's uncertainty at how to celebrate the god, given

---

[36] Contemporary readers could have noted the resemblance between Apollo's aid and that afforded to Delos in a very concrete sense by Ptolemy Philadelphus and his fleet, cf. Meillier, *op. cit.* (n. 3 above) 186. Here, as in the fight against the Gauls (v. 171 ff.), Apollo and Philadelphus share a "common labor".

the great multitude of possibilities (πῶς τ' ἄρ' σ' ὑμνήω πάντως εὔυμνον ἐόντα; "how, then, shall I hymn you, who are worthy to be hymned in all ways?" v. 19), Callimachus counters with εἰ δὲ λίην πολέες σε περιτροχόωσιν ἀοιδαί, / ποίη ἐνιπλέξω σε; ("if so many songs encircle you, / with what sort shall I entwine you?" v. 28-29). And where the earlier poet had passed to his chosen theme with the words ἢ ὡς σε πρῶτον Λητὼ τέκε ("shall I sing of how Leto first bore you?" v. 25), Callimachus substitutes ἢ ὡς τὰ πρώτιστα μέγας θεὸς... / νήσους εἰναλίας εἰργάζετο ("shall I sing of how the great god first... / made the islands in the sea?" v. 30-32). This latter echo is particularly striking as the introductory formula ἢ ὡς with some form of πρῶτον appears in early hexameter poetry *only* in the *Homeric Hymn to Apollo*. There it is used twice, and that conspicuously: once to introduce the Delian section, once the Pythian (v. 25; v. 214). Not Apollo, then, Callimachus seems to be saying in using the very words of the *Hymn to Apollo,* but something different is to be our theme.

Launching us back into time, he shifts the scene to a primordial age before islands existed, and we learn of their violent origins (a νησογονία) at the hands of Poseidon, who pried them up from the landscape with his trident and rolled them into the sea, rooting them to the seabed so that they would forget the mainland (v. 30-35). "Ein groteskes Bild", as Wilamowitz pungently described it (*HD* II 65). But this monstrous act is all the more sinister for the detail that the trident was made by the Telchines.

These malicious wizards would later represent Callimachus' literary opponents in the prologue to the *Aetia,* where they are called "hostile to the Muse" (fr. 1.2). It is not inconsistent with that characterization that they should appear in our hymn as the instruments of ἀνάγκη: brute force (ἀνάγκη) and its correlate, threat of force, are quite deliberately the first impressions we are given of this earlier time. They characterize the age before Apollo's birth and they are the means by which Hera and her henchmen, Ares and Iris, attempt to prevent him from being born.[37] The result, as will be seen, is chaos. An ancient tradition held that the present age was preceded by a reign of Ἀνάγκη, in which violence thrived and there was no place for the Muse (cf. Plato *Symposium* 195b-197b; contemporary with Callimachus cf. Simias' *Wings;* for ἀνάγκη and poetry cf. Plut. *Mor.* 745 G ἄμουσον γὰρ ἡ Ἀνάγκη,

---

[37] We note the similarity between Poseidon's violent prying up of the islands (ἐκ νεάτων ὤχλισσε v. 33), and Ares' threats to drag Peneios up from the depths (βυσσόθεν ἐξερύσειε v. 127) and bury him with a mountain (Παγγαίου προθέλυμνα κάρηατα μέλλεν ἀείρας v. 134).

μουσικὸν δ' ἡ Πειθώ). Such is the world before the advent of Apollo and it is to this museless environment that the Telchines belong.

Only Delos was not afflicted by ἀνάγκη (v. 35), but floated free (ἄφετος) on the sea. As we saw in discussing the Pindaric model for this myth (p. 100 f. above), her name at this time was Asteria because she fled the advances of Zeus, leaping from the heavens ἀστέρι ἴση (v. 38) in order to remain pure. This trait of purity, we should recall, was *not* a feature of the island in the Homeric Hymn. Yet Callimachus adopts precisely this motif from Pindar and, as we shall see, now makes it *functional*, activating it as that which makes her a suitable birthplace for his patron, Apollo.[38] Free from care, she roams the sea on a zig-zag course, visiting her friends (v. 49-50, 197-198) or simply drifting with the waves (v. 192-194). But though free, her life is aimless; she has no proper place in the world. Indeed, her exultant words upon having become Apollo's birthplace, i.e. Delos (καὶ ἔσσομαι οὐκέτι πλαγκτή, "and I shall no longer be a wanderer" v. 273), clearly show that her previous nomadic existence is not to be viewed in a positive light.[39] On the contrary, Asteria's wanderings resemble Leto's search for a place to give birth (v. 68-204) or the chaotic flight of the localities (v. 70 ff.). All mirror the age prior to Apollo's birth. The wanderings cease and Asteria finds her niche only upon volunteering herself to Leto as Apollo's birthplace. Then, in stark contrast to the islands which were rooted in the sea by force, she strikes her own roots (v. 54). The sailors rename her Delos, since she no longer wanders ἄδηλος on the sea (v. 51-53).

The question raised by the island's paradoxical present-day status as depicted in vv. 11-27 has thus been answered. We know now why Apollo confers upon Delos such extraordinary honor that - in spite of

---

[38] For the importance of purity as an attribute of Callimachean poetry cf. esp. H. 2.110-112. Asteria's purity is stressed here in the word ἄφετος (v. 36), which is used especially of sacred flocks allowed to roam freely without having to work, cf. Plat. *Crit.* 119d, *Prot.* 320a, etc.; at Eur. *Ion* 822 it is used to describe Ion himself as dedicated to Apollo at Delphi. Cf. also Io in Aesch. *PV* 666. Asteria's purity is stressed again at v. 98, cf. p. 117 f.

[39] This is borne out by the larger context of the island's words, which come immediately after her transformation from Asteria to Delos. Here, and nowhere else in the hymn, the island describes herself: "αὕτη ἐγὼ τοιήδε· δυσήροτος" (v. 268). This self-revelation recalls another one in both situation and words, namely that of Odysseus when he-like Delos-, after years of wandering, attains his proper place in the world (cf. Delos' καὶ ἔσσομαι οὐκέτι πλαγκτή v. 273) and, setting aside his previous identity, can reveal himself for the first time to a member of his household, to Telemachus (*Od.* 16.205-206): ἀλλ' ὅδ' ἐγὼ τοιόσδε, παθὼν κακά, πολλὰ δ' ἀληθείς, / ἤλυθον εἰκοστῷ ἔτει ἐς πατρίδα γαῖαν. Thus, through the parallel with Odysseus' situation, Asteria's many years of wanderings are given a negative stamp.

her wretched physical circumstances-she is preeminent not only among her immediate neighbors, the Cyclades (v. 2 ff.), but among even the very greatest islands whenever they go in procession to the house of Okeanos and Tethys: she was Apollo's birthplace. The next part of the poem, its narrative core (v. 54-259), now takes us a logical step further, explaining how she came to be so. It thereby provides us with an *aition* of the previous section (v. 28-54), just as that section had of the one prior to itself (i. e. v. 11-27). Accordingly, the γοναὶ Δήλου of the previous section give way to the γοναὶ Ἀπόλλωνος (cf. diagram p. 146).

The reason for Apollo's birth on Delos was Hera's wrath, as we see in the transitional phrase, οὐδ' Ἥρην κοτέουσαν ὑπέτρεσας ("nor did you tremble before Hera in her anger" v. 55). For while it is this goddess' hostility which motivates Leto's wanderings and frames the entire section (cf. the corresponding οὐδ' Ἥρη νεμέσησεν, "nor did Hera begrudge it [*scil.* Apollo's birth]" v. 259), yet Hera cannot bring herself to hate Asteria (v. 244 ff.): "I am not at all distressed by Asteria...but I honor her exceedingly because she did not trample my bed" (Ἀστερίῃ δ' οὐδέν τι βαρύνομαι... ἀλλά μιν ἔκπαγλόν τι σεβίζομαι, οὕνεκ' ἐμεῖο / δέμνιον οὐκ ἐπάτησε). In other words, while those women who bear Zeus' children provoke Hera's wrath (v. 55-57), Asteria's demonstrated purity pacifies the angry goddess. Thus, not only does it make her suitable to Apollo, it is the *sine qua non* for his birth. In Callimachus' view, only the small and pure can overcome the more established powers that rely for their effect on force.

Asteria's success against the proponents of force is inseparable from the similar success represented by Apollo's birth. Here, Callimachus deviates significantly from the *Homeric Hymn to Apollo*. In the older poem, Hera tried to obstruct Apollo's birth mainly because she was jealous of her husband's affair. Callimachus deliberately sets himself off from that version by referring to that traditional motivation ("she [*scil.* Hera] brayed dreadfully at all those laboring women who gave birth to children for Zeus", ἡ μὲν ἁπάσαις / δεινὸν ἐπεβρωμᾶτο λεχωίσιν αἳ Διὶ παῖδας / ἐξέφερον v. 55-57) but insisting that Leto's case is different: "but at Leto especially, because she alone was going to bear to Zeus a son more beloved than Ares", Λητοῖ δὲ διακριδόν, οὕνεκα μούνη / Ζηνὶ τεκεῖν ἤμελλε φιλαίτερον Ἄρεος υἷα. In this way, Callimachus makes the Ἀπόλλωνος γοναί into a myth of succession in the style of Hesiod.

With the phrase τεκεῖν ἤμελλε (v. 58), the poet pointedly refers to several works: first to *Homeric Hymn to Apollo* (v. 99-101), where Hera prevents Eileithyia from going to Leto: ἥ μιν ἔρυκε / ζηλοσύνῃ ὅτ' ἄρ' υἱὸν ἀμύμονά τε κρατερόν τε / Λητὼ τέξεσθαι καλλιπλόκαμος τότ' ἔμελλεν, i. e. as mentioned above, Hera is more jealous because of Zeus' infidelity than because of the particular son to be born to him. The remaining passages all have to do with myths of succession. Thus in Hes. *Th.* 468-9, Rhea was about to bear Zeus (Δί' ἔμελλε.../ τέξεσθαι), but feared for his life, since Cronos had learned that he was destined to be overcome by one of his sons, κρατερῷ περ ἐόντι (465). He thus kept a careful watch (οὐκ ἀλαὸς σκοπιὴν ἔχεν v. 466) and swallowed his children as they were born. In our poem, Hera knows that her strong son, Ares, is to be supplanted by Apollo and hence keeps watch (σκοπιὴν ἔχεν v. 59) in order to prevent his birth. A similar instance may be seen in Hes. *Th.* 888, where Metis was about to bear Athene (ἀλλ' ὅτε δή ῥ' ἤμελλε θεὰν γλαυκῶπιν 'Αθήνην / τέξεσθαι) when Zeus swallowed her in jealousy because παῖδα θεῶν βασιλῆα καὶ ἀνδρῶν / ἤμελλεν τέξεσθαι ὑπέρβιον ἦτορ ἔχουσα, i.e. she was going to bear Zeus' replacement. Callimachus changes this to Ares' replacement. Yet again in the *Iliad* (19.98 ff.) we hear that when Alcmene was about to bear Herakles (ἤματι τῷ ὅτ' ἔμελλε βίην Ἡρακληείην / 'Αλκμήνη τέξεσθαι), Hera tricked Zeus into swearing that a son born on that day would rule over all men, but then prevented Herakles from being born until Eurystheus had come to the world. From this last example it becomes clear that Hera is no mean foe: she has played this game before, and won.

Callimachus thus sets his version of Apollo's birth squarely in the tradition of succession myths, and in this way he shifts the focus of the hymn: Ares and the barbarous, brutalizing force he represents, must in this poem be overcome by the god of song and his allies. Apollo needs the tiny island in order to realize his victory, and the island, in turn, becomes significant (that is, becomes δῆλος) because the god comes into existence through her. For Callimachus, Apollo becomes effective in the world through that which is small and pure.

In order to protect the interests of her son, Ares, Hera attempts to prevent Apollo's birth. She stations herself in heaven, setting Ares to guard the mainland from atop Mt. Haimos in his barbarous northern homeland, while Iris guards the islands from atop Mt. Mimas. Together, they intimidate the localities into refusing asylum for Leto.

Accordingly, wherever Leto appears, the localities flee. In the *Homeric Hymn to Apollo,* Leto's wanderings were set out in an impressive catalogue (v. 30-44), comprising the Aegean islands and coasts, the area in which the worship of Delian Apollo was of immediate significance.[40] The Hellenistic author, however, was not constrained by regional boundaries, and thus an unadorned narrative such as that in the Homeric Hymn would almost demand elaboration. Apart from suiting his poetic purpose, this framework would appeal to Callimachus' geogra-

---

[40] Cf. T. Allen and E. E. Sikes, *The Homeric Hymns* (New York 1904) 63; G. Nagy, *The Best of the Achaeans* (Baltimore 1979) 6-7.

phical/ethnological interests (he was the author of Περὶ τῶν ἐν τῇ οἰκουμένῃ ποταμῶν, Κτίσεις νήσων καὶ πόλεων καὶ μετονομασίαι, and Θαυμάτων τῶν εἰς ἅπασαν τὴν γῆν κατὰ τόπους ὄντων, cf. Pfeiffer, Test. 1.18 ff.). Thus, in our hymn, the story of Leto's journey (v. 70-204) is more ecumenical and almost nine times as long as its archaic counterpart. Yet in spite of its length it retains none of the monumentality (which, as we saw in ch. 1, was one of the hallmarks of the *oral* heritage) found in the catalogue in the Homeric Hymn. Rather it becomes a subtly variegated account, with shifting dynamics, where learned enumeration alternates with colorful narrative digression - in short, a characteristic example of Hellenistic "poikilia".

Furthermore, whereas in the *Homeric Hymn to Apollo* Leto follows (with some deviation) a regular path around the Aegean - from Crete to Athens; along the Western and Northern shore to Asia Minor; southward down the coast to the island Karpathos; then westward again to the Cyclades and Delos -, in Callimachus she proceeds by fits and starts: first (briefly v. 70-74) to Arcadia, then (in an extended narrative v. 75-99) north to Boeotia, then (briefly v. 100-102) doubling back to Achaia, and finally (in a lengthy section v. 103-152) turning north again to Thessaly (cf. diagram p. 146). In one respect, to be sure, the goddess' itinerary is more regular than it had been in the Homeric Hymn. There, she had leaped indiscriminately between mainland and islands; here, she strictly adheres to the scholarly/geographical distinction between the two realms - a distinction (set up through the separate domains of Ares and Iris) which, though it might be natural for mortal journeys, is strikingly artificial for divine ones.

The catalogue of places in the Homeric Hymn provided Callimachus further with the germ of a thought which he now makes central to his poem. At v. 47-48 of the *Homeric Hymn to Apollo* we hear that the localities "trembled and feared, and none dared to receive Phoebus" (αἱ δὲ μάλ᾽ ἐτρόμεον καὶ ἐδείδισαν, οὐδέ τις ἔτλη / Φοῖβον δέξασθαι). To Callimachus, the author of Περὶ Νυμφῶν, this brief description was an invitation to play with the tradition that all places have their eponymous gods from whom they are virtually indistinguishable - and play he did! For Callimachus mischievously presses this conception to its humorous extreme, thereby showing that it is problematical: what, asks the poet, if an entire landscape suddenly took to its heels and no place was left for Apollo's birth?[41]

---

[41] Cf. E. Howald and E. Staiger, *Die Dichtungen des Kallimachos* (Zürich 1955) 100; B. Snell, *Die Entdeckung des Geistes*[4] (Göttingen 1975) 249. Callimachus similarly dramatizes a religious-historical problem in H. 3, namely that of Artemis' ambivalence as huntress and city goddess, setting it in the form of a dialogue between Artemis παῖς and father Zeus, cf. Wilamowitz, *Glaube der Hellenen* II (Nachdr. Darmstadt 1959) 146 n. 1.

The groundwork for this amusing, yet unsettling, experiment was already laid (as we saw, p. 110 f.) in the opening sections of the poem. Now, as Leto turns this way and that, Callimachus toys with his reader's phantasy, leaving him delightfully uncertain whether, for instance, Mt. Helikon itself is running away, or just its divinity. In this way he generates a sense of utter chaos (typical of a time in which Apollo has not yet come into the world, and Hera, Ares and Iris are still in control), bringing the uncertainty he has caused with this fleeing landscape to a climax when the nymph Melie is sent reeling from the dance upon seeing her tree endangered by the flight of Mt. Helikon (v. 79-82). Here, in unprecedented fashion, as though no longer able to bear the uncertainty, the poet breaks into the narrative and demands that his Muses set him straight: "did trees really come into being at the same time as nymphs?", i. e. is the life of a place and its god really one? Whether or not the subsequent couplet (v. 84-85) is the Muses' reply (cf. chapter 1, p. 41 f.), it only compounds the uncertainty.

In the midst of such doubts, an unambiguous voice suddenly makes itself heard: that of Apollo from his mother's womb (v. 86-98). Already in full command of his mantic powers, and hence cognizant of his mother's plight, he lashes out against the fleeing Thebe, prophesying that she will soon feel the effects of his arrows; for she is to be the birthplace of the ill-fated Niobids – but not of him.

For Callimachus, the Niobe myth has a special point, since it contraposes quantity (Niobe's many children) to quality (Leto's two).[42] As the κακόγλωσσος γυνή (v. 96), Niobe plays the same role as the slanderous Telchines (fr. 1.11) and Momos in *H.* 2.106, both of whom likewise criticize on the basis of sheer quantity. The prophecy, and the whole first stage of Leto's journey, culminate in the words εὐαγέων δὲ καὶ εὐαγέεσσι μελοίμην ("being pure myself, may I be a care to the pure" v. 98).

---

[42] Theocritus too had said (17.43-44) that evil, unloving women have easy births (ῥηίδιοι δὲ γοναί, cf. Archilochus *P. Köln* II 58.27) and children who do not resemble their father (τέκνα δ' οὐ ποτεοικότα πατρί). To these he opposed Ptolemy Philadelphus, who was πατρὶ ἐοικώς and παῖς ἀγαπητός (v. 63-64), the "beloved" or "only" true son (cf. *LSJ* and W. Bauer, *Griechisch-Deutsches Wörterbuch des Neuen Testaments*[5] [Berlin 1958] s.v. ἀγαπητός) i. e. legitimate heir to the throne. Callimachus also stresses Philadelphus' likeness to Soter (ὁ δ' εἴσεται ἤθεα πατρός v. 170) implying, though not actually stating explicitly, as in Theocritus, that he is the product of true love and thus his father's rightful successor. What is only implicit for Philadelphus is, however, present in the case of his counterpart, Apollo, who is more beloved (φιλαίτερον v. 58) to Zeus than is Ares, and whose birth is a model of δυστοκία. On the subject of the birth of the "beloved" (*scil.* "only") son, cf. L. Koenen, "Die Adaption ägyptischer Königsideologie am Ptolemäerhof", *Egypt and the Hellenistic World,* Proc. Intl. Colloq. Leuven (Leuven 1983) 161-164.

Thebes and the other localities are foils for Asteria, whose "purity" is a match for Apollo's.[42a]

Leto now doubles back to Achaia in the northern Peloponnese (v. 100-102), but once again the localities (Helice and Bura) flee. Her wanderings grow ever more labyrinthine as she heads north to Thessaly, turning now to Anaurus in the east, now north-west to Larissa; eastwards again to the cliffs of Cheiron (Mt. Pelion); again north-west to the river Peneios. And just as the first stage of Leto's journey had reached its climax with a longer episode (i.e. with Apollo's prophecy against Thebe), so the second culminates in her extended encounter with Peneios (v. 105-152, cf. diagram p. 146 below).[43]

The river at first remains silent, despite Leto's pleas. He is only able to muster the courage to speak once she has already turned again for help to Mt. Pelion. The opening words of his speech are revealing: Λητοῖ, Ἀναγκαίη μεγάλη θεός ("Leto, Force is a great god" v. 122). Like the other localities (except Asteria v. 35), he is subject to force. Indeed, for him it is a "great god".[43a] Once again we are made aware that the dominant force of the age is ἀνάγκη.

Torn between fears that Ares will desiccate his streams, and the noble impulse to aid a needy goddess, Peneios ultimately collects himself and calms his waters for Leto. But he makes his decision under duress, oblivious to any honor that he could receive as Apollo's birthplace. He fears that he will suffer for his action and that, forever drained of his streams, he will be called the most dishonored of rivers: καὶ μόνος ἐν ποταμοῖσιν ἀτιμότατος καλέεσθαι (v. 131). Finally Leto tells him not to suffer on her account and lets him return to his flight (v. 150-152).

Like Thebe, at the end of the first stage of Leto's wanderings, Peneios is foil for Asteria (though the river, through his kindness, is clearly a more positive foil). For Asteria will not have to be begged (or even asked). She will offer herself willingly and fearlessly because she is φιλόμολπε (v. 197, that is, entirely aware of what sort of god will be

---

[42a] We note how Iris tries to impugn this purity by calling her πόντοιο κακὸν σάρον, "the evil rubbish of the sea" v. 225.

[43] The scene is vividly mimetic, with pathetic speeches (cf. esp. the short, simple sentences of Peneios' inner monologue, v. 122-132) and characters reminiscent, as Cahen observed (ad v. 106-152) of New Comedy: Leto, the long-suffering mother; Peneios, the simple, unassuming man (scil. river) who displays unexpected heroism in a crisis; Ares, the thunderous, but inarticulate soldier (a character which, however, does not appear in Menander). For the scene's ironic use of elevated diction, cf. K.J. Mckay, *Erysichthon, A Callimachean Comedy,* Mnemosyne Suppl. 7 (1962) 178-181.

[43a] Cf. the-deliberately?-vague designation of Poseidon, likewise a wielder of force, as μέγας θεός v. 30.

born on her soil). Her streams will not dry up, but rather overflow with gold (v. 263). And far from becoming ἀτιμοτάτη, she will be νησάων ἁγιωτάτη (v. 275).

In the third stage of her journey, Leto turns to the islands (v. 153 ff. cf. diagram p. 146 below). Her route is every bit as erratic as before. With Iris pressing the islands to flight, Leto must turn from the Echinades, off the western coast of Greece near Acarnania, northwestwards to Corcyra, and then, in an enormous leap, to Cos in the eastern Aegean. Thus, the chaotic effect continues to mount.

Against this backdrop, the lucid voice of Apollo is heard once again from his mother's womb (v. 162ff.). He restrains her from going to Cos, not because the island is unworthy, but because another god (θεὸς ἄλλος v. 165), Ptolemy Philadelphus, is destined to be born there. Cos is the third in the series of foils which, if we look back, can be seen to grow ever more positive. Callimachus, it seems, is gradually building towards the ideal birthplace for Apollo.

The song-god ends his prophecy with an address to Philadelphus (v. 188-190): ἐσσόμενε Πτολεμαῖε, τά τοι μαντήια Φοίβου. / αἰνήσεις μέγα δή τι τὸν εἰσέτι γαστέρι μάντιν / ὕστερον ἤματα πάντα ("O future Ptolemy, these are Phoebus' prophecies to you. / And you will greatly praise the prophet still in the belly / all the days to come"). With αἰνήσεις κ.τ.λ. we recall the prooimion. There, Delos was the first to praise Apollo 'as a god' (v. 6 καὶ ὡς θεὸν *ἤνεσε πρώτη*) and the god would praise Callimachus for celebrating Delos (v. 9-10 ὡς ἂν Ἀπόλλων / Κύνθιος *αἰνήσῃ* με φίλης ἀλέγοντα τιθήνης). The implication, as we recall, was that anyone disparaging the hymn would be acting in defiance of the god; the hymn itself thus ensured its own reception. Here, it is Apollo who first praises Ptolemy "as a god", thereby implying that the king will commend not just "the prophet still in the belly" but the poet as well: for it is his poem that preserves (*sic*) and publishes the prophecy. As in the case of the prooimion then (cf. p. 110 above), the poem's reception within the poem is the model for its actual reception by the reader.

As soon as he has finished his prophecy about Philadelphus, Apollo finally points his mother towards that birthplace that truly suits him. It is, of course, Asteria. The god describes Asteria to his mother, and his description reveals why the island appeals to him. It is "slender" (ἀραιή v. 191). The scholia say λεπτή. "Slenderness" is, for Callimachus, a pregnant concept, as we know from the *Aetia* prologue (fr. 1.24, 11). It is only natural that the Callimachean god of song should be attracted to such an island and not to those that were once mountains, ripped out of the earth by the μέγας θεός, Poseidon, with a weapon made by the Telchines. The monstrous image of enormous earth-masses pried up and rolled into the sea, stands in sharpest contrast to Asteria, who is so slender and delicate that the god compares her to an asphodel blown this way and that over the waves: ἀλλὰ παλιρροίῃ ἐπινήχεται ἀνθέρικος ὥς, / ἔνθα νότος, ἔνθ' εὖρος, ὅπῃ φορέῃσι θάλασσα ("but she swims in the current like an asphodel, whither the South Wind, whither the East Wind, whither the sea might carry her" v. 193-194). In the *Homeric Hymn to Apollo,* Delos is barren and poor (cf. v. 54-55, 72), but nowhere delicate and slender. It is precisely these characteristics that Callimachus adds.[44]

With the striking repetition, ὅπῃ φορέῃσι θάλασσα / τῇ με φέροις ("whither the sea might carry her, carry me there"), Callimachus suggests the similarity that attracts Apollo to Asteria: a tiny god and a tiny island, both borne this way and that through the world. He thereby follows the principle of ὅμοιον ὁμοίῳ, which was likewise operative in the programmatic verse: εὐαγέων δὲ καὶ εὐαγέεσσι μελοίμην v. 98. Following this request, the god explains his choice: κείνην γὰρ ἐλεύσεαι εἰς ἐθέλουσαν ("for when you shall come to her, she will be willing" v. 195). Thus, just as the world willingly accepts Ptolemaic rule (v. 167), so Asteria, unaffected by ἀνάγκη, will accept Leto and Apollo. At these words, the remaining islands flee, and Callimachus now addresses himself directly to Asteria: The contrast to the other islands is all the more glaring through the asyndeton which the position of the vocative, Ἀστερίη φιλόμολπε, before σὺ δ', brings about. The poet calls her φιλόμολπε as though to explain her willingness to receive Leto. She is able to offer the god of song a birthplace because she is graced with the decisive characteristic: she loves song. In contrast to the *Homeric Hymn to Apollo,* there is never a moment's doubt as to her appropriateness to Apollo. The god chooses her himself (cf. n. 35 above).

With the most affecting humor, Callimachus describes how Asteria swims down from Euboea, trailing Geraistian sea-weed, and, upon seeing the laboring goddess, comes to a halt (v. 200). In defiance of Hera's threats, she courageously offers herself to Leto. Through this crucial act, Callimachus creates the central paradox of his poem: all places (islands, rivers, mountains, etc.), which by nature ought to be fixed, are on the run; only Asteria, the one who, by nature, is free to roam, comes to a halt.

The god of song selects his conduit into the world as a poet might the particular metrical shape or genre most suited to his content. In Callimachus' view, he must come into the world only through this delicate, song-loving medium and, correspondingly, only the slender island,

---

[44] The description is actually taken not from the *Homeric Hymn to Apollo,* but from *Od.* 4.845 ff.; ἔστι δέ τις νῆσος μέσσῃ ἁλὶ πετρήεσσα…Ἀστερίς, οὐ μεγάλη.

undefiled by force, will suit the god. This relationship is almost like that between inspiration and form. The power of Apollo - and this means here the power of his music - becomes active through that which is small and pure. By means of that power Asteria is transformed, filled with poetic life, made Δῆλος, the subject of song - here specifically the subject of this hymn. This is the birth of the poet's theme, the birth of Delos. In the meeting of these two, then, Callimachus describes nothing less than the creation of his poem. Moreover, inasmuch as Delos embodies Callimachean ideals more generally, this description extends to the rest of his works as well. The birth of Delos may thus be viewed as depicting the realization of Callimachean song.

A closer look at the comparison of Asteria with the asphodel (ἀνθερικος ὥς v. 193) supports this view. Callimachus is here clearly alluding to a unique Homeric simile in which the raft of Odysseus is compared to thistlestalks (*Od.* 5.327-332):[45]

> τὴν δ' ἐφόρει μέγα κῦμα κατὰ ῥόον ἔνθα καὶ ἔνθα.
> ὡς δ' ὅτ' ὀπωρινὸς βορέης φορέῃσιν ἀκάνθας
> ἂμ πεδίον, πυκιναὶ δὲ πρὸς ἀλλήλῃσιν ἔχονται,
> ὣς τὴν ἂμ πέλαγος ἄνεμοι φέρον ἔνθα καὶ ἔνθα
> ἄλλοτε μέν τε Νότος Βορέῃ προβάλεσκε φέρεσθαι,
> ἄλλοτε δ' αὖτ' Εὖρος Ζεφύρῳ εἴξασκε διώκειν.

> And a great wave swept it along the current here and there.
> And as when in late summer the north wind sweeps thistles
> over the plain, and they stick to one another in bunches,
> so the winds swept it along the sea here and there,
> and now the South Wind tossed it over to the North to be carried,
> and then again the East Wind gave way in the chase to the South.

Why did Callimachus substitute the asphodel for thistlestalks? Several reasons suggest themselves: 1) According to Plutarch (*Sept. Sap. conv.* 14), this plant was given as an offering to Apollo on Delos: ἱστόρησε παρ' αὐτοῖς (scil. the Delians) εἰς τὸ ἱερὸν κομιζόμενα τῆς πρώτης ὑπομνήματα τροφῆς καὶ δείγματα μετ' ἄλλων εὐτελῶν καὶ αὐτοφυῶν μαλάχην καὶ ἀνθέρικον. The asphodel is thus associated with Apollo, and it is not surprising that he should compare the island which is most pleasing to him as a birthplace to that plant.

2) In the *Works and Days* (v. 40-41), Hesiod criticizes the kings for their greed: νήπιοι, οὐδὲ ἴσασιν ὅσῳ πλέον ἥμισυ παντός, / οὐδ' ὅσον ἐν μαλάχῃ τε καὶ ἀσφοδέλῳ μέγ' ὄνειαρ. The asphodel is here the poor but worthy plant which illustrates the concept that half is more than the whole. Such a connotation accords well with Callimachus' preference

---

[45] It is comparable only to *Od.* 5.368 ff.

for the "small" art-form and his admiration for Hesiod (cf. esp. *Ep.* 27 and fr. 2).

3) Callimachus' birthplace was Cyrene, and his writings abound with Cyrenaic stories and rites (cf. Pfeiffer p. XXXVIII; the extent of his identification with his native land is well illustrated by *H.* 2.71). As Williams points out (*ad H.* 2.88), Cyrene was called both Κυράνα and Κύρα, and according to V. Bertoldi (in *Mélanges Boisacq,* vol. 1 = Brussels, Univ. Libre, Inst. de philol. et d'hist. orient., annuaire 5, 1937 cf. esp. p. 59-63) followed by F. Chamoux (*Cyrène sous la monarchie des Battiades,* Paris 1953, p. 126-127), this name originally came from the native Libyan word κύρα, which according to Dioskourides (*Mat. Med.* II 169 RV, ed. Wellmann I 235) meant "asphodel": ἀσφόδελος· οἱ δὲ ναρθήκιον, Ῥωμαῖοι ἀλβούκιουμ, Ἄφροι κύρα. Cyrene would thus be the "city of Asphodels", an appropriate name since the asphodel is particularly common to this area (cf. Chamoux, *op. cit.*). Already Herodotus notes that Libyan nomads made their portable huts out of this plant (IV 190): οἰκήματα δὲ σύμπηκτα ἐξ ἀνθερίκων ἐνειρμένων περὶ σχοίνους ἐστί, καὶ ταῦτα περιφορητά, and according to Diodorus (20.57), these nomads were called Ἀσφοδελώδεις, "those like the asphodel".

In comparing Asteria to an asphodel, Callimachus thus linked her with Cyrene. If our suggestion is correct that Callimachus saw Delos as a metaphor for his own poetry, then that link would be quite natural: Delos, the embodiment of Callimachean ideals, is like that which grows in (and gives its name to) the poet's native city.[45a]

The realization of Callimachean song is part of the new order that comes with Apollo's birth, and it helps overturn the old. To Callimachus, the most significant representative of the old order is Ares. He constructs his poem in such a way that Ares is the force that must, by various means, be overthrown. Thus, just as Apollo's birth defeats the war-god on a mythic level, so on a literary one the creation of Delos overcomes the old (poetic) order in which Ares is the favorite son: i.e. that order which favors heroic epic. The supporters of the old order

---

[45a] In this light, we might now give serious consideration after all to the suggestion that the MSS readings of καύριος, καύθιος or κάνθιος in v. 10 of the hymn are indeed corruptions from Καρνεῖ' (C. Haeberlin, *Philol.* 46 [1888] 69) or Κάρνεος (C. Gallavotti, *Par. Pass.* 8 [1953] 467) rather than from Κύνθιος as proposed by Lascaris. Mineur's objection (*ad* Κύνθιος v. 10) that "mention of Ἀπόλλων Καρνεῖος is quite out of place in a hymn to Delos, which contains no further references to Callimachus' Cyrenean origin" is evidently groundless - for Cyrene *is* present, albeit obliquely, at that moment when Asteria is characterized by the god. The fact that that god may actually have been invoked in his Cyrenean aspect would give added point to his description and would continue the theme of ὅμοιον ὁμοίῳ which we saw above, p. 120. Cf., however, our discussion of this passage above, p. 111.

possess precisely those traits that Callimachus assailed in his literary opponents: they are impure,[46] and slanderous, and they value quantity over quality;[47] they engage in monstrous acts of force[48] and make dreadful noise.[49]

Callimachus provides a clue that his subject - at least in part - is poetry by giving the warrior-god a distinctly epic coloring. It is significant that, in his first appearance in the poem, this god is referred to as θοῦρος Ἄρης (v. 64), an unashamedly stock Homeric epithet, and as such "quite exceptional" in Callimachus (thus Mineur *ad loc.*). In addition, he is given two horses (v. 64, a rare Callimachean use of the dual, cf. Mineur *ad loc.*) as in Homer (*Il.* 5.356 ff. in collocation with θοῦρος Ἄρης v. 355. Otherwise, Ares usually has four horses cf. "Hes." *Scut.* 109, 191; Pind. *P.* 4.87; *H. H.* 8.7-8, etc.). From the very start, then, Ares exhibits the marks of martial-epic tradition. But further, the poet connects this god with a literary device which is one of the most striking features of heroic epic, the extended simile (v. 141-147 cf. H. Fränkel, *Dicht. u. Phil.* p. 44 "eines der auffallendsten Stilelemente in den Epen, besonders der Ilias"). The terrible noise that arises when Ares strikes his shield with his spear is compared to the din of Hephaestus' workshop when Briareus, the giant trapped beneath Mt. Aetna, shifts positions, causing volcanic eruptions that make the furnaces roar. Although this image is dependent on Pindar's description of the serpent Typhon beneath Mt. Aetna (*P.* 1.15-28),[50] its form is taken from epic. In the Homeric Hymns, extended similes are virtually nonexistent (the longest is *H. H. Dem.* 174-175); they are likewise rare in Hesiod (cf. West *ad Th.* 594 ff.). In the pseudo-Hesiodic *Shield*, by contrast, they are plentiful as soon as the poem turns to violent themes: Herakles' battle with Cycnus (v. 374-379, 386-392, 402-412, 421-423) and his father Ares (v. 426-433, 437-441). Callimachus was fond of Hesiod and the Homeric Hymns, but deeply averse to any attempt at reproducing the scope and matter of heroic epic. It is not surprising then that he should use only few extended similes.[51] The longest is, in

---

[46] Cf. The discussion of εὐαγέων δὲ καὶ εὐαγέεσσι μελοίμην above p. 101, 113, 118.

[47] Cf. Niobe p. 117 above, and also Iris' description of Asteria v. 255.

[48] Cf. Poseidon p. 112 f., particularly his connection with the Telchines; and Ares p. 118 above. Contrast Callimachus' childlike, slender verse, p. 94 above.

[49] Hera "brays" like an ass at Zeus' mistresses (v. 56), cf. also the poet with the voice of an ass, fr. 192.11; also Ares below, v. 133-147. Callimachus rejected the μέγα ψοφέουσαν ἀοιδήν fr. 1.19, saying βροντᾶν οὐκ ἐμόν.

[50] Callimachus similarly had v. 23 ff. in mind for his description of Poseidon rolling the islands into the sea, εἰσεκύλισε θαλάσσῃ v. 33.

[51] They are listed in Lapp, *De Callimachi Cyrenaei Tropis et Figuris*, (Diss. Bonn 1965) p. 88-89. On similes in Hellenistic epic, cf. H. Drögemüller, *Die Gleichnisse im hellenistischen Epos* (Diss. Hamburg 1956).

fact, this one; the second-longest, also in our hymn, is that in which Iris is compared to a watchful hunting dog at her mistress' throne (v. 228 ff.).[52] Further, the invading Gauls are compared to snowflakes (v. 175, a common simile in the *Iliad,* cf. 3.222, 12.156, 278, 19.357) and the mass of stars in the sky (v. 176).

What is striking is that in each case a malevolent character, or force, is characterized in a way that is unmistakably associated with heroic epic.[53] Ares, i.e. war, is the heroic topic *par excellence*. On Delos, the subject matter of such epic is excluded: the war-cry, death and the horses of war (οὐδέ σ' Ἐνυώ / οὐδ' Ἀίδης οὐδ' ἵπποι ἐπιστείβουσιν Ἄρηος v. 276-277). Nor does the island even possess those accouterments that evoke warfare: she is fortified neither by ramparts (πύργοισι περισκεπέεσι v. 23) or walls (τείχεα v. 25). Thus, if Callimachus saw in Delos a metaphor for his own poetry, then perhaps Ares and his associates embody the hackneyed heroic style that he rejected.[54]

This is not to say that Callimachus repudiates *Homer,* or that he fails to give his due to earlier poetry. The fact that Callimachus' poem is unthinkable without the model of the *Homeric Hymn to Apollo* shows the depth of his respect and veneration for those great antecedents. Each generation, however, must bring Apollo into the world in its own way, transforming and making productive for the here and now those paradigms that succeeded in the past. This is what Pindar had done in

---

[52] Cf. Drögemüller's excellent analysis, *op. cit.* (n. 51 above) 41-43: "Der Leser ...entsinnt sich, daß in dem vv. 59-66 der Dichter in einem eigens neu und gut erfundenen Bild Ares und Iris als Wächter der Hera auf den Thrakischen Haimos und den kleinasiatischen Mimas gesetzt hat, und daß entsprechend dem schrecklichen Toben des Kriegsgottes (133-147) nun ja auch Iris in Aktion treten mußte. Und wie dort das ungeheure Getöse im Gleichnis – auch akustisch – ... verdeutlicht wird, so wird hier die Szene im Gleichnis visuell verdeutlicht."

[53] A similar line of interpretation has been pursued by N. Hopkinson in his commentary, *Callimachus: Hymn to Demeter* (Cambridge 1984) 6-7, where Iliadic features are seen to put a character in a negative light: "She (*scil.* the priestess) warns (*scil.* Erysichthon) against incurring the goddess's anger and finishes with the resounding Iliadic ἐκκεραΐζεις (49) to stress the unnatural violence of desecration.

The narrative continues on an Iliadic plane, rising to match Erysichthon's ferocity in reply with an epic simile of the type usually associated with hand-to-hand combat (50-2). With a look more fearsome than that of a Tmarian lioness Erysichthon rejects 'Nicippe' with a cento of Homeric verbal violence".

[54] For the advent of a new sort of poetry seen in terms of the overthrow of an old divine order for a new one cf. Timotheos *PMG* 796.

Callimachus' poetry is emphatically not of the sort that Aristophanes calls Ἄρεως μεστόν (*Ran.* 1021). Rather, the *Hymn to Delos* falls into the traditional category of songs that renounce the themes of war for other kinds: thus, e.g. Anacr. *el.* 2 (West), Ibycus *PMG* 282, Stesich. *PMG* 210, Xenoph. fr. 1.13-24 (West), Dionysius Chalcus fr. 2 (West). In general cf. W. Slater, "Peace, the Symposium and the Poet", *ICS* 6.2 (1981) 207 with n. 13.

setting his version of Apollo's birth off from that of the Homeric Hymn (cf. p. 104 f. above). Yet he had done so with a polemic that never so much as mentioned what those "well-worn wagon-tracks of Homer" (*Pae.* 7 b.11) actually were. The *Homeric Hymn to Apollo* is present in Pindar's poem in none but the most unspecific terms. Callimachus, by contrast, refers to his models incessantly, comprehensively – an instance of that very different relationship towards the literary past which, as we saw in ch. 2, the poets of his time developed. That is, by permeating his poem with its Homeric antecedant, creating in effect "a modern counterpart" (Herter, *op. cit.* p. 59 = 379) to it, Callimachus demands of his readers another kind of activity altogether, for he compels them, as Pindar had not, to compare the two poems in detail, to discover what was new by noticing deviations in the specifics of narrative and diction. Prominent among these differences is that Callimachus incorporates within his adaptation of the Homeric Hymn, his primary model, the Pindaric tale of Asteria. And this, in turn, contributes to that central transformation, namely of a *Hymn to Apollo* into a *Hymn to Delos,* and of giving to Delos those qualities that bespeak his poetic programme: the god of song will come into the world only through that which is slender, pure and free from war.

Once Asteria becomes fixed in one place, she is called Delos again (v. 251, the first time since v. 40). With this moment, the power of Ares is broken, the chaos and confusion that had characterized the previous age disappear: for the birth of music on Delos in the person of Apollo transforms and orders the world. A regular, circling motion sets in, with Delos at its axis.

This circling motif appears already at the start of the poem – in that portion that deals with Delos today (v. 11–29). There, the island is surrounded by the rushing sea (ὁ, *scil.* the sea, δ' ἀμφί ἑ πουλὺς ἑλίσσων v. 13) and by Apollo's protective might (v. 27). The image of encirclement continues (*pace* Mineur *ad* v. 28) with the striking use of περιτροχόωσιν for songs: "but if so many songs *encircle* you" (εἰ δὲ λίην πολέες σε περιτροχόωσιν ἀοιδαί v. 28), and with the image of the wreath of song for Delos in the next line: "with what sort shall I entwine you?" (ποίῃ ἐνιπλέξω σε; v. 29).[55] Thus, in the course of the first twenty nine lines, Delos' physical circumstances merge almost imperceptibly with its position as a focal point of veneration.

This blending of the physical and musical within the circling motif is now continued, but with the added knowledge that it reflects the harmony brought about by Apollo's birth. All things revolve about his

---

[55] For the metaphor see Pindar's *Olympian 1* v. 100 ff.: ἐμὲ δὲ στεφανῶσαι κεῖνον... μολπᾷ χρή, cf. also *P.* 12.5 *I.* 4.44.

birthplace: first the swans heralding his birth in song (v. 250-251 ἐκυκλώσαντο...ἑβδομάκις περὶ Δῆλον); then the yearly processions arrive from the four corners of the earth (v. 278 ff.);[56] next, the Cyclades themselves are explained as a chorus surrounding Delos (v. 301 κύκλον ἐποιήσαντο καὶ ὡς χορὸν ἀμφεβάλοντο) and they provide a model within the environment for the chorus of youths and maidens who make Delos ἀμφιβόητον (v. 303), for the Athenian chorus led by Theseus (κύκλιον ὠρχήσαντο v. 313) and finally for the simple mariners who circle the Delian altar (v. 321).[57]

---

[56] According to Plut. de Mus. 1136 a, the procession of the ἀπαρχαί was musical.

[57] The circling motif plays a similar role in the last part of the *Hymn to Artemis*. There, after Artemis has assumed her rightful place among the gods on Olympus (the equivalent of Apollo's birth here), her nymphs dance in her cult-sites (170 αἱ νύμφαι σε χορῷ ἔνι κυκλώσονται). As here, the dance serves to shift the focus of the poem from the goddess herself to her companions and the cultic observance she receives. The mythical dance of the nymphs around Artemis finally becomes the cultic dance of the Amazons around her statue at Ephesus (v. 240 περὶ, *scil.* βρέτας,...ὠρχήσαντο and v. 241-242 κύκλῳ / στησάμεναι χορὸν εὐρύν), and this in turn is the model for the Artemesium of Ephesus itself (v. 248-249 κεῖνο...περὶ βρέτας εὐρυ θέμειλον / δωμήθη). The motif thus frames and organizes the entire last section of the poem.

This resemblance between the *Hymn to Artemis* and the *Hymn to Delos* has led me to suspect that the two poems were originally companion pieces, the one perhaps written for Arsinoe, the other for Philadelphus.

Other similarities: Like our hymn, the *Hymn to Artemis* is closely modelled on the *Homeric Hymn to Apollo* (cf. Bornmann p. XVI-XVII and F. Dornseiff, *Philol. Wochenschr.* 56 [1936] 733 ff.). Both poems contain a description of Hephaestus' workshop in which heavy stress is laid on the terrible noise (*H.* 4.141-146, *H.* 3.51-56). In each case, moreover, this noise is caused by terrifying mythical giants: In the fourth hymn, the movements of Briareus, pinned beneath Mt. Aetna, cause the volcanic eruptions that fuel the forges of Hephaestus; in *H.* 3, the monstrous Cyclopes, big as the crags of Ossa, make even distant places ring with their hammering (*H.* 3.56-61):

> ...αὖε γὰρ Αἴτνη,
> αὖε δὲ Τρινακρίη, Σικανῶν ἕδος, αὖε δὲ γείτων
> Ἰταλίη, μεγάλην δὲ βοὴν ἐπὶ Κύρνος ἀύτει,
> εὖθ' οἵγε ῥαιστῆρας ἀειράμενοι ὑπὲρ ὤμων
> ἢ χαλκὸν ζείοντο καμινόθεν ἠὲ σίδηρον
> ἀμβολαδὶς τετύποντες ἐπὶ μέγα μυχθίσσειαν.

Just so Ares, about to rip up the peaks of Pangaeum, strikes his shield on high, causing even distant places to tremble at the dreadful din (*H.* 4.136-140):

> ὑψόθε ἐσμαράγησε καὶ ἀσπίδα τύψεν ἀκωκῇ
> δούρατος· ἡ δ' ἐλέλιξεν ἐνόπλιον· ἔτρεμε δ' Ὄσσης
> οὔρεα καὶ πεδίον Κραννώνιον αἵ τε δυσαεῖς
> ἐσχατιαὶ Πίνδοιο, φόβῳ δ' ὠρχήσατο πᾶσα
> Θεσσαλίη· τοῖος γὰρ ἀπ' ἀσπίδος ἔβραμεν ἦχος.

It is precisely the noise in Hephaestus' workshop to which this din is compared (cf. esp. ἔβραμεν-βρέμουσιν v. 144). In each case, only one character is courageous enough to

The chorus of Athenians celebrated their escape from the deadly labyrinth and its denizen, the minotaur (v. 310-311 οἱ χαλεπὸν μύκημα καὶ ἄγριον υἷα φυγόντες / Πασιφάης καὶ γναμπτὸν ἕδος σκολιοῦ λαβυρίνθου). Their dance, the so-called Geranos, was said to reflect the twists and turns of the labyrinth (cf. Plut. *Thes.* 21, Pollux 4.110. On the Geranos generally cf. P. Bruneau, *Récherches sur les Cultes de Délos* [Paris 1970] 19-23, 29-32), the journey through which was an encounter with death[58] and brute bellowing force. In the dance, the victory over death was affirmed. This dance helps us to understand the other dances that begin with Apollo's birth. All of them affirm the harmony of the new order and its victory over the violence and fear in the old. In retrospect, the chaotic flight of the localities and Leto's tortuous wanderings were also journeys through a labyrinth.[59] In either case, force is supplanted by music.

The circular motion that characterizes the new order is adapted from the very ancient notion of the circle as the most perfect of forms. This notion was, of course, pre-philosophical,[60] but it was most systematically developed in philosophy. There, because it has neither beginning nor end, the circle was widely used to describe the eternal.[61] In Plato,

---

stand up to this noise: while all other localities flee, Peneios stands his ground; although her companions are terrified, Artemis boldly confronts the Cyclopes.
  Both poems describe the god's defense of his chief shrine against barbarian attack. In the *Hymn to Delos* (v. 171-187), the assault of the Celtic hordes on Delphi, ἰσάριθμοι / τείρεσιν (v. 175-176), is thwarted by Apollo. Theirs is a κακὴ ὁδός, since it is a one-way journey to destruction; in the *Hymn to Artemis* (v. 251-258), the Cimmerians under the command of Lygdamis attack Ephesus, ψαμάθι ἴσον, but for them too there is no homecoming, for Artemis' bow deters them (v. 255). Just as, in our hymn, the god's protection creates an environment in which poetry can flourish, so in the *Hymn to Artemis* (v. 129-137) the city favored by the goddess is the best location for the poet.
  These are only the most striking correspondances.
  [58] Cf. J. Layard, *Eranos Jb.* 5 (1937) 241-291; D. C. Fox, *Paideuma* 1 (1940) 381-394; K. Kerenyi, *Labyrinthstudien*² (Zürich 1950).
  [59] In the verse about the labyrinth, v. 311, the lack of harmony appears even in the meter. As H. Fränkel observed ("Der homerische und kallimacheische Hexameter", in *Wege und Formen frühgriechischen Denkens* [Munich 1968] 130 n. 4) there is an uncharacteristic and unharmonious word-break after σκολιοῦ, following a hephthemimeres (this occurs elsewhere in Callimachus only at *H.* 1.36, 94). In his words, "ein krummer Vers für das 'krumme' Labyrinth." Cf. however Mineur p. 40 # 4.2.2 (7).
  [60] Cf. W. Burkert, *Lore and Science in Ancient Pythagoreanism* (Harvard 1972) 331-332, 168 n. 18, 169 n. 23. The circle was an ordering device already in the notion of an earth bounded by the ocean stream: thus already the view of the world on the shield of Achilles (*Il.* 18.487 ff.), cf. W. Schadewaldt, *Die Anfänge der Philosophie bei den Griechen* (Frankfurt 1978) 54; cf. also Herodotus' derisive comments about the many map-makers who depict the world in this way (IV 36).
  [61] On this question generally, cf. R. Mondolfo, *L'Infinito nel Pensiero dell' Antichità Classica* (Florence 1956). Cf. also C. Kahn, "Anaximander and the Arguments concerning

where speculation on the eternal, circular motion reaches its peak, we find the creator god of the *Timaeus* confronted with an original chaos which he wishes to make as much like himself as possible (*Tim.* 30a). He thus brings order to the disorderly and irregular motions,[62] and out of the chaos creates the animal (τὸ ζῷον 33b), giving it the motion most closely related to "mind" and "reason", i.e. the circular motion.[63]

By pursuing philosophy, in Plato's view, a man cultivates his reason and is thus able to rid himself of irrational motions, growing ever closer to the divine movement of the universe.[64] In Callimachus' grand conception, it is poetry - not mind - that brings this eternal motion to the world and thus transforms it.

Apollo, Egypt and the Reign of Ptolemy Philadelphus

The very heart of the *Hymn to Delos* has ostensibly nothing to do with the theme of poetry which has concerned us thus far. It deals with kingship. Yet here too the poem describes a victory over the forces of Ares: the Κελτὸν Ἄρηα (v. 173) that threatened Delphi in 279/8, and Egypt a few years later (cf. below).

Beginning with line 162, Apollo prophesies a second time from the womb. This time, however, he penetrates right to the present. He holds

---

the "Ἄπειρον", *Festschr. E. Kapp*, 19-29; M. Kaplan, "ἄπειρος and circularity", *GRBS* 16.2 (1975) 125-140. On Alcmaion and circularity in Greek thought, cf. W. K. C. Guthrie, *A History of Greek Philosophy* I (Cambridge 1967) 350-357.

[62] οὕτω δὴ πᾶν ὅσον ἦν ὁρατὸν παραλαβὼν οὐχ ἡσυχίαν ἄγον ἀλλὰ κινούμενον πλημμελῶς καὶ ἀτάκτως, εἰς τάξιν αὐτὸ ἤγαγεν ἐκ τῆς ἀταξίας (*Tim.* 30a). Cf. also 52 d ff. where the chaos is compared to a winnowing fan in which all sorts of grain is jumbled about every which way. At Arist. *Met.* 1072b 3 ff. the unmoved mover produces circular motion which, as the primary and most perfect (cf. *Phys.* 265a 13 ff.), tries to imitate the perfection of the unmoved mover.

[63] κίνησιν γὰρ ἐπένειμεν αὐτῷ τὴν τοῦ σώματος οἰκείαν, τῶν ἑπτὰ τὴν περὶ νοῦν καὶ φρόνησιν μάλιστα οὖσαν· διὸ δὴ κατὰ ταὐτὰ ἐν τῷ αὐτῷ καὶ ἐν ἑαυτῷ περιαγαγὼν αὐτὸ ἐποίησε κύκλῳ κινεῖσθαι στρεφόμενον, τὰς δὲ ἐξ ἁπάσας κινήσεις ἀφεῖλεν καὶ ἀπλανὲς ἀπηργάσατο ἐκείνων. Cf. also *Laws* 897 d ff.

[64] The same is true to a lesser extent for music (*Tim.* 47 c-d) which, though belonging to the realm of the senses, and being of secondary importance compared to mind, is related to the revolutions of the soul. When properly used (which, Plato makes clear, it is not), it can promote those movements and so bring us into greater harmony with the revolutions of the universe: ὅσον τ᾽ αὖ μουσικῆς φωνῇ χρήσιμον πρὸς ἀκοὴν ἕνεκα ἁρμονίας ἐστὶ δοθέν. ἡ δὲ ἁρμονία, συγγενεῖς ἔχουσα φορὰς ταῖς ἐν ἡμῖν τῆς ψυχῆς περιόδοις, τῷ μετὰ νοῦ προσχρωμένῳ Μούσαις οὐκ ἐφ᾽ ἡδονὴν ἄλογον καθάπερ νῦν εἶναι δοκεῖ χρήσιμος, ἀλλ᾽ ἐπὶ τὴν γεγονυῖαν ἐν ἡμῖν ἀνάρμοστον ψυχῆς περίοδον εἰς κατακόσμησιν καὶ συμφωνίαν ἑαυτῇ σύμμαχος ὑπὸ Μουσῶν δέδοται· καὶ ῥυθμὸς αὖ διὰ τὴν ἄμετρον ἐν ἡμῖν καὶ χαρίτων ἐπιδεᾶ γιγνομένην ἐν τοῖς πλείστοις ἕξιν ἐπίκουρος ἐπὶ ταὐτὰ ὑπὸ τῶν αὐτῶν ἐδόθη (*Tim.* 47 c-d).

his mother back from Cos because another god (θεὸς ἄλλος v. 165) is destined to be born there: the supreme son of the Saviours (v. 166), Ptolemy Philadelphus. Just as Callimachus had turned from his own time to the mythical past in order to show how Delos was born as a fixed entity, so now Apollo reaches into the future (the poet's present) to show why he cannot be born on Cos, but on Delos. These are complementary acts, playing upon the tradition that prophetic and poetic knowledge embrace the past, present and future.[65] But more, they reflect an attempt to abolish the temporal disjunction between the modern world and its distant cultural roots: Callimachus bridges the gulf by conspicuously integrating his own age together with its cultural assumptions – such as divinity of kings – into the vision of the past. That is, the new Ptolemaic realm already belongs, in a projected (embryonic) state, to the discourse of the tradition. Such play with time, whereby the poet juxtaposes disparate events and has the past reach into the present, occurs in ritual as well – a fact Callimachus will presently exploit.

Apollo now predicts his famous singlehanded victory over the Gauls when they marched on Delphi in the winter of 279/8.[66] Although this attack was a well documented event (cf. Nachtergael, *op. cit. ad* n. 2, p. 15-125), Callimachus includes a detail that appears in no other source: the Gauls struck at precisely the time when the ritual celebration of Apollo's mythic victory over Python – an equally barbarous force – was being performed.[67]

---

[65] Cf. West *ad Th.* 32; E. Heitsch, *Gymnasium* 78 (1971) 426 ff.

[66] For the date, cf. above p. 91. The Gallic invasions of the Greek mainland and Asia Minor seem to have inspired a considerable body of poetry with its own conventions and stock phrases: Cf. Callimachus' *Galatea* fr. 378-379 with G. Petzl, *ZPE* 56 (1984) 141-144; the elegy P. Hamburgensis: *De Galatis* (Powell p. 131-132 = *SH* 958), cf. W. Richter, *Maia* 15 (1963) 93-119 and A. Barigazzi, *Rh.M.* 117 (1974) 221-246, who considers it as Aratus' *Hymn to Pan* (since the Gauls "panicked") written for Antigonos Gonatas' victory in 276; *SH* 969, an elegy on a third century Florence papyrus, first published by N. Terzaghi, "Un Nuovo frammento di Callimaco?", *Studie in onore di A. Calderini e R. Paribeni* II (Milan 1957) 127, cf. W. Peek, *Maia* 15 (1963) 199-210; the *Delphic Paeans* (Powell p. 141 and 150); an epigram by Anyte (22 Page = *AP* VII 492) about three girls who choose death rather than submit to the Γαλατῶν ὕβριν v. 2, n. b. the phrase Κελτῶν..."Ἄρης v. 4. For Gauls in the art of this time, cf. H. Kyrieleis, *Antike Plastik* (1974) 136 n. 11.

[67] It may indeed have coincided if we assume that the Dorian procession (discussed below) was just *leaving* Delphi rather than returning (as Pfeiffer thought, cf. app. crit. *ad* v. 177b). This would fit better with the logic of the ritual since the procession followed directly on Apollo's fight with the serpent and traced the path of the wounded monster (Plut. *q.gr.* 293 c). Further, the miraculous hail and snow with which the Gauls are said to have been defeated (Diod. XXII 9.3; Paus. X 23.3; Schol. Callim. H. 4.175-87; Iust. XXIV 8.10) suits the beginning of the procession more than its return shortly before the Pythian games, which came at the end of August (cf. W. Burkert, *Homo Necans* [Berkeley 1983]

As Pfeiffer recognized in his critical apparatus, the fragmentary verses 177 a-b almost certainly refer to the Dorian procession sent to the valley of Tempe every eight years as part of the Septerion festival, in order to bring back laurel for the victors of the Pythian games. This festival commemorated Apollo's victory over Python[68] and, whatever its original significance might have been (cf. W. Burkert, *Homo Necans* [Berkeley 1983] 127-130), by the time of Ephorus in the fourth century B.C. its rites were seen as a re-enactment of Apollo's battle with the serpent.[69] A hut or tent,[70] thought to represent Python's home,[71] was erected on a threshing floor; a table was set up inside it. Youths of the Labyadae clan accompanied a young boy, carrying lighted torches for a

---

130 n.77). This order of events largely removes Mineur's chronological objections, "The Boys and the Barbarians", *Mnem.* 32 (1979) 120-127. For a thoroughgoing discussion of the chronology cf. Koenen, *op. cit.* (n.42 above) 178 n.98.

Such criteria, however, may not be decisive since 1) Callimachus had, as our discussion will show, ample reason for tampering with dates so as to make the Septerion coincide with the attack of the Celts (*pace* Mineur, *op. cit.* esp. p.125-126) and 2) the Gallic attack, as presented by Callimachus, falls easily into a mythical pattern of barbarian invasions against Delphi. We should therefore be cautious about drawing far-reaching chronological conclusions. For a comparable prophecy by a god concerning such an invasion, cf. Eur. *Ba.* 1330 ff., where Dionysus predicts the metamorphoses of Cadmus and Harmonia (a daughter of Ares!) into serpents who will lead a barbarian horde against Greece, and plunder Delphi. This attack will cause them a νόστον ἄθλιον, just as it causes the Gauls a κακὴν ὁδόν in our hymn (v.185, cf. the barbarians of *H.* 3.251 ff., esp. οὐ γὰρ ἔμελλεν …νοστήσειν, v.255, 258). Likewise, that the barbarians are countless, appears traditional, cf. *H.* 4.175-176 ἰσάριθμοι τείρεσιν, *H.* 3.253 ψαμάθῳ ἴσον, Eur. *Ba.* 1335 ἀναρίθμῳ στρατεύματι, cf. Dodds *ad* v.1330-1339. The victory over the barbarians at Delphi was thus, for Euripides, a victory over a serpent similar to Apollo's triumph over Python.

On the historical side, a prophecy predicting disaster for a planned Persian attack on Delphi is recorded in Hdt.IX 42. The miraculous deliverance of Delphi from barbarian attack is likewise a traditional motif. Herodotus (VIII 35-39) tells of how, when Xerxes attacked the shrine, the sacred arms suddenly appeared before the temple and the Persians were greeted with lightning and boulders which tumbled down on them of their own accord. Upon fleeing, they were pursued by the mythical warriors, Phylacus and Antonoos. In Theognis 773-782, Apollo is called on to confound the Persian threat to the Megarid in 479 B.C.: αὐτὸς δὲ στρατὸν ὑβριστὴν Μήδων ἀπέρυκε (v.775, cf. B.A. Van Groningen, *Theognis: Le premier livre* [Amsterdam 1966] 301-302). Thus, such invasions were quickly transformed into mythic events.

[68] The principle sources are Plut. *def. orac.* 417 e-418 d, *quaest. gr.* 293 c, Theopompus *FGrHist.* 80 = Ael. *v.h.* 3.1, Plut. *de Mus.* 1136, Ephorus *FGrHist.* 70 F 31 b = Strabo 422.

[69] This myth was clearly of current interest in Ptolemaic circles. Strabo (421 f.) records that Timosthenes, an admiral under Philadelphus, composed the "pythian nome", whose various parts were meant to reflect the stages of Apollo's fight with the dragon. The piece was regularly performed at the Pythian games.

[70] Plut. *de def. orac.* 418 a calls it καλία; Ephorus, *op. cit.*, σκηνή.

[71] Thus Ephorus, *op. cit.* Plutarch, *op. cit.*, disputes this view, but this only indicates that it was prevalent.

secret attack on the structure. They upset the table, set the hut on fire and fled (cf. Python's death in the *Homeric Hymn to Apollo,* where the serpent is made to rot in the searing heat of the sun, v. 363-374, whence it takes its name: Πυθώ). This act was followed by the procession to the river Peneios in the valley of Tempe, where the participants sought purification, as Apollo had done after slaying Python. By making Apollo's triumph over the Gauls coincide with this ritual re-enactment of his victory over Python, Callimachus clearly identifies the two. They are different aspects of the same fight, periodically waged by Apollo against those who threaten his sacred domain.[72]

Callimachus identifies yet another victory with this one. Apollo states that his struggle against the Κελτὸν Ἄρηα will be a ξυνὸς ἄεθλος (v. 171) together with the "other god", Ptolemy Philadelphus,[73] and that each will have his share of trophies (v. 185 ff.): τέων (*scil.* the enemy shields) αἱ μὲν ἐμοὶ γέρας, αἱ δ' ἐπὶ Νείλῳ / ἐν πυρὶ τοὺς φορέοντας / ἀποπνεύσαντας ἰδοῦσαι / κείσονται βασιλῆος ἄεθλια πολλὰ καμόντος. The event that Callimachus is referring to is recorded in only two other sources: the scholia to our passage and Pausanias I 72. According to these, Ptolemy hired four thousand Gallic mercenaries, survivors of the invasion of 279/8, to fight against his half-brother Magas, king of Cyrene, who was about to attack Egypt. Philadelphus ultimately did not have to fight since a rebellion by Libyan tribes forced Magas to abort his plans. But the Gauls, we are told, mutinied and Philadelphus lured them to a deserted island in the Sebennytic branch of the Nile and burned them (ἐν πυρὶ... ἀποπνεύσαντας v. 186; κατέκαυσεν αὐτοὺς ἐκεῖσε, schol. *ad* v. 175-187. According to Pausanias, the mercenaries killed one another or died of starvation). Although, rationally speaking, the value of Philadelphus' victory was negligible (cf. Fraser, *op. cit.,* 660), Callimachus casts it as the equivalent of Apollo's at Delphi. It is thus likewise a repetition of the primeval victory over Python. Indeed, the fiery death of the Gauls may recall the burning of the hut in the Septerion as well as Python rotting in the sun.

It might seem that Callimachus has exaggerated a minor event out of all proportion. But the equivalences are more easily understood if we recall that the court-poet was writing to please a king who, because he was obliged to rule a large native majority, had adopted many of the traditional forms of Egyptian kingship. The mythological material of our hymn, while thoroughly Greek in origin, was accordingly chosen

---

[72] The identification of a victory over barbarians with that over a serpent is expressly made in the Euripides passage cited in n. 67.
[73] Cf. *H.* 2.27 where Callimachus says the same thing more generally: ὅστις ἐμῷ βασιλῆϊ καὶ Ἀπόλλωνι μάχοιτο.

and tailored so as to reflect the new realities of royal statecraft. Put somewhat differently, the poem attempts to interpret in Greek terms and for a Greek audience a conception of monarchy which, in some of its most conspicuous features, was shaped by Egyptian custom.[74] In that conception, the identification of the king with Apollo was a given. For as ruler of Egypt, Ptolemy was the incarnation of Horus, the god that, as early as Herodotus (II 144, 156), was considered the equivalent of Apollo. Thus, not only is there a single foe, the "Celtic Ares", but those opposing it, though nominally distinct (cf. θεὸς ἄλλος v. 165), are the embodiments of a single salutary force which might sometimes be called Apollo, sometimes Ptolemy.[75] Every Egyptian king had to earn his right to the throne by re-enacting the mythical victory of Horus over Seth, thus bringing order to the world and freeing it from chaos.[76] During his reign, the king was expected to maintain that order against renewed opposition. Seth and his followers might threaten chaos in the guise of political enemies within the state, or as foreign invaders, or simply in the cult-ceremonies that preceded the king's coronation.[77]

---

[74] The fundamental discussion of this phenomenon is that of R. Merkelbach, "Das Königtum der Ptolemäer und die Hellenistischen Dichter" in *Alexandria, Kulturbegegnungen dreier Jahrtausende im Schmelztiegel einer mediterranen Großstadt, Aegyptiaca Treverensia: Trierer Studien z. Gr.-Röm. Ägypten I* (1981) 27–35, esp. 29–30.

[75] Such identification, not just similarity, is as much a part of Greek thought as of Egyptian, cf. e.g. Pind. *P.* 9.63 ff., where the Horae take Aristaios on their knees and feed him ambrosia: θήσονταί τέ μιν ἀθάνατον, / Ζῆνα καὶ ἁγνὸν Ἀπόλλων᾽, ἀνδράσι χάρμα φίλοις, / ἄγχιστον ὀπάονα μήλων, / Ἀγρέα καὶ Νόμιον, τοῖς δ᾽ Ἀρισταῖον καλεῖν, cf. Fränkel's comments on this passage: "[Es ist] fast ein Schock für uns, daß dieser Gott auch noch zugleich ein Sohn Apollons, und (ein) Apollon, und (ein) Zeus sein soll. Die Stelle zeigt drastisch, wie wenig strikte Geltung…die Aufgliederung des Göttlichen in gesonderten Personen hatte, wenn sogar die großen Olympier ihre individuellen Namen mit dritten teilen konnten, und somit auch miteinander. So lebendig war also bei dem Dichter und seinem Publikum das Bewußtsein, daß man mit dem Namen eines Gottes nicht eine Person meinte, sondern eine wirkende Macht." (*Dicht. u. Phil.* [Munich 1962] 504 n. 5). Cf. Wil. *op. cit.* (n. 41 above) 244; A. D. Nock, *Essays* I (Cambr. Mass. 1972) 34 ff.; H. W. Pleket, *Lampas* 12 (1979) 126 ff. and R. Merkelbach, *op. cit.* (n. 74 above) 33: "Die mehrfachen Parallelen von Apollon und Ptolemaios…lassen keinen Zweifel, daß der Hörer eine Art von Identität der beiden Götter verstehen sollte, jene Identität des mythischen Denkens, welche von den ephemeren Einzelheiten absieht und auf das Gleiche achtet, welches zugrunde liegt. Der ägyptische Name des Apollon ist ja Horos, und Ptolemaios als König Ägyptens war ebenfalls Horos, wie jeder König des Nillandes."

[76] For the contendings of Horus and Seth generally cf. P. Chester Beatty I, translated in M. Lichtheim, *AEL* II, 214 ff. For the Pharaoh as Horus, cf. e.g. E. Hornung, *Geschichte als Fest* (Darmstadt 1966) 13, 24, 29 and H. Frankfort, *Kingship and the Gods* (Chicago 1948) 37 ff. The role of Ptolemaic kingship ideology in our hymn is discussed by L. Koenen, *Chr. d'Eg.* 34 (1959) 110 ff. and *ICS* 1 (1976) 134 n. 29 and "Die Adaption Ägyptischer Königsideologie" *op. cit.* (n. 42 above).

[77] On these different aspects of Seth, cf. H. Te Velde, *Seth, God of Confusion* (Leiden 1967) and E. Hornung, "Seth, Geschichte und Bedeutung eines aegyptischen Gottes", *Symbolon* NF 2 (1974) 49–64.

What mattered was not the magnitude of the historic event, but that the king appeared in a role which affirmed the legitimacy of his reign and its strength.[78] In this light, it is striking that descriptions of the Pharaonic victory as Horus over Seth in Egyptian literature often take the form of *post eventum* prophecies such as the one in our hymn.[79] Further, the fact that Apollo acts from the womb, something he does not do in any Greek tradition, seems calculated to recall the common Egyptian belief that gods and kings were active already before they were born.[80] Finally, in burning the Gauls, Philadelphus availed himself

---

[78] Thus, according to the Rosetta stone (*OGIS* 90 v. 23 ff.) Ptolemy V Epiphanes defeated rebels in Lykopolis during the Nile-flood before being crowned: καὶ τοὺς ἐν αὐτῆι ἀσεβεῖς πάντας διέφθειρεν καθάπερ ['Ερμ]ῆς καὶ Ὧρος ὁ τῆς Ἴσιδος καὶ Ὀσίριος υἱὸς ἐχειρώσαντο τοὺς ἐν τοῖς αὐτοῖς τόποις ἀποστάντας πρότερον, cf. R. Merkelbach, *Isisfeste* (Meisenheim 1963) 23; or the Raphia decree (217 B.C.) in which statues of Ptolemy IV Philopator as "Πτολεμαίου Ὧρου τοῦ ἐπαμύνοντος τῶι πατρὶ καλλινίκου" are set up after he defeated Antiochus (according to the Demotic version, "just as Horus, the son of Isis, had slaughtered his enemies", cf. H. Thissen, *Studien zum Raphiadekret* [Meisenheim 1966] 22, 55). On the continuance of these traditional kingship practices in Ptolemaic times, cf. E. Hornung, *op. cit.* (n. 76 above) 28–29; H. Kyrieleis, *op. cit.* (n. 66 above) 133 ff.; L. Koenen, *Eine agonistische Inschrift*, *op. cit.* (n. 3 above); and R. Merkelbach, *op. cit.* (n. 74 above) 35: "Zwar wollten die Griechen in Alexandrien Griechen bleiben und nicht zu Ägyptern werden; aber die Verhältnisse waren derart, daß ein Ausgleich gefunden werden mußte. Die zentrale Position im Aufbau des Staates kam dem König zu, und damit war ein starker Einfluß der ägyptischen Wirklichkeit gegeben; denn Ägypten ist ein Land, in welchem Planwirtschaft – nämlich in der Bewässerung des Ackerlandes und seiner Vermessung – in beträchtlichem Maß notwendig ist. In sehr vielen Punkten blieb den Ptolemäern gar nichts anderes übrig als die traditionellen Lösungen der Ägypter zu übernehmen. So war an der einflußreichsten Stelle des gesamten Staates, im Königtum, eine Anpassung an die ägyptischen Vorstellungen ganz unumgänglich."

[79] A famous example is the prophecy of Neferti, cf. M. Lichtheim, *AEL* I 139–145; W. Helck, *Die Prophezeiung des Nfrti*, Kl. Äg. Texte (Wiesbaden 1970); and the different interpretation of H. Goedicke, *The Protocol of Neferyt* (Baltimore 1977).

[80] Examples in Greek myth (Dionysus in Aeschylus' *Semele*, Schol. in Ap. Rh. 1.636 = Aesch. p. 335 Radt; Akrisios and Proitos, Apollod. 2.2), are rare in comparison with the wealth of Near Eastern and especially Egyptian material. For our purposes, the Egyptian examples are especially significant since they belonged to Callimachus' immediate environment: According to Plutarch (*de Iside* 12, 356 A), Isis and Osiris made love before they were born; and Seth is said to have "devised evil before he came forth from the womb" (*Urk.* VI 39, cf. J. G. Griffiths, *Plutarch's de Iside et Osiride* [Univ. of Wales Press 1970] 307). Philostratus tells of Proteus, who is specifically called Αἰγύπτιος δαίμων and Αἰγύπτιος θεός, announcing his own birth (*Vit. Apollon. Tyan.* I.4). As divine incarnations of Horus, the Egyptian pharaohs naturally incorporated this motif into their kingship ideology, cf. the Cuban Stele (A. Hermann, *Die ägyptische Königsnovelle*, Leipzig. ägypt. Stud. 10 [Glückstadt-Hamburg-New York 1938] 17): "Du (*scil.* Ramses II) hast schöne Pläne gemacht, als du noch im Ei warst"; cf. also a papyrus (*P. Berl.* P 3029, in Lichtheim, *AEL* I 116) where Sesostris the First proclaims "I conquered as a fledgling, I lorded in the egg. He fashioned me as palace-dweller, an offspring not yet issued from the thighs"; etc.

of a traditional method by which Egyptian Pharaohs disposed of their enemies.[81]

The early Ptolemies actively cultivated and adapted themselves to Egyptian religious and political institutions, particularly in the capital (cf. H. Volkmann, *RE* XXIII 2 "Ptolemaios" p. 1631-1632, 1658-1662), and it was imperative to them that the Greek population not be offended by, or reject, this policy.[82] The problem may be seen from the

---

[81] Cf. E. Hornung, "Altägyptische Höllenvorstellungen", *Abh. d. Sächs. Akad. Leipzig, philol.-hist. Kl.* 59 (1968) 27, who cites the following: King Merenptah (1224-1204), who burned a large number of war-captives; Prince Osorkon II, who sentenced political prisoners to death by burning in 829 B.C.; the pharaoh Bocchoris who, according to Manetho (fr. 66 Loeb ed.) was burned to death by Shabaka, the victorious king of Ethiopia; Cambyses, who, according to Hdt. III 16, removed the body of the pharaoh Amasis from its tomb and burned it; Euergetes II, who killed his enemies in 127/6 by setting a stadium on fire where they were gathered. Finally, Plutarch (*de Iside* 73), quoting Manetho, records that every year two men were burned as "Typhonians", i.e. followers of Seth, in mid-summer. Cf. also the Egyptian "island of flames", where the dead were judged and, if guilty burned. Cf. generally Koenen, "Die Adaption ägyptischer Königsideologie", *op. cit.* (n. 42 above) 180-181.

[82] This view has been attacked by C. Préaux (*Le Monde Hellénistique* [Paris 1978] esp. 545-586), who argues primarily on the basis of documentary papyri from smaller towns, that the Egyptian and Greek systems were kept entirely separate.

It may be that the early Ptolemaic policy of reconciling the two cultures ultimately failed, but it is hard to deny that such a policy existed. I have already raised this possibility with regard to the organization of the Alexandrian Museum (ch. 1 n. 7a above). With regard to sovereignty, the inscriptions cited in n. 78 clearly attempt to communicate Egyptian kingship beliefs in Greek to a Greek audience – what is more, they do so, unlike the poems we have been discussing, with an unabashedly Egyptian nomenclature. A similar attempt at reconciliation may be seen in the Ptolemaic Oinochoai described by D. Burr-Thompson (*Ptolemaic Oinochoai and Portraits in Faience: Aspects of the Ruler Cult* [Oxford 1973] 119-120).

Perhaps the most impressive emblem of the royal union of the two cultures is the famous river-boat of Ptolemy IV (cf. Callixenus in Athenaeus 206a ff.). The two principal rooms on this boat were decorated in Corinthian and Egyptian style respectively. An illuminating analysis of this pairing is given by J. Onians, *Art and Thought in the Hellenistic Age* (London 1979) 71: "Another distinctive feature of Ptolemy's boat was a dining-room, built, according to the text, entirely 'in the Egyptian manner', that is with black and white banded columns whose capitals were shaped like rose blossoms and decorated with lotus flowers and palm blooms. The forms thus corresponded quite closely to column types based on vegetable forms with which we are familiar from early times in Egypt. As this room together with the Corinthian oikos seems to have been the most magnificent on the boat, Ptolemy appears to have shown a considerable respect for Egyptian forms, especially since the setting here is not some ancient temple precinct where it would be necessary to continue the tradition of pharaonic art, but a private environment where few concessions to public demands would be necessary. Probably the existence of the two rooms on the boat is a demonstration of how far the Macedonian royal family in Egypt felt its loyalties divided between two cultures. The need to acknowledge the traditional needs of both Greek and Egyptian subjects had already induced Ptolemy I to inaugurate the worship of a new deity, Serapis, embodying features of Osiris and Apis as well as of Dionysus

case of Philadelphus' marriage to his sister Arsinoe, a most conspicuous concession to Egyptian kingship practices.[83] When the poet Sotades attacked this marriage in verse ("you thrust the prick into an unholy hole", εἰς οὐχ ὁσίην τρυμαλίην τὸ κέντρον ὠθεῖς, Powell p. 238), he was swiftly and cruelly punished (cf. Fraser, *op. cit.*, 117-118). Theocritus, by contrast, justified the marriage by reference to the "sacred marriage", ἱερὸς γάμος, of Zeus and Hera (17.130 ff.).

Callimachus similarly chose to cast the view of kingship, which the Ptolemies were eager to promote, in terms acceptable to Greeks, yet true to the native influence that was now a reality of government. The battle against the Gauls was thus not only a struggle against the forces of Ares. It could at once be seen as the re-enactment of Horus' victory over Seth, or a re-enactment of the primeval victory of Apollo over Python. In any case, the result was a harmonious world, ruled of its own accord – without threats or ἀνάγκη – by Ptolemy Philadelphus: "under whose crown it shall come not unwilling to be ruled by a Macedonian" (ᾧ ὑπὸ μίτρην / ἵξεται οὐκ ἀέκουσα Μακηδόνι κοιρανέεσθαι v. 166-167).[84]

---

and Pluto. The shrine of Serapis at Memphis with its mixture of Greek and Egyptian architectural and sculptural styles reveals the same artistic eclecticism as Ptolemy's boat."

[83] For this practice cf. *Lex. d. Ägypt.*, W. Helck and W. Westendorf ed. (Wiesbaden 1975) s.v. Geschwisterehe; cf. also H. Thierfelder, *Die Geschwisterehe im hellenistisch-römischen Ägypten* (Münster 1960).

[84] As soon as we see the various strata within the poem, the innovations in Callimachus' version of the Ἀπόλλωνος γοναί fall into place. For instance, the notion that Apollo should eclipse his belligerent elder half-brother, Ares (cf. p. 114f. above), bears a strong resemblance to the official Egyptian kingship myth: the king in his role as Horus had to defeat his elder brother Seth, the god of chaos and war, before acceding to the throne. Seth denied that Horus was the legitimate heir and threatened him even before he was born. Cf. n. 76 and the sarcophagus text (Cairo # 16/17 in RU 204/5) cited by T. Hopfner, *Plutarch über Isis und Osiris* I (Prague 1940) 85-86. Seth is elsewhere seen as the uncle of Horus, but in the Chester Beatty Papyrus cited in n. 76, as well as in the earliest traditions he was considered Horus' elder brother, cf. Lichtheim, *AEL* II, 223 n. 8.

The rivalry between Ares and Apollo is also strangely analogous to the situation of Ptolemy Philadelphus with respect to his elder half-brother Keraunos (cf. Mineur p. 98 ad v. 58). Like Apollo, Philadelphus was characterized by his love for music (Theocritus calls him φιλόμουσος, 14.62, which is hardly surprising since the king was a student of Philetas of Cos), while Keraunos was headstrong and contentious, like Ares. Indeed, Keraunos got his name, according to Pausanias, διὰ τὸ ἄγαν τολμηρόν (X 19.7) and his eagerness for any violent undertaking (I 16.2 cf. also H. Heinen, *Untersuchungen zur hellenistischen Geschichte des 3. Jahrhunderts v. Chr.*, Historia Einzelschr. 20 [Wiesbaden 1972] 7). Because of his superior talent, Philadelphus was favored by Ptolemy Soter as successor to the throne, becoming co-regent at age twenty three, while Keraunos eventually left for the north to rule Macedonia.

The situation is likewise reflected in two passages from the *Hymn to Zeus*, v. 57-59: ἀλλ' ἔτι παιδνὸς ἐὼν ἐφράσσαο πάντα τέλεια· / τῷ τοι καὶ γνωτοὶ προτερηγενέες περ ἐόντες / οὐρανὸν οὐκ ἐμέγηραν ἔχειν ἐπιδαίσιον οἶκον. and v. 66-67: οὔ σε θεῶν ἐσσῆνα

Callimachus allows this Egyptian background to appear somewhat more explicitly elsewhere in the poem. Scholars, for instance, had long puzzled over Apollo's statement (v. 168) that Philadelphus would rule over ἀμφοτέρη μεσόγεια, taking the phrase to mean "both continents" – an alleged reference to Africa and Asia, though only a tiny fraction of the latter continent was part of Ptolemy's realm (cf. Mineur *ad loc.*). Recently, however, two scholars have suggested independently of one another that ἀμφοτέρη μεσόγεια can more plausibly be interpreted as "both inland regions" (the usual sense of μεσόγεια), and that this denotes Upper and Lower Egypt.[85] In fact, "Lord of the two (*scil.* upper and lower) lands" was one of the conventional titles of the Egyptian pharaoh. It appears, then, that that most Greek of gods, Apollo, addresses Ptolemy in terms suggestive of traditional pharaonic nomenclature.[86]

The Egyptian undercurrent comes to the surface most explicitly, however, in the details of Apollo's birth.[87] The description largely follows the model of the *Homeric Hymn to Apollo*. There (v. 18-19), Leto leaned back against Mt. Kynthos, near the palm tree, next to the streams of Inopus: κεκλιμένη πρὸς μακρὸν ὄρος καὶ Κύνθιον ὄχθον, / ἀγχοτάτω φοίνικος ὑπ' Ἰνωποῖο ῥεέθροις. Here, she sits down next to the streams of Inopus and leans back against the trunk of the palm tree (v. 206 ff.): ἕζετο Ἰνωποῖο παρὰ ῥόον…ἀπὸ δ' ἐκλίθη ἔμπαλιν ὤμοις / φοίνικος ποτὶ πρέμνον. But Callimachus makes a significant addition: referring to the tradition that many rivers were connected underground,[88] he says that the Inopus flows deepest when the Nile comes

---

πάλοι θέσαν, ἔργα δὲ χειρῶν, / σή τε βίη τό τε κάρτος, ὃ καὶ πέλας εἶσαο δίφρου. Keraunos left Egypt (heaven) to rule Macedonia, just as Poseidon and Hades left to rule over other provinces, cf. D. W. Tandy, *Callimachus Hymn to Zeus* (Diss. Yale 1979) 15-16.

[85] Cf. L. Koenen, *op. cit.* (n. 42 above) 186-187 and Mineur (*ad* v. 168) who apparently did not yet know of Koenen's publication.

[86] Koenen, *op. cit.* (n. 42 above) 187, suggests that the subsequent description of Ptolemy's realm ("both inland regions and the islands which lie by the sea, as far as where the end of the earth is and from whence swift horses carry the sun" v. 168-170) likewise contains a traditional Egyptian component: "Bei dem Gegensatzpaar Festländer-Inseln möchte man aber zunächst griechische Denkweise vermuten. Jedoch spricht beispielsweise schon Sinuhe von den 'Göttern Ägyptens und der Inseln des Meeres'…König Echnatons (1364-1347) Herrschaftsgebiet ist umschrieben als 'der Süden wie der Norden, der Westen und die Inseln inmitten des Meeres'; es reicht 'so weit die Sonne scheint'."

[87] For this section cf. also the discussion of R. Merkelbach, *op. cit.* (n. 74 above) 32.

[88] This tradition probably goes back to the idea that all rivers have their source in Oceanos (*Il.* 21.192-197, cf. Xenophanes *DK* fr. 30), or alternately Acheloos (cf. Schol. T to *Il.* 21.195). The first reference to such underground connections applied to a particular river is in Ibycus *PMG* 322, where the Asopos is said to come to Sicyon (near Corinth) from Phrygia; and *PMG* 323, where the poet told of a victor in the Olympics who threw a golden bowl into the Alpheios and it surfaced in the Syracusan spring Arethousa. The

down with swelling stream from Aethiopia: ὅν τε βάθιστον / γαῖα τότ' ἐξανίησιν, ὅτε πλήθοντι ῥεέθρῳ / Νεῖλος ἀπὸ κρημνοῖο κατέρχεται Αἰθιοπῆος. Callimachus thus links Delos, as Apollo's birthplace, to Egypt.[89] We saw how Apollo's prophecy concerning the Celts was a *temporal* bridge, spanning the gulf between Greek past and Ptolemaic present; this link with the Nile is a *spacial* bridge (or tunnel) connecting the alien African land with a familiar cultural hub of the old Greek world.

But Callimachus goes even further. For at Apollo's birth, the Inopus floods like the Nile (v. 263): πλήμυρε βαθὺς Ἰνωπός. This is clear from the unmistakable verbal echoes of the above-mentioned passage in which the Nile's swelling streams are explicitly mentioned. πλήμυρε v. 263 thus recalls πλήθοντι v. 207, and βαθύς v. 263 recalls βάθιστον v. 206.[90] Our poet thus deliberately - startlingly - makes Apollo's birth coincide with the Nile-flood. This coincidence was clearly not fortuitous since, according to Egyptian belief, the Nile flood came at the same time as the birth of Horus (i. e. Apollo), and just as Apollo's birth in our poem is a victory over Ares, so the flooding of the Nile was thought to reflect the victory of Horus over Seth.[91] Further, the Nile-flood was a favored time for coronations[92] - i. e. the moment at which the Egyptian king became Horus and established order in the world following a period of chaos.[93]

The link to Egypt is yet greater when we recall that there was also an Egyptian tradition about a floating island, which was well known to the

---

connection between the Alpheios and Arethousa, which was especially renowned, appears also in Pind. *N.* 1.1 (with schol.), *P.* 2.12 (with schol.), Callimachus fr. 407.45-50, *AP* XI 220, Ovid *Met.* 5.572-641, Paus. V 7.2-3, Schol. to *Od.* 3.489, Serv. *ad Ecl.* 10.4, *ad Aen.* 3.694, 1.445. The orator Zoilos said that the Alpheios came from Tenedos (cf. Strabo 432). According to Philostratus (*Vit. Ap.* I 20.2) and Paus. (II 5.3), the Euphrates was linked to the Nile.

[89] For the connection between the Nile and the Inopus, cf. also the *Hymn to Artemis* v. 171 Αἰγυπτίου Ἰνωποῖο, Lyc. 574-576 (with schol.), Paus. II 5.3, Strabo 6.271, Pliny *N. H.* 2.229.

[90] Cf. schol *ad H.* 3.171 Ἰνωπὸς ποταμὸς Δήλου· Αἰγύπτιος δὲ διὰ τὸν Νεῖλον, ὅτι καὶ αὐτὸς ἐκεῖ πλημυρεῖ. For πλημυρέω as a term for the Nile-flood, cf. Preisigke, *Wörterbuch* s. v., D. Bonneau, *La Crue du Nil* (Paris 1964) 61 n. 4, 62 n. 1, cf. also the *Hymn to Zeus* v. 18-41 where the flooding of Arcadia at the birth of Zeus may be meant to recall the Nile-flood, cf. esp. ἄβροχος v. 19, which was a technical term for land that was not reached by the Nile-flood (*Wörterbuch* I and IV s. v.). Zeus was even identified with the Nile, cf. Parmenon of Byzantium (*SH* 604 A v. 1): Αἰγύπτιε Ζεῦ Νεῖλ', and already Pindar *P.* 4.56: Νείλοιο... Κρονίδα.

[91] Cf. R. Merkelbach, *op. cit.* (n. 74 above) 30, 28 n. 90 and 21-22; T. Hopfner, *op. cit.* (n. 84 above) 86.

[92] E. g. the Rosettana cited in n. 78 and H. Frankfort, *op. cit.* (n. 76 above) 102-106.

[93] Cf. E. Hornung, *op. cit.* (n. 76 above) 24, 26-27; H. Frankfort, *op. cit.* (n. 76 above) 150.

Greeks. The 6th cent. B.C. historian Hecataeus (*FGrHist.* F305) was the first to mention Chemmis, the floating island sacred to Apollo.[94] In the 5th cent., Herodotus (II 156) described it in more detail, explaining why it began to float:

> λόγον δὲ τόνδε ἐπιλέγοντες οἱ Αἰγύπτιοί φασι εἶναι αὐτὴν πλωτήν, ὡς ἐν τῇ νήσῳ ταύτῃ οὐκ ἐούσῃ πρότερον πλωτῇ Λητώ, ἐοῦσα τῶν ὀκτὼ θεῶν τῶν πρώτων γενομένων, οἰκέουσα δὲ ἐν Βουτοῖ πόλι, ἵνα δή οἱ τὸ χρηστήριον τοῦτο ἐστί, Ἀπόλλωνα παρ' Ἴσιος παρακαταθήκην· δεξαμένη διέσωσε κατακρύψασα ἐν τῇ νῦν πλωτῇ λεγομένῃ νήσῳ, ὅτε τὸ πᾶν διζήμενος ὁ Τυφῶν (*scil.* Seth) ἐπῆλθε, θέλων ἐξευρεῖν τοῦ Ὀσίριος τὸν παῖδα...τὴν δὲ νῆσον διὰ τοῦτο γενέσθαι πλωτήν (cf. also Pomp. Mela I 55)
>
> The story told by the Egyptians to show why the island moves is this: when Typhon came seeking through the world for the son of Osiris, Leto, being one of the eight earliest gods, and dwelling in Buto where this oracle of hers is, received Apollo in charge from Isis and hid him for safety in this island which was before immovable but is now said to float...On account of this the island started to float.

As to the fact that in Greek tradition Delos *ceased* floating with Apollo's advent, whereas in the Egyptian version it only *began* to float at that time, Callimachus might humorously have referred the reader to Herodotus' statement that Egyptians simply do everything backwards (II 35.2 ff.): τὰ πολλὰ πάντα ἔμπαλιν τοῖσι ἄλλοισι ἀνθρώποισι ἐστήσαντο. In any case, Chemmis was of enduring importance in Egyptian kingship ideology since the Pharaoh was often designated as "Horus in Chemmis"[95] and many – including Ptolemy X Soter II – claimed to have been brought up there like Horus.[96] There was even a coronation in Chemmis.[97]

Thus, in his story of Delos, Callimachus once again disposes his myth in such a way that it is meaningful both from the standpoint of Egyptian kingship practices as well as from a Greek perspective. From either perspective the poet seems to be telling the same story again and again. The defeat of Ares through Apollo's birth at the Nile-flood is

---

[94] ἐν Βούτοις περὶ τὸ ἱερὸν τῆς Λητοῦς ἔστι νῆσος Χέμβις ὄνομα, ἴρη τοῦ Ἀπόλλωνος, ἔστι δὲ ἡ νῆσος μεταρσίη καὶ περιπλεῖ καὶ κινέεται ἐπὶ τοῦ ὕδατος.

[95] Cf. *Urk.* IV, S. 239; S. 16, 15; S. 157, 12; cf. M. Münster, *Untersuchungen zur Göttin Isis,* Münchner Ägyptol. Stud. 11 (1968) 122 n. 1345.

[96] Cf. J. Bergman, *Ich bin Isis* (Uppsala 1968) 137–140; A. Wiedman, *Herodots zweites Buch* (Leipzig 1890) 558, who cites Thutmes III (Mar. Karnak 16.47), Thutmes IV (Lepsius, *Denkmäler aus Ägypten und Äthiopien* [Berlin 1849–1858] III, 68.4), Ameneses (Lepsius, *op. cit.* III 201 a), Ptolemy X Soter II (Lepsius, *op. cit.* IV 41 c).

[97] Cf. *Urk.* IV S. 16, 15 where Ahmose takes up the crowns in Chemmis, cf. J. Bergman, *op. cit.* (n. 96 above) 138 n. 3.

simply another aspect of the victory over the Κελτὸν ”Αρηα by Apollo and Philadelphus. The function of the king in creating and maintaining order in the real world is the same as that of Apollo (and Horus) in myth.

Apollo, Philadelphus and Callimachean Poetry

It remains to ask in what way the political order of Apollo and Philadelphus corresponds to the new poetic order created by the birth of Delos (that is, Callimachean poetry). In other words, how does Apollo's role as ally of kings relate to his role as patron of song? We have already seen in our discussion of how Callimachus used the *Theogony* of Hesiod for his *Hymn to Zeus* (cf. ch. 2 p. 76 f. above) that the Muse's gift can be given to singer and sovereign alike. In a development of this theme, political and musical harmony came to be viewed as merely different aspects of a single force.

The traditional union of these two aspects would have been familiar to Callimachus, if from no other source, then through various odes of Pindar. In particular we may look to *Pythian 5*, since this is a poem for an athlete from Callimachus' home town, Cyrene, and contains – as one Pindaric scholar has recently put it[98] – 'more precise reference to the customs and geography of the city' celebrated than any other extant poem by Pindar. Here, political and musical harmony are concomitant gifts of Apollo.[99] This is the god 'who dispenses cures to men and women from painful diseases, and gave them the lyre, and bestows the Muse on those he wishes, bringing love of order without war into their minds" (ὅ καὶ βαρειᾶν νόσων / ἀκέσματ' ἄνδρεσσι καὶ γυναιξὶ νέμει, / πόρεν τε κίθαριν, δίδωσί τε Μοῖσαν οἷς ἂν ἐθέλῃ, / ἀπόλεμον ἀγαγών / ἐς πραπίδας εὐνομίαν v. 63-67). Musical and political harmony are here made virtually synonymous through the pun "Apollon/ἀπόλεμον" (cf. Slater, *op. cit.* [n. 54 above] 208).

The situation is similar in Pindar's *Pythian 1* – which Callimachus draws on more than once in our hymn (cf. the discussion of the Ares-simile and n. 50). There, in the words of E. Fraenkel (*Horace* [Oxford 1957] 278), "the power of music, this present music and music in general, is effective throughout the world: it puts out the fire of that warrior thunderbolt, it lulls the eagle on the sceptre of Zeus into slumber; even the violent Ares leaves the battle and lets his heart enjoy profound

---

[98] M. Lefkowitz, "Pindar's Pythian V", *Pindare*, Fond. Hardt XXXI (1984) 33.
[99] For allusions to this poem in Callimachus' *Hymn to Apollo* cf. Williams ad H. 2.71, 74.

sleep".[100] The enemies of Zeus upon the earth, or the monster Typhos trapped beneath Mt. Aetna, are struck with terror by the beautiful sounds. For Callimachus too, the music of Apollo brings peace and subdues the war-god, but it does more: it defeats the power of Ares altogether. Ares is barred from Callimachus' song, that is, from Delos, and Callimachean poetry generally shuns the themes of war. To speak here of 'Callimachus' song' or 'the music of Apollo' is, of course, slightly misleading. We recall from chapter 1 that the dissemination of verse had changed profoundly since the time of Pindar, and we know, therefore, that even as our poet mines the past for this theme, the power of music has shifted its traditional locus: from audible song to legible page. This knowledge inevitably colors our understanding. The grandeur of the image notwithstanding, for instance, we might be tempted to see in the stable circling motion launched by Apollo's birth on his sacred island a reflection of the scholar/poet's organizing zeal, the cataloguer's rage for order.

In the new order established by the song-god's birth, Delos becomes a fixed entity and a constant source of song. It is exalted and, in turn, provides the world with a stable focal point. But this order, once established, must be maintained against the periodic encroachments of barbarism and chaos. In defeating the Gauls, Apollo and Philadelphus do just that. They (re)create an harmonious political environment in which this *Hymn to Delos* (and Callimachean poetry generally) could be written and thrive and enjoy a prominent position. The hymn thus describes the conditions it needs to exist: a world made safe for Callimachean song. This world is not subject to ἀνάγκη, but is ruled of its own accord (οὐκ ἀέκουσα v. 167). In the poetry of Callimachus, it finds its appropriate voice. Delos is not impressed by force, but willingly submits to Apollo (ἐθέλουσαν v. 195). The very existence of this poem testifies to the success of Ptolemaic rule.

Here too, for the connection to the contemporary political setting, Callimachus could look to Pindar's first Pythian Ode as a model. For there, after describing the effect of music on the gods and on the monsters subdued by Zeus, Pindar prays that Hieron, having subdued the barbarian Etruscans and Carthaginians, be able to lead his people σύμφωνον ἐς ἡσυχίαν (v. 70). As Fraenkel points out (*op. cit.* 280), the metaphor of "harmonious" (σύμφωνος) peace, though applied to polit-

---

[100] Fraenkel's statement must be modified slightly inasmuch as it is not all music that has this effect, but specifically Apollonian. As H. Fränkel observed (*Dicht. u. Phil., op. cit.* [n. 75 above] 521 ff.), the harmonious picture in *P.* 1 has its violent counterpart in the Dithyramb (fr. 70 b v. 5 ff.) where the thunderbolt and the spear of Ares are participants in the wild dance.

ical peace, "still retained its full meaning and its close association with the skill and wisdom of Apollo and the Muses... Just as the monsters whom Zeus defeated threatened the world with chaos, so did the barbarians whom Hieron defeated. Out of such a defeat may there again, as in the old days, grow a rule of order and harmony". The "lyres beneath the roof" (φόρμιγγες ὑπωρόφιαι v. 97) of Hieron's house, which play to celebrate his victory, confirm that "the golden lyre of Apollo" (χρυσέα φόρμιγξ Ἀπόλλωνος v. 1) is indeed at work in the realm. As in the case of Ptolemy's victory over the Gauls, "Hieron has himself created the precondition for his own praise".[101]

Callimachus never directly links the king and Delos, either as a political entity or as the theme of song. As we saw in chapter two (p. 81 f. above), that former kinship of the political and of the poetic sphere, of sovereign and singer, which had been acted out in the public arenas provided by the political institutions of the city-state, had – with the rise of absolute monarchy and the rigidly centralized authority of the Hellenistic kingdoms – become progressively more tenuous. The worlds of government and of song had grown apart. Yet Callimachus suggests a subtle interdependence beneath the surface: the Inopos and the Nile, Delos and Egypt, were after all connected by a subterranean link. In retrospect we see that submerged associations of this kind are part of a larger pattern in this hymn – one of play between that which is δῆλον and ἄδηλον (Callimachus' own terms for the "now you see it, now you don't" quality of his theme). Thus, just as Callimachus was at pains to establish an inconspicuous link between Egypt and Delos, so he does not advertise his esteem for the king in any open or direct way. His encomium emanates rather from one who is ὑποκόλπιος, beneath the surface of his mother's womb, as yet unborn. Perhaps the hymn contains in these examples a metaphor for its own allegory, that is of Delos as embodying Callimachean principles, its birth as the realization of Callimachean song, and of the Egyptian substratum which informs, as we have argued, the hymn's view of kingship.

---

[101] Thus Slater (*op. cit.* [n. 54 above] 211). We said earlier that the regular, circling motion of the world was an emblem for the new musical order established by Apollo through Delos. This motion may also reflect the general aspects of Apollo's power. Such an interpretation would not have surprised Callimachus' audience. It appears to have been topical. The Egyptian priest Manetho, Callimachus' contemporary, wrote of how the Egyptians call the magnet "the bone of Horus", but iron "the bone of Typhon" (*scil.* Seth). The iron is sometimes attracted by the magnet, sometimes repelled. Manetho continues, οὕτως ἡ σωτήριος καὶ ἀγαθὴ καὶ λόγον ἔχουσα τοῦ κόσμου κίνησις ἐπιστρέφεταί τε καὶ προσάγεται μαλακωτέραν ποιεῖ, πείθουσα τὴν σκληρὰν ἐκείνην καὶ τυφώνειαν (Manetho in Plut. *de Iside* 62). The power of Horus (that is, Apollo) is equated with the "salutory, good and rational movement of the world" which mollifies Seth.

Callimachus ends his poem on a disarmingly humorous note with the strange rites of the sailors, created as παίγνια by Asteria for the baby Apollo. This ending reminds us that the very earnest themes with which we have been concerned are also, to a significant extent, beneath the surface. The dominant impression throughout is rather that of a *grammaticus ludens* wittily and learnedly transforming a traditional theme from venerable models into something better suited to the Age, and aimed to delight his peers - the *grammatici ludentes* of Alexandrian Museum. It is largely in this sense that the Homeric Hymn and the *Hymn to Delos* are - despite the latter's constant reference to the former - worlds apart. Yet I would stress that the playful and childlike are at home in this new world, not helpless like children, but strong in their laughter and wit. The closing invocation (v. 325) illustrates this point. By using the Ionic form ἱστίη and modifying it with the hapax εὐέστιε, Callimachus creates an amusing sound-play on the word "hearth". One could be tempted to think that this alone might have prompted the poet to call Delos "the hearth of the islands" (ἱστίη ὦ νήσων v. 325).

The scholia, however, explain the appropriateness of this image: the hearth is an altar that stands in the middle of every house; thus Delos stands at the center of the Cyclades like a hearth and an altar. But not only houses had hearths. A city had a "common hearth" (Arist. *Pol.* 1322 b 26) and the eternal flame at Delphi was sometimes considered the hearth for all of Greece (cf. Plut. Aristid. 20.4-8; thus W. Burkert, *Griechische Religion der archaischen und klassischen Epoche* [Stuttgart 1977] 264-265).

Perhaps Callimachus wished to make a similar claim for Delos (cf. Kuiper, *op. cit.* p. 190). According to Philostratus' *Heroicus* (ed. Kayser p. 235), the Lemnians purified their island every year and extinguished all fire for nine days. Then, sending a θεωρίς to Delos, they would get new fire and, upon returning, said that this moment signalled for them the beginning of a new life (cf. W. Burkert, *Homo Necans, op. cit.,* 192). By calling Delos the hearth of all islands, Callimachus could stress its great prestige as a place of pilgrimage and source of life for people (and poets) throughout the world. Such a meaning would certainly not have been lost on the Ptolemies, who controlled the island at this time.

The image is appropriate for other reasons as well. It underlines the purity and strength of Callimachean song. Like Delos, the goddess Hestia was famous for her chastity (cf. her decision to remain a virgin forever, *H. H. Aphr.* 21-32). Further, as Plato mentions in the *Phaedrus* (247 a), the hearth is immovable and Hestia does not participate in the procession of the gods.[102] Although at the poem's start, Delos was depicted leading the procession of islands (v. 16–22), Callimachus now lays stress on something else: the slender entity through which Apollo enters the world has become the *recipient* of processions. It has won a permanent place in the landscape and in song, from which, like the hearth, it cannot be shaken.

---

[102] Cf. the discussion of Hestia by J-P Vernant, "Hestia-Hermes: The religious expression of space and movement among the Greeks" *Soc. Sci. Inform.* 8 (1969) 131–168 = *Mythe et pensée chez les Grecs: études de psychologie historique* (Paris 1969) 97–143.

Conclusion

Tradition and originality, the interplay of present and past, are a concern of poets in any Age. "Each work of art," as G. B. Conte has said,[1] "is the result of conflict at all levels between originality and convention and between the new and traditional structures that shape literary memory. The literary memory becomes active and present when poets accept and welcome the norms of tradition." It is no surprise then that modern "Homeric" scholarship has focused as unerringly on these questions as has the study of Hellenistic literature.[2] Yet it has long been recognized that in the Age after Alexander's conquests – in large part *because of* Alexander's conquests and the new world that they ushered in – this issue became more pressing than ever before. "Now for the first time the Greeks were convinced that the old order of things in the political as well as in the intellectual field, in their whole way of life indeed, was gone forever. They became conscious of a definitive break between the mighty past and a still uncertain present." (Pfeiffer, *Hist.* p. 87). In such circumstances there was enormous opportunity for innovation, yet at the same time a strong pull towards the past. Both tendencies are embodied in the person of the well-read Muse: if, on the one hand, she is a novel figure in her emphatically literate erudition, retrospection is by the same token her central concern.

In treating these themes, we are dealing of course with critical commonplaces. Yet it has been the aim of this study to raise such commonplaces above the level of intuition (where scholars of this period have generally been content to leave them), to give them substance, and to demonstrate their interrelationship. Thus chapter one addressed the well-known "bookishness" of the Age by pursuing – as had hitherto not been done – the book itself, the activities of reading and writing as literary themes, thereby revealing that the poets of the time had developed a new and revolutionary self-image. We observed here an engaging receptivity to the new and a willingness to experiment. Chapter two dealt, on the other hand, with the noted sense of epigonality among the Hellenistic authors, and with their proverbial allusiveness to earlier literature – two themes that have traditionally been treated separately, but

---

[1] *The Rhetoric of Imitation* (Ithaca 1986) 91.
[2] I need only point to the collection of essays in the Wege der Forschung volume, *Homer, Tradition und Neuerung,* ed. J. Latacz (Darmstadt 1979).

which I argued must be seen as functions of each other. The first of these themes was shown to be powerfully expressed in the proliferation at this time of poems for the dead, fictitious epitaphs for the great literary personages of the past: the old poetic world was defunct, the new generation born after the fact. Yet the Hellenistic poets devised ways to overcome the perceived rift between themselves and the heritage, to revive the past into their own Age: full-scale resurrection was one means to this end; pervasive allusion another. While chapters one and two dealt with the poet's relation to present and past respectively, chapter three presented a synthesis of these themes in a new interpretation of the *Hymn to Delos*. Here we saw how Callimachus continuously and comprehensively evoked his chosen models, the *Homeric Hymn to Apollo* and Pindar's poems about Asteria, compelling his readers to reconstitute these antecedent texts – and so establish continuity with the past – even as they experienced his own. But this is also a poem in which the contemporary world is strongly present. For the hymn reflects Callimachus' characteristically Alexandrian aesthetic concerns. And even as the poet connects his king with the familiar political world of old Hellas, we find traces of the very different world with which he was in constant daily contact, namely that of Egypt. This should remind us that the poets who came to Alexandria were essentially foreigners, and it was to a foreign way of life that they were constantly exposed. Set thus on an alien shore, they looked back to their ancestral world with something more than mere nostalgia, for their identity – as is so often the case with immigrants – was stubbornly bound up with their heritage. Yet at the same time there was no escaping the new world of which they were a part. It is this situation, with its necessary and productive ambivalence, that is everywhere present in their works.

Structural Diagram of the Hymn to Delos

1-10 Prooimion: τὴν ἱερὴν Δῆλον, Ἀπόλλωνος κουροτρόφον

11-27: Delos today: The fundamental paradox

    11-15: The wretched island πόντῳ ἐνεστήρικται - ἀμφί...ἑλίσσων
    16-22: Delos preeminent among the great islands
    23-27: Apollo protects Delos: ἀμφιβέβηκεν

  28-54: γοναὶ Δήλου

    28-29: Transition: Choice of theme, πολέες σε περιτροχόωσιν ἀοιδαί
    30-35a: Poseidon's creation of islands, πρυμνόθεν ἐρρίζωσε
    35b-40: the contrast of Asteria
    41-50: Asteria's wanderings
    51-54: Asteria as Apollo's birthplace,
        change of name, mooring: ποδῶν ἐθήκαο ῥίζας

    55-259: γοναὶ Ἀπόλλωνος

      55-58: Transition: Hera's wrath: οὐδ' Ἥρην κοτέουσαν
      59-69: Hera's guards: Ares (ἤπειρος), Iris (νῆσοι)

      70-74: Leto's wanderings: Arcadia
      75-99a: Leto's wanderings: Boeotia
          Apollo's 1st prophecy: Thebes

      99b-102: Leto's wanderings: Achaea
      103-152: Leto's wanderings: Thessaly
          Peneios episode
          Ares-simile

      153-204: Leto's wanderings: the islands
          Apollo's 2nd prophecy: Cos, Ptolemy, kingdom
          Celts (ξυνὸς ἄεθλος), Celt-simile
          Asteria πλαζομένη

      205-214: Leto on Asteria
      215-248: Hera intermezzo
          Iris-simile
      249-259: The birth: οὐδ' Ἥρη νεμέσησεν
          κύκνοι...ἐκυκλώσαντο...περὶ Δῆλον

  260-274: γοναὶ Δήλου

    260-263: The island becomes golden
    264-274: Delos exultant: poverty vs. Apollo Δήλιος
        Mooring (καὶ ἔσσομαι οὐκέτι πλαγκτή)
        Apollo's recognition of Delos

275-324: Delos today: νησάων ἁγιωτάτη. *The* τιμαί

    275-277: Delos Ἀπόλλωνος κουροτρόφος
    278-299: ἀπαρχαί
    300-315: χοροί· νῆσοι κύκλον ἐποιήσαντο - (παῖδες) κύκλιον ὠρχήσαντο
    316-324: Rites: σέο βωμὸν...ἑλίξαι

325-326: Salutation. Delos as ἱστίη νήσων

Bibliography

Allen, T., and Sikes, E. E., *The Homeric Hymns* (New York 1904).
Austin, J. N., "Theocritus and Simonides," *TAPhA* 98 (1964) 1-21.

Bagnall, R., *The Administration of the Ptolemaic Possessions outside Egypt* (Leiden 1976).
Barigazzi, A., "Un frammento dell' inno a Pan di Arato," *RhM* 117 (1974) 221-246.
Barrett, W. S., *Euripides Hippolytus* (Oxford 1964).
Bauer, L. J., *Callimachus, Hymn IV: An Exegesis* (Diss. Brown Univ. 1970).
Bauer, W., *Griechisch-Deutsches Wörterbuch des neuen Testament* (Berlin 1958).
Beloch, K. J., *Griechische Geschichte* IV 2 (Berlin 1927).
Benveniste, E., *Le vocabulaire des institutions indo-européenes* (Paris 1969).
Bergman, J., *Ich bin Isis* (Uppsala 1968).
Bertoldi, V., in *Mélanges Boisacq*, vol. 1 = Brussels, Univ. Libre, Inst. de philol. et d'hist. orient., annuaire 5 (1937).
Bie, O., *Die Musen in der antiken Kunst* (Berlin 1887).
Bing, P., review of Mineur *AJPh* (forthcoming).
-, "The Alder and the Poet. Philetas 10 (p. 92 Powell)," *RhM* 129 (1986) 222-226.
-, "Kastorion of Soloi's Hymn to Pan," *AJPh* 106.4 (1985) 502-509.
-, "Callimachus' Cows. A Riddling Recusatio," *ZPE* 59 (1984) 1-8.
Birt, Th., *Die Buchrolle in der Kunst* (Leipzig 1907).
Bloom, H., *The Anxiety of Influence* (Oxford 1973).
Blum, R., *Kallimachos und die Literaturverzeichnung bei den Griechen* (Frankfurt 1977).
Boardman, J., "The Islands," *CAH* III 1 (Cambridge 1984) 754-778.
Bonneau, D., *La crue du Nil* (Paris 1964).
Bornmann, F., *Callimachi Hymnus in Dianam* (Florence 1968).
Bowman, A. K., "The Vindolanda writing tablets and the development of the Roman form" *ZPE* 18 (1975) 237-252.
-, and Thomas, J. D., "The Vindolanda writing tablets and their significance. An interim report," *Historia* 24 (1975) 463-478.
Bowra, C. M., *Pindar* (Oxford 1964).
Boyancé, P., *Le culte des Muses chez les Philosophes Grecs* (Paris 1937).
Brink, C. O., "Ennius and the Hellenistic worship of Homer," *AJPh* 93 (1972) 457-567.
Bruneau, P., *Recherches sur les cultes de Délos a l'époque Hellénistique et a l'époque impériale* (Paris 1970).
Bulloch, A. W., "Hellenistic Poetry" in *Camb. Hist. of Class. Lit.* I (Cambridge 1985).
-, "The Future of a Hellenistic Illusion. Some observations on Callimachus and religion," *MH* 41 (1984) 209-230.
Burkert, W., *Lore and Science in Ancient Pythagoreanism* (Harvard 1972).
-, "Die Leistung eines Kreophylos. Kreophyleer, Homeriden und die archaische Heraklesepik," *MH* 29 (1972) 74-85.
-, *Griechische Religion der archaischen und klassischen Epoche* (Stuttgart 1977).
-, *Homo Necans* (Berkeley, 1983).
Burr-Thomas, D., *Ptolemaic Oinochoai and Portraits in Faience: Aspects of the Ruler Cult* (Oxford 1973).

Cahen, E., *Callimaque et son Œuvre Poétique* (Paris 1921).
-, *Les Hymnes de Callimaque* (Paris 1930).

Calderini, A., *Dizionario dei Nomi Geografici e Topografici dell' Egitto Greco-Romano* I 1 (Cairo 1935).
Cazzaniga, I., "Un epigramma di Fileta," *RFIC* 40 (1962) 238-248.
Chamoux, F., *Cyrène sous la monarchie des Battiades* (Paris 1953).
Christ, W., and Schmid, W., *Geschichte der griechischen Literatur* II 1 (Munich 1920).
Clayman, D. L., *Callimachus' Iambi* (Leiden 1980).
Conte, G. B., *The Rhetoric of Imitation* (Ithaca 1986).
Couat, H., *Alexandrian Poetry under the first three Ptolemies*, (transl. J. Loeb, New York 1931).
Cunningham, I. C., *Herodas' Mimiambi* (Oxford 1971).
Daremberg, Ch., and Saglio, Edm., *Dictionaire des Antiquités Grecques et Romaines* IV 2 (Paris 1911).
Davison, J. A., "Quotations and allusions in Early Greek Literature," *Eranos* 53 (1955) 125-140 = *From Archilochus to Pindar* (New York 1968) 70-85.
Degani, E., "Note sulla fortuna di Archiloci e di Ipponatte in epoca Ellenistica," in *Poeti greci giambici ed elegiaci*, ed. Degani (Milan 1977) 106-126.
Denniston, J. D., *The Greek Particles*² (Oxford 1954).
Diels, H., and Kranz, W., *Die Fragmente der Vorsokratiker*, 3 vols. (Berlin 1951).
Dodds, E. R., *Euripides Bacchae* (Oxford 1960).
Dornseiff, F., "Kallimachos' Hymnos auf Artemis," *Philol. Wochensch.* 56 (1936) 733-736.
Dover, K. J., *Theocritus. Select Poems* (London 1971).
Drögemüller, H., *Die Gleichnisse im hellenistischen Epos* (Diss. Hamburg 1956).
Erbse, H., "Zum Apollonhymnus des Kallimachos," *Hermes* 83 (1955) 411-428.
Farnell, L. R., *Critical Commentary to the Works of Pindar* (London 1932).
Fehling, D., *Die Wiederholungsfiguren und ihr Gebrauch bei den Griechen vor Gorgias* (Berlin 1969).
Fox, D. C., "Labyrinth und Totenreich," *Paideuma* 1 (1938/40) 381-394.
Fränkel, H., *Wege und Formen frühgriechischen Denkens* (Munich 1968).
-, *Dichtung und Philosophie des frühen Griechentums* (Munich 1976).
Frankfort, H., *Kingship and the Gods* (Chicago 1948).
Fraser, P. M., *Ptolemaic Alexandria* 3 vols. (Oxford 1972).
Friedländer, P., "Das Proömium der Theogonie," *Hermes* 49 (1914) 1-16 = *WdF Hesiod* 277-294.
von Fritz, K., "Das Proömium der hesiodischen Theogonie," *Festschr. Snell* (Munich 1956) 29-45 = *WdF Hesiod* 295-315.
Gabathuler, M., *Hellenistische Epigramme auf Dichter* (St. Gallen 1937).
Gallavotti, C., "Review of Pfeiffer vol. 2," *Par. Pass.* 9 (1953) 464-472.
Gentili, B., "Oralità e scrittura in Grecia," in *Oralità Scrittura Spettacolo*, ed. M. Vegetti (Torino 1983) 37-43.
Giangrande, G., "The Utilization of Homeric Variants by Apollonius Rhodius: A Methodological Canon of Research," *QUCC* NS (1973) 73-81 = *Scripta Minora Alexandrina* I (Amsterdam 1980) 1-9.
-, "Arte allusiva and Alexandrian epic poetry," *CQ* 17 (1967) 95-97 = *Scripta Minora Alexandrina* I 11 ff.
-, "Sympotic Literature and the Epigram," in *L'Épigramme Grecque*, Entretiens Hardt 14 (1967) 93-174.
Goedicke, H., *The Protocol of Neferyt* (Baltimore 1977).
Goldhill, S., "Framing and Polyphony: Readings in Hellenistic Poetry," *Proc. Camb. Philol. Soc.* 212 (1986) 25-52.
Goody, J., and Watt, I., "The Consequences of Literacy," in *Literacy in Traditional Societies*, ed. J. Goody (Cambridge 1968) 27-68.

Gow, A. S. F., and Page, D. L., *The Greek Anthology, Hellenistic Epigrams* 2 vols. (Cambridge 1965).
-, *The Greek Anthology. The Garland of Philip* 2 vols. (Cambridge 1968).
Gow, A. S. F., *Theocritus* 2 vols. (Cambridge 1952).
Griffiths, A. H., "Six Passages in Callimachus and the Anthology," *BICS* 17 (1970) 32-43.
Griffiths, F. T., "The date of Callimachus' Hymn to Delos," *Maia* 29-30 (1977/8) 95-100.
-, *Theocritus at Court* (Leiden 1979).
Griffiths, J. G., *Plutarch de Iside et Osiride* (Univ. of Wales Press 1970).
Groeneboom, P., *Aeschylus Prometheus* (Groningen 1928, repr. 1966).
Guthrie, W. K. C., *A History of Greek Philosophy* I (Cambridge 1962).
Habicht, Chr., *Gottmenschentum und die griechischen Städte*, Zetemata 14 (1956).
Haeberlin, C., "Zu Kallimachos," *Philologus* 46 (1888) 69.
Harder, R., "Bemerkungen zur griechischen Schriftlichkeit," *Die Antike* 19 (1943) 86-108 = *Kleine Schriften* (Munich 1960) 57-80.
Harvey, A. E., "Homeric epithets in Greek lyric poetry," *CQ* 51 (1957) 206-223.
Havelock, E. A., *Preface to Plato* (Cambridge Mass. 1963).
-, *The Literate Revolution in Greece and its Cultural Consequences* (Princeton 1982).
-, *The Muse Learns to Write* (New Haven 1986).
Heinen, H., *Untersuchungen zur hellenistischen Geschichte des 3. Jahrhunderts v. Chr.* Historia Einzelschr. 20 (Wiesbaden 1972).
Heitsch, E., *Die griechischen Dichterfragmente der römischen Kaiserzeit* Abh. d. Ak. d. Wiss. in Göttingen. phil. hist. Kl., dritte Folge 49 (1961, 1).
-, "Sein und Gegenwart im frühgriechischen Denken," *Gymnasium* 78 (1971) 421-437.
Helck, W., *Die Prophezeiung des Nfrti*, kl. Äg. Texte (Wiesbaden 1970).
-, and Westendorf, W., *Lexikon d. Ägyptologie* (Wiesbaden 1975).
Henrichs, A., "Thou shalt not kill a tree," *Bull. Amer. Soc. of Papyr.* 16 (1979) 35.
Herington, J., *Poetry into Drama* (Berkeley 1985).
Hermann, A., *Die ägyptische Königsnovelle*, Leipzig. ägypt. Stud. 10 (Glückstadt-Hamburg-New York 1938).
Herter, H., "Kallimachos und Homer," *Xenia Bonnensia. Festschr. z. 75jährigen Bestehen des Philologischen Vereins und Bonner Kreises* (Bonn 1929) 50-105 = *Kleine Schriften* (Munich 1975) 371-416.
-, "Kallimachos aus Kyrene," *RE* Suppl. V (1931) 386-452.
-, "Review of Cahen, *Callimaque* and *Les Hymnes de Callimaque*, and Couat, *Alexandrian Poetry*," *Gnomon* 12 (1936) 449-459.
-, "Kallimachos," *Bursian Jahresbericht* 255 (1937).
-, "Kallimachos aus Kyrene," *RE* Suppl. XIII (1973) 184-266.
Hiltbrunner, O., "Ovids Gedicht vom Siegelring und ein anonymes Epigramm aus Pompei," *Gymn.* 77 (1970) 283-299.
Hopfner, T., *Plutarch über Isis und Osiris* I (Prague 1940).
Hopkinson, N., *Callimachus, Hymn to Demeter* (Cambridge 1984).
-, "Callimachus' Hymn to Zeus," *CQ* 34 (1984) 139-148.
Hornung, E., *Geschichte als Fest* (Darmstadt 1966).
-, "Altägyptische Höllenvorstellungen," *Abh. d. Sächs. Akad. Leipzig*, philol.-hist. Kl. 59 (1968) 27.
-, "Seth. Geschichte und Bedeutung eines ägyptischen Gottes," *Symbolon* NF 2 (1974) 49.
Howald, E., and Staiger, E., *Die Dichtungen des Kallimachos* (Zürich 1955).
Immerwahr, H. R., "Book Rolls on Attic Vases," in *Classical Mediaeval and Renaissance Studies in Honor of Berthold Louis Ullman*. I ed. Ch. Henderson (Rome 1964) 17-48.
-, "More Book Rolls on Attic Vases," *Ant. K.* 16 (1973) 143-147.
Jacobs, F., *Animadversiones in epigrammata Anthologiae Graecae* I 1 (Leipzig 1798).

Jacoby, F., *Die Fragmente der griechischen Historiker* (Berlin 1923-1930, Leiden 1940-1958).
Jacques, J. M., "Sur un acrostiche d'Aratos (Phen. 783-787)," *Rev. d. Ét. Anc.* 62 (1960) 48-61.
Janko, R., "The Structure of the Homeric Hymns: A Study in Genre," *Hermes* 109 (1981) 9-24.
Jehasse, L., *La Nécropole Préromain d'Aléria* Gallia Suppl. 25 (Paris 1973).
Jung, F., *Hipponax redivivus* (Bonn 1929).
Kahn, C., "Anaximander and the Arguments Concerning the Apeiron," *Festschr. E. Kapp* (Hamburg 1958) 19-29.
Kaplan, M., "Apeiros and Circularity," *GRBS* 16.2 (1975) 125-140.
Kassel, R., and Austin, C., *Poetarum Comicorum Graecorum Fragmenta* (Berlin 198-...).
Keefe, D. E., "Gallus and Euphorion," *CQ* 32 (1982) 237-238.
Kerenyi, K., *Labyrinthstudien* (Zürich 1950).
Kern, O., *Die Religion der Griechen* III (Berlin 1926, repr. 1963).
Köhnken, A., "Envy's Retort to Apollo," *AJPh* 102 (1981) 411-422.
Koenen, L., "Ein einheimischer Gegenkönig in Ägypten," *Chr. d'Egypt* 34 (1959) 103-119.
-, "Egyptian Influence in Tibullus," *ICS* 1 (1976) 127-159.
-, *Eine agonistische Inschrift aus Ägypten und frühptolemaische Königsfeste* (Meisenheim 1977).
-, "Die Adaption ägyptischer Königsideologie am Ptolemäerhof," in *Egypt and the Hellenistic World. Proceedings of the International Colloquium Leuven 24-26 May 1982* (Leuven 1983) 143-190.
-, "A supplementary note on the date of the Oracle of the Potter," *ZPE* 54 (1984) 9-13.
Körte, A., and Händel, P., *Die Hellenistische Dichtung* (Stuttgart 1960).
Kroll, W., "Kastorion," *RE* Suppl. IV (1924) 880.
Kuchenmüller, G., *Philetae Coi Reliquiae* (Berlin 1928).
Kuiper, K., *Studia Callimachea* I (Leiden 1896).
Kumpf, M., *The Homeric Hapax Legomena and their Literary Use by Later Authors, especially Euripides and Apollonius of Rhodes* (Diss. Ohio State Univ. 1974).
Kyrieleis, H., "ΚΑΘΑΠΕΡ ΕΡΜΗΣ ΚΑΙ ΩΡΟΣ," *Antike Plastik* 12 (1973) 133-147.
Lachmann, K., *Berichte über die Verhandlungen der Akademie der Wissenschaften* (1846) = *Betrachtungen über Homer's Ilias* 3 (1874).
Landfester, M., *Das griechische Nomen "philos" und seine Ableitungen* (Hildesheim 1966).
Latacz, J., *Kampfparänese, Kampfdarstellung und Kampfwirklichkeit in der Ilias, bei Kallinos und Tyrtaios* (Munich 1977).
-, "Tradition und Neuerung in der Homerforschung," in *Homer,* Wege der Forschung CDLXII (Darmstadt 1979).
Layard, J., "Der Mythos der Totenfahrt auf Malekula," *Eranos Jb.* 4 (1937) 241-291.
Lefkowitz, M., "Pindar's Pythian V," in *Pindare,* Fond. Hardt XXI (1984) 33-69.
LeGrand, Ph., E., *Étude sur Théocrite,* Bibliotheque des écoles Francaises d'Athenes et de Rome 79 (Paris 1898, repr. 1968).
-, "Problèmes alexandrins: Pourquoi furent composés les hymnes de Callimaque?" *REA* 3 (1901) 281-312.
Lehnus, L., *L'Inno a Pan di Pindaro* (Milano 1979).
Lepsius, R., *Denkmäler aus Ägypten und Äthiopien* (Berlin 1849-1858).
Lewis, N., *Greeks in Ptolemaic Egypt* (Oxford 1986).
Lichtheim, M., *Ancient Egyptian Literature* 3 vols. (Berkeley 1973-1980).
Livrea, E., "Der Liller Kallimachos und die Mausefallen," *ZPE* 34 (1979) 37-42.
-, "Review of Supplementum Hellenisticum," *Gnomon* 57 (1985) 592-601.
Lloyd-Jones, H., "The Seal of Poseidippus," *JHS* 83 (1963) 75-99.
-, "A Hellenistic Miscellany," *SFIC* 77 (1984) 52-72.

-, and Parsons, P., *Supplementum Hellenisticum* (Berlin 1983).
Long, A. A., "Timon of Phlius," *Proc. Cambr. Philol. Soc.* 24 (1978) 68-91.
Luppe, W., "Review of P. Oxy. vol. 38-39," *Gnomon* 46 (1974) 641-651.
Lynch, J. P., *Aristotle's School* (Berkeley 1972).
Mair, A. E., *Callimachus, Hymns and Epigrams* (Loeb Classical Library 1955).
Maas, P., *Greek Metre* (Oxford 1962).
Maass, E., *Aratea* (Berlin 1892).
-, *De tribus Philetae carminibus* Ind. Lect. Marp. (1895).
Maehler, H., *Die Auffassung des Dichterberufs im frühen Griechentum* (Göttingen 1963).
Mancini, A. C., *Ann. d. Sc. Norm. Sup. di Pisa*, Cl. di Lett. e filos., ser. III 2 (1972) 502-505.
-, *Pap. Lett. Greci,* ed. Carlini etc. (Pisa 1978).
Martin, R. P., "Hesiod, Odysseus, and the instruction of princes," *TAPhA* 114 (1984) 29-48.
McKay, K. J., *Erysichthon, A Callimachean Comedy* Mnem. Suppl. 7 (Leiden 1962).
McLennan, G. R., *Callimachus, Hymn to Zeus, Introduction and Commentary* (Rome 1977).
Meiggs, R., *Trees and Timber in the Ancient Mediterranean World* (Oxford 1982).
Meillier, C., *Callimaque et son temps* (Lille 1979).
Meincke, A., *Philologicarum exercitationum in Athenaei Deipnosophistae* (1843).
Meineke, W., *Untersuchungen zu den enkomiastischen Gedichten Theokrits* (Diss. Kiel 1965).
Merkelbach, R., "Sappho und ihr Kreis," *Philologus* 101 (1957) 1-29.
-, *Isisfeste* (Meisenheim 1963).
-, "Das Königtum der Ptolemäer und die Hellenistischen Dichter," in *Alexandria, Kultur im Schmelztiegel einer mediterranen Großstadt. Aegyptiaca Treverensia: Trierer Studien z. Gr. Röm. Ägypten* 1 (1981) 27-35.
Meyer, H., *Hymnische Stilelemente in der frühgriechischen Dichtung* (Würzburg 1933).
Mineur, W. H., "The boys and the barbarians. Some remarks on Callimachus H. 4.177," *Mnem.* 32 (1979) 119-127.
-, *Callimachus, Hymn to Delos. Introduction and Commentary* (Leiden 1984).
Misgeld, W. R., *Rhianos von Bene und das historische Epos im Hellenismus* (Diss. Köln 1968).
Momigliano, A., *Terzo Contributo alla Storia Degli Studi Classici e dell Mondo Antico* (Rome 1966).
Mondolfo, R., *L'Infinito nel Pensiero dell' Antichità Classica* (Florence 1956).
Most, G. W., "Callimachus and Herophilus," *Hermes* 109 (1981) 188-196.
Müllenhoff, K., *Deutsche Altertumskunde* I (Berlin 1870).
Münster, M., *Untersuchungen zur Göttin Isis,* Münchner Ägyptol. Stud. 11 (1968).
Murray, O., *Early Greece* (Sussex 1980).
Murray, P., "Poetic Inspiration in Early Greece," *JHS* 101 (1981) 87-100.
Nachtergael, G., *Les Galates en Grèce et les Sôteria de Delphe,* Academie Royale de Belgique, Memoires de la classe des Lettres, collection in 2. serie, T. LXIII, Fascicule 1 (1977).
Nagy, G., *The Best of the Achaeans* (Baltimore 1979).
Naveh, J., *Early History of the Alphabet. An Introduction to West Semitic Epigraphy and Palaeography* (Leiden 1982).
Nilsson, M. P., *Die Hellenistische Schule* (Munich 1955).
Nock, A. D., *Essays* I (Cambridge Mass. 1972).
Norden, E., *Agnostos Theos* (Leipzig 1913).
Oehler, J., "Skytale," *RE* III A (1927) 691-692.
Ogilvie, R. M., "The Song of Thyrsis," *JHS* 82 (1962) 106-110.
Ohlert, K., *Rätsel und Rätselspiele der alten Griechen* (Berlin 1912).
Ong, W. J., *Literacy and Orality* (New York 1982).

Onians, J., *Art and Thought in the Hellenistic Age: The Greek World View 350-50 B.C.* (London 1979).
Page, D. L., *Select Papyri III. Literary Papyri (Poetry)* (Cambridge Mass. 1942).
-, "Archilochus and the Oral Tradition," in *Archiloque*, Entretiens Hardt X (Geneva 1964) 117-179.
-, *Further Greek Epigrams* (Cambridge 1981).
Papastavrou, H., "Asteria," *Lex. Icon. Myth. Class. II* 1 (Zürich 1984) 903-904.
Parsons, P. J., "Callimachus: Victoria Berenices," *ZPE* 25 (1977) 1-50.
Pasquali, G., "Arte Allusiva," *Italia che scrive* 25 (1942) 185 ff. = *Stravaganze quarte e supreme* (Venice 1951) 11-20 = *Pagine stravaganti* II (Florence 1968) 275-283.
Peek, W., "Papyrus-Fragmente einer alexandrinischen Elegie," *Maia* 15 (1963) 199.
Petzl, G., "Kein Umsturz beim Galater-Überfall auf Delphi," *ZPE* 56 (1984) 141-144.
Pfeiffer, R., *Kallimachos Studien* (Munich 1922).
-, "Ein neues Altersgedicht des Kallimachos," *Hermes* 63 (1928) 302-341 = *Ausg. Schriften* (Munich 1960) 98-132.
-, *Callimachus* 2 vols. (Oxford 1949, 1953).
-, "The Image of the Delian Apollo and Apolline Ethics," *Journal of the Warburg and Courtauld Institutes* 25 (1952) 20-32 = *Ausg. Schr.* (Munich 1960) 55-71.
-, "The Future of Studies in the Field of Hellenistic Poetry," *JHS* 75 (1955) 69-73 = *Ausg. Schriften* (Munich 1960) 148-158.
-, *History of Classical Scholarship* (Oxford 1968).
Pickard-Cambridge, A., *The Dramatic Festivals of Athens*[2] (Oxford 1968).
Platthy, J., *Sources on the Earliest Greek Libraries* (Amsterdam 1968).
Pleket, H. W., *Lampas* 12 (1979) 126.
Poliakoff, M., "Nectar, Springs and the Sea: Critical Terminology in Pindar and Callimachus," *ZPE* 39 (1980) 41-47.
Porson, R., *Euripides Hecuba* (Leipzig 1824).
Préaux, C., *Le monde hellénistique* 2 vols. (Paris 1978).
Preisigke, F., *Wörterbuch der griechischen Papyruskunde* (Berlin 1925-1971).
Powell, J. U., *Collectanea Alexandrina* (Oxford 1925).
Pucci, P., *Hesiod and the Language of Poetry* (Baltimore 1977).
Quaegebeur, J., "Reines Ptolémaiques et Traditions Égyptiennes," in *Das Ptolemäische Ägypten* ed. H. Maehler and V. M. Strocka (Mainz 1978) 245-262.
Race, W. H., "Aspects of Rhetoric and Form in Greek Hymns," *GRBS* 23 (1982) 5-14.
Reinach, A., "Les Galates en Égypte," *REA* 13 (1911) 33-74.
Reinsch-Werner, H., *Callimachus Hesiodicus: die Rezeption der hesiodischen Dichtung durch Kallimachos von Kyrene* (Berlin 1976).
Rhodes, P. J., *A Commentary on the Aristotelian Athenaion Politeia* (Oxford 1981).
Rice, E. E., *The Grand Procession of Ptolemy Philadelphus* (Oxford 1983).
Richter, W., "Eine Elegie des Musaios von Ephesos auf Attalos I.?" *Maia* 15 (1963) 93-119.
Riele, G. J. M. J. Te, "Deux épigrammes trouvées en Arcadie," *Chiron* 14 (1984) 235-243.
Rissman, L., *Love and War. Homeric Allusion in the Poetry of Sappho* (Meisenheim 1984).
Rösler, W., "Die Entdeckung der Fiktionalität in der Antike," *Poetica* 12 (1980) 283-319.
-, "Schriftkultur und Fiktionalität. Zum Funktionswandel der griechischen Literatur von Homer bis Aristoteles," in *Schrift und Gedächtnis. Beiträge zur Archäologie der literarischen Kommunikation* eds. A. and J. Assmann, and Chr. Hardmeier (Munich 1983) 109-122.
-, "Alte und neue Mündlichkeit. Über kulturellen Wandel im Antiken Griechenland und heute," *Der altsprachliche Unterricht* 28 (1985) 4-26.
Rosen, H. B., "Die Ausdrucksform für 'veräußerlichen' und 'unveräußerlichen Besitz' im Frühgriechischen. Das Funktionsfeld von homerischen Philos," *Lingua* 8 (1959) 264-293.

Roussel, P., "Inscriptions anciennement découvertes à Délos," *BCH* 31 (1907) 335-377.
Russell, D. A., "De imitatione," in *Creative Imitation and Latin Literature* eds. D. West and T. Woodman (Cambridge 1979).
Sansone, D., *Aeschylean Metaphors for Intellectual Activity,* Hermes Einzelschr. 35 (1975).
Schadewaldt, W., "Der Umfang des Begriffs der Literatur in der Antike," in *Literatur und Dichtung,* ed. H. Rüdiger (Stuttgart 1973) 12-25.
-, *Die Anfänge der Philosophie bei den Griechen* (Frankfurt 1978).
Schlatter, G., *Theokrit und Kallimachos* (Diss. Zürich 1941).
Schmidt, V., "Zu Pindar," *Glotta* 53 (1975) 36-43.
Schubart, W., "Posidippus Redivivus," *Symbolae Philologicae O. A. Danielsson octogenario dicata* (Uppsala 1932) 290-298.
-, *Das Buch bei den Griechen und Römern*[3] (Heidelberg 1962).
Schwinge, E. R., "Wilamowitz Verständis der hellenistischen Poesie," in *Wilamowitz nach 50 Jahren* (Darmstadt 1985) 151-177.
Seek, G. A., *Das griechische Drama* (Darmstadt 1979).
Segal, C., "Greek Tragedy: Writing, Trust, and the Representation of the Self," in *Mnemai. Classical Studies in Memory of Karl K. Hulley,* ed. H. D. Evjen (Chicago 1984).
Sethe, K., and Helck, W., *Urkunden des ägyptischen Altertums* IV Fasc. 1-22 (Leipzig, Berlin 1906-1958).
Skutsch, O., *The Annals of Q. Ennius* (Oxford 1985).
Slater, W. J., *Lexicon to Pindar* (Berlin 1969).
-, "Simonides' House," *Phoenix* 26 (1972) 232-240.
-, "Peace, the Symposium and the Poet," *ICS* 6.2 (1981) 205-214.
Smiley, M. T., "Callimachus' Debt to Pindar and Others," *Hermathena* 18 (1919) 46-72.
Snell, B., "Identifikationen von Pindarbruchstücken," *Hermes* 73 (1938) 424-439.
-, *Poetry and Society* (Bloomington 1961).
-, *Szenen aus griechischen Dramen* (Berlin 1971).
-, *Die Entdeckung des Geistes*[4] (Göttingen 1975).
Stephan, G. M., "The Coronis," *Scriptorium* 13 (1959) 3-14.
Tandy, G. M., *Callimachus' Hymn to Zeus* (Diss. Yale 1979).
Tarn, G. M., *Antigonos Gonatas* (Oxford 1913).
Terzaghi, N., "Un Nuovo frammento di Callimaco?" *Studie in onore di A. Calderini e R. Paribeni* II (Milano 1957) 127-135.
Thierfelder, H., *Die Geschwisterehe im hellenistisch-römischen Ägypten* (Münster 1960).
Thissen, H., *Studien zum Raphiadekret* (Meisenheim 1966).
Thomas, R., "Virgil's Georgics and the Art of Reference," *HSCP* 90 (1986) 171-198.
Treu, M., "Selbstzeugnisse alexandrinischer Dichter," *Miscellanea di studi allesandrini in memoria di A. Rostagni* (Torino 1963) 273-290.
-, "Review of C. M. Bowra's Pindar," *Gymn.* 74 (1967) 149-153.
Van Groeningen, B. A., *Theognis: Le premier livre* (Amsterdam 1966).
Velde, H. Te, *Seth. God of Confusion* (Leiden 1967).
Vernant, J.-P., "Hestia-Hermes: The religious expression of space and movement among the Greeks" *Soc. Sci. Inform.* 8 (1969) 131-168 = *Mythe et pensée chez les Grecs: études de psychologie historique* (Paris 1969) 97-143.
Vogt, E., "Das Akrostichon in der griechischen Literatur," *A & A* 13 (1967) 80-95.
Volkmann, H., "Ptolemaios," *RE* XXIII 2 (1959) 1599ff.
Wernicke, K., "Apollon," *RE* II 1 (1895) 1-111.
West, M. L., *Hesiod. Theogony* (Oxford 1966).
-, *Greek Metre* (Oxford 1982).
-, *The Orphic Poems* (Oxford 1983).
White, H., *New Essays in Hellenistic Poetry* (Amsterdam 1985).
Wiedman, A., *Herodots zweites Buch* (Leipzig 1890).

Wilamowitz-Moellendorff, U. von, *Homerische Untersuchungen*, vol. 7, Philol. Unters. (1884).
-, *Die Ilias und Homer* (Berlin 1916).
-, *Griechische Verskunst* (Berlin 1921).
-, *Pindaros* (Berlin 1922).
-, *Hellenistische Dichtung in der Zeit des Kallimachos* 2 vols. (Berlin 1924).
-, *Der Glaube der Hellenen* 2 vols. (Berlin 1931/2, repr. Darmstadt 1959).
-, *Kleine Schriften* VI (Berlin 1971).
Will, E., *Histoire Politique du Monde Hellénistique* (Nancy 1979).
Williams, F., *Callimachus. Hymn to Apollo. A Commentary* (Oxford 1978).
Wölke, H., *Untersuchungen zur Batrachomyomachie* (Meisenheim 1978).
Wörrle, M., "Epigraphische Forschungen zur Geschichte Lykiens," *Chiron* 8 (1978) 201-246.
Xanthakis-Karamanos, G., *Studies in Fourth Century Tragedy* (Athens 1980).
Zanker, G., "The Nature and Origin of Realism in Alexandrian Poetry," *A & A* 29 (1983) 125-145.
-, *Realism in Alexandrian Poetry* (Kent 1986).
Ziegler, K., *Das hellenistische Epos: ein vergessenes Kapitel der griechischen Dichtung* (Leipzig 1934, rev. 1966).
-, "Zum Zeushymnus des Kallimachos," *RhM* 68 (1913) 336-354.

Index Locorum

Passages treated in detail are indicated in bold print

Aceratus
  AP VII 138.3-4 = *FGE* p. 3:   33
Aeschylus
  Choe. 450:   12 n. 5
  Eum. 273-275:   12 n. 5
  PV 666:   133 n. 38
  Semele (p. 335 Radt) = Schol. in Ap. Rh. 1.636:   133 n. 80
Alcaeus, *fr.* 58.12 (L-P):   21 n. 22
Alcaeus of Messene
  AP VII 536 = 13 G-P: 71 n. 33
  AP VII 536.6 = 13.6 G-P: 63
Alcman
  PMG 2 iv. 5:   100
  PMG 12.8:   100
Anacreon
  El. 2 (West):   124 n. 54
  PMG 356 b: 21 n. 22
Anacreontea
  1 (West):   71 n. 33
  22 (West):   31 n. 44
AP
  V 83:   31 n. 44
  V 84:   31 n. 44
  V 223:   88 n. 65
  V 283:   88 n. 65
  VII 153:   25 n. 33
  IX 190 = Page, *FGE* p. 345:   29 n. 40
  XI 220:   137 n. 88
  XIV 45:   33 n. 52
  XIV 60:   33 n. 52
Antipater of Sidon
  AP VII 23 = 13 G-P: 59
  AP VII 26 = 14 G-P: 59
  AP VII 26.1-4 = 14.1-4 G-P: **62–63**
  AP VII 27 = 15 G-P: 59
  AP VII 29 = 16 G-P: 59
  AP VII 30 = 17 G-P: 59
Anyte
  AP VII 492 = 22 Page = 23 G-P: 129 n. 66
Apollodorus, 2.2:   133 n. 80
Apollonius of Rhodes
  3.1340-1344:   87 n. 62
  4.1423-1430:   **43–44**

Aratus, *Phaenomena* 783-787:   29 n. 39
Archilochus
  fr. 120 W = 117 Tarditi: 21
  fr. 185 W = 188 Tarditi: **28–29 n. 39**
  P. Koeln II 58.27:   117 n. 42
Aristides, XXXI 2 p. 212 (Keil):   69
Aristophanes
  Eccl. 683 f.:   45 n. 72
  Ran. 1021:   124 n. 54
Aristotle
  Ath. Pol. 63.2-4:   45 n. 72
  Met. 1072 b 3 ff.:   128 n. 62
  Phys. 265 a 13 ff.:   128 n. 62
  Poet. 10, 1452 a 21:   50
  Poet. 1458 a 26 f.:   88
  Pol. 1322 b 26:   142
Asclepiades
  AP VII 11 = 28 G-P: 29 n. 40
  AP IX 63 = 32 G-P: 20, **29–30**
Astydamas, Page *FGE p. 33-34* = Snell *TrGF* 1, 60 T 2 a: **60–62**
Athenaeus
  I 3 a-b: 47 n. 74
  III 98 c: **73**
  (Callixenus), 206 a ff.:   **134–135 n. 82**
  X 454 f. (Kastorion of Soloi):   23 f.
Bacchylides
  5.9:   20
  5.91-93:   78 n. 43
  11.58:   100
  fr. 65.14:   105 n. 30
  Scholia in fr. 23 (Cassandra), lines 16-19:   **97 n. 12**
Batrachomyomachia, 1-3:   **19**
Boïskos of Kyzikos, *SH* 233:   **22–23**
Callimachus
  Aetia
  fr. 1.2:   112
  fr. 1.5:   50, 94
  fr. 1.6:   46
  fr. 1.11:   117, 119
  fr. 1.17:   46, 94
  fr. 1.19:   46, 50, 123 n. 49
  fr. 1.20:   46, 94
  fr. 1.23-24:   46, 94, 119
  fr. 1.25-28:   94

fr. 2:   70–71, 122
fr. 7.13–14:   **18**
fr. 64:   **67–70**
SH 254–269:   23, 47
fr. 75.64–66:   **18–19**
fr. 75.76–77:   **27–28**
fr. 86–89:   109 n. 35
fr. 92:   33 n. 52 a
fr. 112.9:   **19 n. 20 a**
Iambi
1,   fr. 191:   **65–67, 70–71**
    fr. 191.26:   14–15
2,   fr. 192.11:   123 n. 49
4,   fr. 194.34 f.:   109 n. 35
8,   fr. 198:   66
12, fr. 202:   66
13, fr. 203:   38
13, fr. 203.63–64:   66
fr. 216:   66
Galatea fr. 378–379:   129 n. 66
Victory of Sosibios fr. 384:   23
fr. 398:   46, 94
fr. 407.45–50:   137 n. 88
fr. 465:   46
fr. 612:   **36**
Athena, Test #23:   88 n. 64
Κτίσεις νήσων ... κ. τ. λ.:   101 n. 20
Hymns
1.1:   81
1.5 f.:   44
1.7–8:   42 n. 67
1.8 f.:   **76–77 n. 42**
1.10:   82
1.18–41:   137 n. 90
1.36:   127 n. 59
1.57–59:   **135–136 n. 84**
1.60 f.:   **77 n. 42**
1.70–75:   **76–77**
1.74–75:   **82**
1.77–78:   **81**
1.79:   **77–78**
1.79–80:   81
1.86–88:   **81–82**
2.27:   131 n. 73
2.59:   102 n. 21
2.71:   122
2.106:   117
2.108 f.:   **55**
2.110–112:   113 n. 38
3.51–56:   **126 n. 57**
3.56–61:   **126 n. 57**
3.137–140:   **18–19**

3.170–182:   **83–89**
3.170:   **126 n. 57**
3.171:   137 n. 89
3.171 (Scholia):   137 n. 90
3.174–175:   84 n. 56
3.183–186:   **36–37**
3.240–242:   **126 n. 57**
3.248–249:   **126 n. 57**
3.251–258:   **127 n. 57**
3.251 f.:   **130 n. 67**
4:   ch. 3 *passim*
4.82–85:   **40–44**
4.84–85:   76 n. 42
5.49–52:   **124 n. 53**
Epigr.
6 Pf. = 55 G–P: **30**
27 Pf. = 56 G–P: 122
27.4 Pf. = 56.4 G–P: **36**
28 Pf. = 2 G–P: 46, 94
Pseudo-Callisthenes, I 32:   **45–46**
Catullus
38.8:   69
50.1–6:   21–22 n. 24
Chairemon, F 14 b (Snell):   15
Choirilos of Samos, *SH* 317:   **13**, 60 n. 17
Cicero, *De Orat.* 1.69:   36
Clement Alex., *Strom.* 1.59:   76 n. 42
Cratinus, *Archilochoi*:   65 n. 23
Crinagoras
    AP IX 239.4 = 7.4 *Garl. Phil.*:   20
    AP IX 513.2 = 49.2 *Garl. Phil.*:   20
    AP IX 545 = 11 *Garl. Phil.*:   29 n. 40
Critias
    DK 88 B 4:   **16**
    DK 88 B 5:   **16**
Democritus, *DK* 68 B 18:   15 n. 8
Diodorus Siculus
    XIX 3.70:   68 n. 29
    XX 57:   122
    XXII 9.3:   129 n. 67
Diogenes Laertius
    III 5:   13
    IX 110:   72 n. 37
    IX 111:   72
Dionysius, *de imit.* p. 205.7 (Usener):   69
Dionysius Chalcus, fr. 2 (West):   124 n. 54
Dioscorides
    AP VII 37 = 22 G–P: **39–40**
    AP VII 707 = 23 G–P: **39–40**
Dioskourides, *Mat. Med.* II 169 RV, (ed. Wellmann, I 235):   122

Ennius, *Annals* fr. ii-x (Skutsch): 70
Ephorus, *FGrHist* 70 F 31 b = Strabo 422: 130 n. 68
Pseud-Epicharmea (Axiopistus?), fr. 1.1-6 (p. 219 Powell): 19 n. 18 a
Epimenides of Crete, fr. 5 (Kinkel): **76–77 n. 42**
Euenus, *AP* IX 251.1 = 1.1 *Garl. Phil.*: **19, 44–45**
Eumelos, fr. 15 (Kinkel): 43 n. 68
Euphorion of Chalkis, fr. 22, 22 b (p. 34 Powell): 58 n. 13
Euphron, fr. 8 (Meineke) = fr. 8 (Kock): 16 n. 12
Eupolis, *Demoi*: 65 n. 23
Euripides
  Alc. 966 f.: 29
  Ba. 1330 ff.: 130 n. 67
  Hipp. 864–865: 29
  Hipp. 877–881: 29
  Hipp. 1253 f.: 33
  Ion 822: 113 n. 38
  I. A. 39: 33
  Rhes. 355: 92 n. 3
  fr. 60.6-7 (Austin) = 369.6-7 (Nauck²): 29
Eustathius, *ad Od.* 18.374: 86 n. 58
Hecataeus, *FGrHist* F 305: 138
Hedylus, 6 G–P = Ath. 11.473: **21**
Hermocles, fr. 1.13 (p. 174 Powell): 92 n. 3
Herodas
  3.92: **28**
  8.59–60: **71 n. 33**
Herodotus
  I 143: 98 n. 14
  I 146: 98 n. 14
  II 35.2: 138
  II 112 f.: 14
  II 144: 132
  II 156: 132, **138**
  III 16: 134 n. 81
  IV 36: 127 n. 60
  IV 190: 122
  VI 98: 100
  VII 228: 68
  VIII 35–39: **130 n. 67**
  IX 42: **130 n. 67**
Hesiod
  Th. 54: 12
  Th. 79–84: **78–79**
  Th. 80–82: **81 n. 51**
  Th. 81–82: **79**
  Th. 93 f.: **79**
  Th. 94 f.: **80**
  Th. 96: 77
  Th. 96: **81 n. 51**
  Th. 96–98: **80**
  Th. 404 f.: 105 n. 30
  Th. 409: 97
  Th. 465–469: **115**
  Th. 888: **115**
  WD 1: 24 n. 30
  WD 40–41: **121–122**
"Hesiod"
  Scut. 105: 54
  Scut. 109: 123
  Scut. 191: 123
  Scut. 374–379: 123
  Scut. 386–392: 123
  Scut. 402–412: 123
  Scut. 421–423: 123
  Scut. 426–433: 123
  Scut. 437–41: 123
  fr. 304 (M–W): **43**
  fr. 357.2 (M–W): 22
Hipponax
  fr. 1 (West) = 17 (Degani): 66
  fr. 12.2 (West) = 20.2 (Degani): 66
  fr. 15 (West) = 18 (Degani): 66
  fr. 20 (West) = 8 (Degani): **71 n. 33**
  fr. 32.4 (West) = 42 ab (Degani): 66, 64 n. 21
  fr. 36.2 (West) = 44.2 (Degani): 66, 64 n. 21
  fr. 37 (West) = 46 (Degani): 66, 64 n. 21
  fr. 84.18 (West) = 86.18 (Degani): 66
  fr. 95.3-4, 15 (West) = 98.3-4, 15 (Degani): 66
  fr. 95 a (West) = 19 (Degani): 66
  fr. 117.4 (West) = 196.4 (Degani): 66, 64 n. 21
  fr. 120 (West) = 121 (Degani): 66, 71 **n. 33**
  fr. 121 (West) = 122 (Degani): 71 **n. 33**
Homer
  Iliad
  1.249: 78
  2.484–492: **11–12**
  2.594–600: 19
  2.750: 24 n. 30
  3.222: 124

4.98-99:   54
5.356 ff.:   123
6.168-169:   11
7.84-91:   71 n. 34
7.371:   53
8.487-488:   53
8.512-515:   53
8.519:   100
8.529:   53
9.88:   53
10.97 f.:   54
10.180 f.:   54
10.416-417:   54
12.2-33:   71 n. 34
12.156:   124
12.278:   124
13.822:   55
13.834:   55
15.393:   55
16.692 f.:   **36-37**
17.719-721:   54
17.723:   55
18.299:   53
18.487 ff.:   127 n. 60
19.9:   54
19.49:   55
19.98 ff.:   **115**
19.357:   124
19.421:   55 n. 8
21.192-197:   136 n. 88
21.195-197:   55-56 n. 11
23.245-248:   71 n. 34
24.1-5:   29 n. 39
Od.
2.312:   54
3.70:   55
3.489 (Scholia):   136 n. 88
4.845 ff.:   120 n. 44
5.47:   29 n. 39
5.327-332:   **121-122**
5.368 ff.:   121 n. 45
6.162 f.:   104
7.113:   86 n. 58
7.159:   55
7.214:   54
8.166-177:   **32 n. 48,** 79 n. 44
8.543:   55
9.27:   110
10.82-86:   **88-89**
10.86 (Scholia):   88
11.36-43:   66
16.205-206:   **113 n. 39**

16.260:   55
17.573:   55 n. 8
20.236:   55
24.80-84:   71 n. 34
Hom. Hymn.
2.174-175:   123
3.18-19:   **136**
3.19:   **111-112**
3.25:   **112**
3.30-44:   **115-116**
3.47-48:   **116**
3.54-55:   **120**
3.72:   **120**
3.99-101:   **114**
3.120-121:   **110**
3.172:   **105 n. 28**
3.363-374:   131
4.529 f.:   29 n. 39
5.21-32:   142
5.166:   54-55
5.264-272:   **42-43**
8.7-8:   123
24.5:   55
Horace
   Car. II 1.38:   69
   Ep. II 1.50:   70
Ibycus
   PMG 282:   124 n. 54
   PMG 322:   136 n. 88
   PMG 323:   136 n. 88
Ion, *fr.* 27.7 (West):   21
Iust., XXIV 8.10:   129 n. 67
Kastorion of Soloi, *SH* 310:   **23-26**
Klearchos, *fr.* 88 (Wehrli):   24
Leonidas of Tarentum
   AP VII 408.1-2 = 58.1-2 G-P: 63
   AP IX 25 = 101 G-P: 29 n. 40
Pseudo-Longinus
   13.2:   63 n. 19
   13.4:   61 n. 18
Longus, 1.14:   31 n. 44
Lucilius, *fr.* 1189 (Marx):   70
Lycophron, 574-576:   137 n. 89
Manetho
   fr. 66 (Loeb ed.):   134 n. 81
   (in Plut. *de Iside* 62):   141 n. 101
Martial, X 1.1:   35
Meleager
   AP IV 1.55 = 1.55 G-P: **22**
   AP V 171 = 35 G-P: 31 n. 44
   AP V 174 = 36 G-P: 31 n. 44
   AP XII 52 = 81 G-P: 31 n. 44

AP XII 52.3-4 = 81 G-P: 31
AP XII 257 = 129 G-P: **33–34**
"Moschus"
  Lament for Bion
  70 ff.: **57**
  87–92: **57–58**
Nossis, *AP* VII 718 = 11 G-P: 39 n. 60
Ophelion, I 415 (Meineke) = 11 p. 294 (Kock): 16 n. 12
Ovid
  Metamorphoses
  5.572–641: 137 n. 88
  8.738 ff.: 43 n. 68
Parmenon of Byzantium, *SH* 604 A v.
  1: 137 n. 90
Paul, *Letter to Titus* 1.12: 76 n. 42
Pausanias
  I 7.2: 92 n. 3
  I 16.2: 135 n. 84
  I 72: **131**
  II 5.3: 137 n. 88, 137 n. 89
  IV 6.1–3: **52**
  IV 20.5: **53**
  V 7.2–3: 137 n. 88
  X 19.7: 135 n. 84
  X 23.3: 129 n. 67
  X 23.9: 91 n. 2
Pherekrates, *Persai* fr. 131.5 (Kock): 21
Philetas 10 (p. 92 Powell): **31–33**
Philikos of Corcyra, *SH* 677: **22**
Philip, *AP* IV 2.3 = 1.3 Garl. Phil.: **22**
Philo of Alexandria, *In Flacc.* 55: 45 n. 71
Philodemus, *AP* XI 41 = 17 Garl. Phil.: **35**
Philostephanus of Cyrene, *FGE* p. 21: 29 n. 39
Philostratus
  Heroicus (p. 235 ed. Kayser): **142**
  Vit. Apoll. Tyan.
  I 4: 133 n. 80
  I 20.2: 137 n. 88
Phrynichus, *fr.* 31–35 (Meineke) = 31–35 (Kock): 16 n. 12
Pindar
  Ol.
  1: 103 n. 24
  1.100 ff.: 125 n. 55
  6.16–17: 78 n. 43
  6.59: 100 n. 16
  6.154: **28–29 n. 39**
  7.54–70: **107–109 n. 35**
  10.1 f.: 12 n. 5

  10.1–3: **28**
  14: 103 n. 24
  Pyth.
  1.1: **139–140**
  1.15–28: 123
  1.23 ff.: 123 n. 50
  1.61: 100 n. 16
  1.70: **140**
  1.97: **141**
  2.12: 137 n. 88
  4.56: 137 n. 90
  4.87: 123
  4.277–278: 78 n. 43
  5: 103 n. 24
  5.63–67: **139**
  6.20 f.: 78 n. 43
  9.63 ff.: **132 n. 75**
  11.63: 24 n. 30
  12.5: 125 n. 55
  Nem.
  1.1: 137 n. 88
  4.6–8: **18**
  8.20–21: 22
  9.53 f.: 20
  Isthm.
  2.34: 105 n. 30
  4.44: 125 n. 55
  6.11: 100 n. 16
  6.66–67: 78 n. 43
  8: 103 n. 24
  8.57: 105 n. 30
  Hymn
  1 *fr.* 33c–33d: **99–103**
  1 *fr.* 33d: 107
  Paean
  5.35–47 = fr. 52e (Snell-Maehler): **97–99**
  5.41: 107
  6 = fr. 52f. (Snell-Maehler): 103 n. 25
  6.126: 100 n. 18
  7b = fr. 52h (Snell-Maehler): **103–107**
  7b.11: 125
  7b.47: 102 n. 22
  10 = fr. 52l (Snell-Maehler): 109 n. 35
  12.8–14 = fr. 52m (Snell-Maehler): **108–109 n. 35**
  12.19: 109 n. 35
  Dithyr. 2.5 f. = fr. 70b (Snell-Maehler): 140 n. 100
  fr.

140b (Snell-Maehler): 103
150 (Snell-Maehler): 36
165 (Snell-Maehler): 43
169 (Snell-Maehler): 103 n. 25
Plato
  Crit. 119 d: 113 n. 38
  Laws 897 d ff.: 128 n. 63
  Ph. 61 a: 13
  Phdr.
  247 a: 102, 142
  264 d: 25 n. 33
  Prot. 320 a: 113 n. 38
  Symp. 195 b–197 b: 112
  Tim.
  30 a: 128
  33 b: 128
  34 a: 128 n. 63
  47 c–d: 128 n. 64
  52 d ff.: 128 n. 62
Pliny, NH 2.229: 137 n. 89
Plut.
  Aristid. 20.4–8: 142
  de def. orac.
  415 c–d: 43
  417 c–418 d: 130 n. 68
  418 a: 130 n. 70
  q. gr. 293 c: 129 n. 67, 130 n. 68
  de Iside
  12, 356 A: 133 n. 80
  62: 141 n. 101
  73: 134 n. 81
  Mor. 745 G: 112–113
  de Mus. 1136 a: 126 n. 56, 130 n. 68
  Sept. Sap. conv. 14: 121
  Thes. 21: 127
Pollianos, AP XI 130.1–2: 50
Pollux, 4.110: 127
Polybius
  II 20.6: 91 n. 2
  III 32.1: 17 n. 14
Polyzelus, 7–10 (Meineke) = 7–10 (Kock): 16 n. 12
Pomp. Mela, I 55: 138
Poseidippus
  SH 705.1: 38
  SH 705.5–6: 15
  SH 705.7–8: 37–38
  SH 705.16–17: 15
  SH 705.18–20: 57
  17.6 G–P: 33
  AP XII 98 = 6 G–P: 37
Quintilian, X 1.64: 69

Rhianos
  fr. 1 (p. 9 Powell): 55 n. 9
  SH 946: 51–56
  SH 947: 52–56
  AP XII 142' = 10 G–P: 31 n. 44
Sappho
  2.5 L–P: 18
  9 L–P: 18
  150.1 L–P: 24 n. 30
Simias of Rhodes
  AP VII 21 = 4 G–P: 59–61
  Wings: 112
Simonides
  PMG 531: 68
  PMG 581: 78 n. 43
  8 (West): 78 n. 43
Solon
  20 (West): 78 n. 43
  20.3 (West): 16
  36.18–20 (West): 16
Sophocles, Triptolemus fr. 597 (Radt): 12 n. 5
Sotades
  fr. 1 (p. 238 Powell): 135
  fr. 15.5–16 (p. 243 Powell): 58 n. 13
Stesichorus
  PMG 187.3: 34
  PMG 210: 124 n. 54
Strabo
  421 f.: 130 n. 69
  6.271: 137 n. 89
  432: 137 n. 88
Straton, AP XII 208: 30–31
Symphosius, XVI (Buecheler): 45
Telekleides, fr. 14–21 (Kock I p. 213–215): 65 n. 23
Theocritus
  1.140: 66 n. 27
  3.12–14: 31 n. 44
  7.47–48: 61
  7.86–89: 61–62
  14.62: 135 n. 84
  15.110–144: 92 n. 3
  16.5–12: 20–21
  16.20: 50
  17.43–44: 117 n. 42
  17.63–64: 117 n. 42
  17.73–75: 81 n. 51
  17.130 ff.: 135
  22.221: 24 n. 30
  Epigr. XVII = AP IX 599 = 15 G–P: 56–57

Epigr. XVIII = *AP* IX 600 = 17 G-P: 56–57
Epigr. XIX = *AP* XIII 3 = 13 G-P: 64
Epigr. XXI = *AP* VII 664 = 14 G-P: 56
Epigr. XXII = *AP* IX 598 = 16 G-P: 56–57
Theognis
  533 (West): 21 n. 22
  773–782: 130 n. 67
Theopompus, *FGrHist* 80 = Ael. *v. h.* 3.1: 130 n. 68
Thucydides
  I 131: 28 n. 39
  II 8.3: 100
  II 102: 105
Timon of Phlius
  SH 775–840: **71–72**
  SH 786: 72 n. 37
Timotheos
  PMG 791.202 f.: 22
  PMG 796: **22**, 124 n. 54
Varro, *De Re Rustica* I 1.4–7: **19 n. 20**
Xenophanes
  fr. 1.13–24 (West): 124 n. 54
  fr. 30 DK: 56 n. 11, 136 n. 88
Xenophon
  Hellenica III 3.8–9: 28 n. 39
  Hellenica V 2.34: 28 n. 39
  Memorabilia IV 2.10: 17 n. 14
Anon.
  PMG 851 b: 22
  SH 979.4–5: 29 n. 39

Carm. Conv.
  PMG 900: 31
  PMG 901: 31 n. 44
Delphic Paeans, (p. 141, 150 Powell): 129 n. 66
GV 945 (Peek): **35**
IG
  ii² 2338 = Snell, *TrGF* I, DID A 1 201: 60 n. 15
  XI 4, 1038 = Durrbach *Choix* #21 (p. 30–31 v. 23–27): 92 n. 3
  XII 5, 1004 = *OGIS* 773: 92 n. 5
OGIS 90 v. 23 ff.: 133 n. 78
*Syll*³
  367: 93 n. 5
  398: 91 n. 2
Urk.
  IV S. 16.15: 139 n. 95, 139 n. 97
  IV S. 239: 139 n. 95
  IV S. 157, 12: 139 n. 95
  VI 39: 133 n. 80
P. Alex. 547: **41 n. 63**
P. Berl. P 3029: 133 n. 80
P. Chester Beatty I: 132 n. 76
P. Hamburg. De Galatis (p. 131–132 Powell) = *SH* 958: 129 n. 66
P. Hibeh 199.11–17: 92 n. 3
PSI inv. 436 = *SH* 969: 129 n. 66
P. Lit. Lond. 11: **34–35**
P. Oxy.
  1800, fr. 1.45 f.: 68 n. 30
  2211.9–10 = Callimachus fr. 64: 68 n. 30
  2225 = Callimachus H. 4.84–85: **41 n. 63**

Subject Index

Acrostics 15, 18, 29 n. 39
Aetiology 70-71
Alexander the Great 14
Alexandria 14
   division into 5 γράμματα 45-46
   Library of 14-15, 40, 44-45
   Museum of 14-15, 40
Allegory 95, 141
Allusion
   in Archaic and Classical poetry 73 n. 38
   in Hellenistic poetry (see also Epicism) 72-90
Anacreon 56-57, 58-59, 62-63, 71 n. 33
Ἀνάγκη 112-113, 118, 120
Antimachus, the Lyde of 29-30
Archilochus 28-29 n. 39, 57, 65 n. 23
"arte allusiva" 74 n. 39
Asphodel 119-122
Asteria 96-110, ch. 3 *passim*
Asyndeton
   with maxims following a question 42 n. 66
   with vocative 120

Birth, ease thereof as showing lack of love between parents 117 n. 42
Books
   and love 30-31
   singing or talking (see also writing-tablets) 29-33
   in vase-painting 16 n. 10
Book-inscriptions 29-30
Book-worms 19, 44-45

Callimachus
   activity in connection with Library 37, 97 n. 12
   poetic programme 46, 86, 94-96
Celts
   attack on Delphi 91-93, 128-131
   mutiny under Ptolemy Philadelphus 131-134
   in Hellenistic poetry 129 n. 66

Chemmis, floating island 137-138
Circling, as motif in Callimachus 125-128, 126 n. 57
Closure, poetic conventions thereof in the Hellenistic Age (see also Coronis) 19 n. 20a
Columns of writing 15, 33
Coronis 33-35
Cows 83-89
Cyrene 122

Daphnis, death of 66 n. 27
Delos
   as emblem of Callimachean song 94-96, 119-124
   free from death and war 124
   impervious to earthquakes 100-103
   Ptolemaic policy concerning 91-93
Delphi, as object of barbarian invasions 129-131, 129 n. 67
Dream-encounters, with past poets 71 n. 33, 72 n. 35

Egypt, traditions of in Callimachus (see also Kings, Marriages, Nile) 14 n. 7a, 131-139
Epic, Hellenistic 50-56
Epicism, non-allusive use thereof 54-56, 72-73
Epimenides of Crete 76 n. 42
Epinician, Hellenistic 23, 82 n. 54
Epitaphs, cf. Sepulchral epigrams

Fetus, already active in the womb in Greek and Egyptian tradition 133 n. 80

γάρ, explaining underlying thought 79
Gauls, see Celts
Gymnasium, importance thereof as bulwark of Greek culture in Hellenistic Age 75 n. 41

Hamadryads, see Tree-nymphs
Hesiod 83-89, 58 n. 13, 121-122
Hestia 102, 142-143

Subject Index

Hipponax 63–67, 71 n. 33
Homer 11–12, 36–37, 29 n. 39, 50, 55 n. 11, 57, 61, 70, 104–105, 124–125
Horus
 Egyptian pharaoh as 131–139
 victory over Seth 131–139
Hymns 23–26, 26–27 n. 38, 93–94 n. 8, ch. 3 *passim*

Katabasis 71–72
Keraunos 135–136 n. 84
Kings
 and Muses 78–82, 139–141
 and poets 37, 77–82, 139–141
 divinity of 78–82, 91–92 n. 3, 128–129
 enemies thereof burned in Egyptian tradition 134 n. 81

Labyrinth 127
Lamentation, for dead poets 57–58
Literacy 10–14, ch. 1 *passim*

Marriages, incestuous 92 n. 3, 135
μή, as substitute for οὐ in Hellenistic period 41 n. 63
Meter, Hellenistic experiments with 22–23
Muses
 writing 15–20
 reading 27–28, 35–37
 plays about 16 n. 12
Museum of Alexandria
 organization thereof 14–15
 connection with Library 14, 40

Names
 divine and mortal 101–102
 μετονομασία 101–102
Nile 136–137
Niobe, as exemplar of preference for quantity over quality 117
Novelty, as poetic theme 22–23, 104–105, 108–110

Oichalias Halosis 30
ὅμοιον ὁμοίῳ 101, 117–118, 120
Orality 10–14, 46–47, 116

Ortygia, as alternate name for Delos 102 n. 21
Ouranopolis, city of glosses 72–73

Pattern-poems (see Technopaignia)
Performance 16–17, 38 n. 59, 59–61, 93–94 n. 8
Peripatos, as model for Alexandrian Museum (see Museum of Alexandria)
φίλος, used of familial bond 80
Phoinix, commander of Akragas 67–70
Pinakes 37, 97 n. 12
Prooimion 15, 19, 70, 110–111
Prophecy, *post eventum*, in connection with Egyptian kingship 133
Ptolemies, see Kings

Quotation 76–83

Reading, effects thereof on reception of poetry 23–27, 59–61
Regional boundaries, ignored in Hellenistic poetry 37–40
Reincarnation 70
Resurrection 65–67, 82–83
Riddles 23–24, 31–33, 88–89
Rivers, subterranean links between 136–137

σελίς, see Columns of writing
Septerion, Delphic festival 129–131
Sepulchral epigrams 39–40, 58–65, 67–70
Similes 123–124
Simonides 20–21, 67–70
σκυτάλη 28–29 n. 39
Sophocles 39–40, 59–61
Succession myths 114–115

Technopaignia 15, 18
Telchines 95, 112–113
Tragedy, revival of 60–62
Tree-nymphs 40–44

Wine and song 21
Writing tablets
 made of alder-wood 31–33
 speaking 29, 31–33
 used metaphorically of mental activity 12 n. 5, 105 n. 31
 wax thereon speaking 33 n. 52